Reading TUTOR 리딩 튜터

Junior 2

Welcome to
Reading Tutor Junior

<리딩튜터 주니어> 시리즈는 오랜 시간 동안 여러분의 사랑을 받아온 중학 독해 전문서입니다. **독해가 즐거워지는 놀라운 경험**을 선사해 드리고자 거듭 변화해 온, **<리딩튜터 주니어>** 시리즈가 더욱 새롭게 탄생했어요. 다채로운 소재로 흥미를 끄는 지문들을 읽다 보면 어느새 즐거운 독해가 만드는 실력의 차이를 실감하게 될 거예요.

구성 체계적인 학습을 위한 시리즈 구성 및 난이도

단어 수와 렉사일(Lexile) 지수를 기반으로 개발되어, 더욱 객관적으로 난이도를 비교·선택하실 수 있습니다.

110-130 words
500L-700L

120-140 words
600L-800L

130-150 words
700L-900L

140-160 words
800L-1000L

특징 독해 실력을 향상하는 <리딩튜터 주니어>만의 특징

- 학생들이 호기심을 가지고 접근할 수 있는 소재를 선정하였습니다.
- 이해력을 높여 독해가 쉬워지도록 Knowledge Bank 코너를 강화했습니다.
- 실질적인 실력 향상을 뒷받침하는 내신 서술형 문제를 더 많이 수록하였습니다.
- 수능 영어 영역에서 다루는 문제 유형을 수록하여 수능의 기초를 다질 수 있도록 하였습니다.

How to Study
Reading Tutor Junior

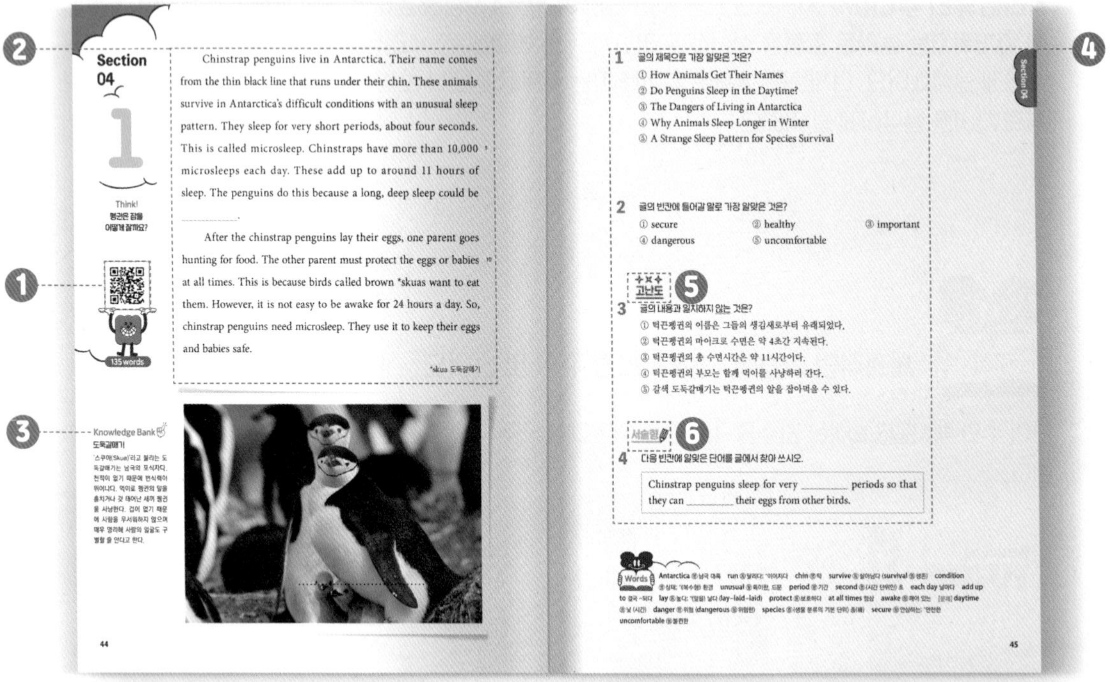

Section 04

1

Think!
펭귄은 잠을 어떻게 잘까요?

135 words

Chinstrap penguins live in Antarctica. Their name comes from the thin black line that runs under their chin. These animals survive in Antarctica's difficult conditions with an unusual sleep pattern. They sleep for very short periods, about four seconds. This is called microsleep. Chinstraps have more than 10,000 microsleeps each day. These add up to around 11 hours of sleep. The penguins do this because a long, deep sleep could be ________.

After the chinstrap penguins lay their eggs, one parent goes hunting for food. The other parent must protect the eggs or babies at all times. This is because birds called brown *skuas want to eat them. However, it is not easy to be awake for 24 hours a day. So, chinstrap penguins need microsleep. They use it to keep their eggs and babies safe.

*skua 도둑갈매기

Knowledge Bank
도둑갈매기
'스쿠아(Skua)'라고 불리는 도둑갈매기는 남극의 포식자다. 천적이 없기 때문에 번식력이 뛰어나다. 먹이로 펭귄의 알을 훔치거나 갓 태어난 새끼 펭귄을 사냥한다. 겁이 없기 때문에 사람을 무서워하지 않으며 매우 영리해 사람의 얼굴도 구별할 줄 안다고 한다.

44

1 글의 제목으로 가장 알맞은 것은?
① How Animals Get Their Names
② Do Penguins Sleep in the Daytime?
③ The Dangers of Living in Antarctica
④ Why Animals Sleep Longer in Winter
⑤ A Strange Sleep Pattern for Species Survival

2 글의 빈칸에 들어갈 말로 가장 알맞은 것은?
① secure ② healthy ③ important
④ dangerous ⑤ uncomfortable

고난도
3 글의 내용과 일치하지 않는 것은?
① 턱끈펭귄의 이름은 그들의 생김새로부터 유래되었다.
② 턱끈펭귄의 마이크로 수면은 약 4초간 지속된다.
③ 턱끈펭귄의 총 수면시간은 약 11시간이다.
④ 턱끈펭귄의 부모는 함께 먹이를 사냥하러 간다.
⑤ 갈색 도둑갈매기는 턱끈펭귄의 알을 잡아먹을 수 있다.

서술형
4 다음 빈칸에 알맞은 단어를 글에서 찾아 쓰시오.
Chinstrap penguins sleep for very ________ periods so that they can ________ their eggs from other birds.

Words

45

❶ QR코드
지문을 읽기 전에 녹음 파일을 듣고, 내용을 미리 파악해 보세요. 또, 학습 후 녹음 파일을 들으면서 복습할 수도 있어요.

❷ Reading
재미있고 상식도 쌓을 수 있는 지문을 읽어 보세요. 영어 독해 실력 향상은 물론, 상식을 넓히고 사고력도 기를 수 있어요.

❸ Knowledge Bank
지문 이해를 돕는 배경지식을 읽어 보세요. 지문이 이해가 안 될 때, 내용을 더 깊이 알고 싶을 때 큰 도움이 될 거예요.

❹ 최신 경향의 문제
최신 학습 경향을 반영한 다양한 문제를 풀어 보세요. 대의 파악부터 세부 정보 파악, 서술형 문제까지 정답을 보지 않고 스스로 푸는 것이 중요해요.

❺ 고난도
조금 어렵지만 풀고 나면 독해력이 한층 더 상승하는 것을 느낄 수 있어요. 한 번에 풀 수 없으면, 지문을 한 번 더 읽어 보세요.

❻ 서술형
서술형 문제로 독해력을 높이는 동시에 학교 내신 서술형 문제에도 대비할 수 있어요.

English Only
각 섹션마다 4개의 지문 중 마지막 지문은 문제가 영어로만 제시되어 있어요. 처음에는 어려울 수도 있지만, 영어 실력 향상에 도움이 될 거예요. 차근차근 해석하며 문제를 풀어 보세요.

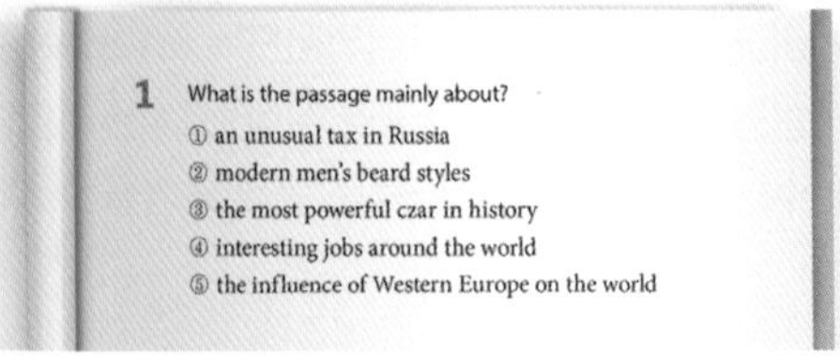

1 What is the passage mainly about?
① an unusual tax in Russia
② modern men's beard styles
③ the most powerful czar in history
④ interesting jobs around the world
⑤ the influence of Western Europe on the world

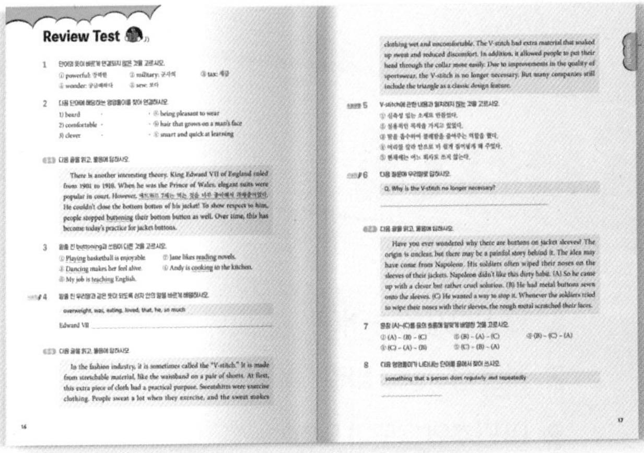

Review Test

각 섹션에서 배운 단어와 숙어를 반복 학습하고, 수능 유형과 최신 내신 기출 서술형 유형을 반영한 문제를 통해 실전 감각을 기를 수 있어요.

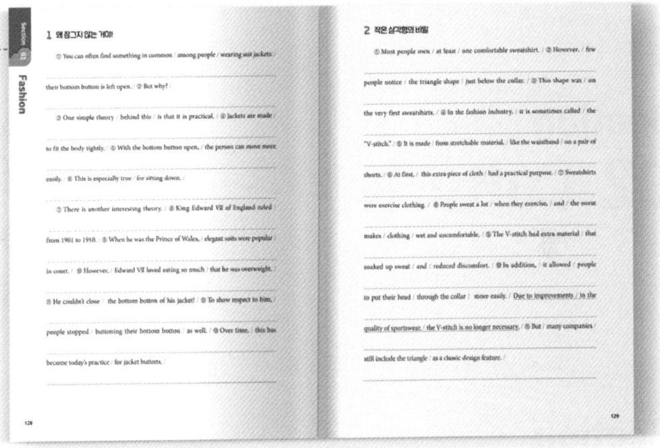

직독직해 워크시트

각 지문의 문장별 직독직해 훈련을 통해 배운 내용을 더 꼼꼼히 복습할 수 있어요.

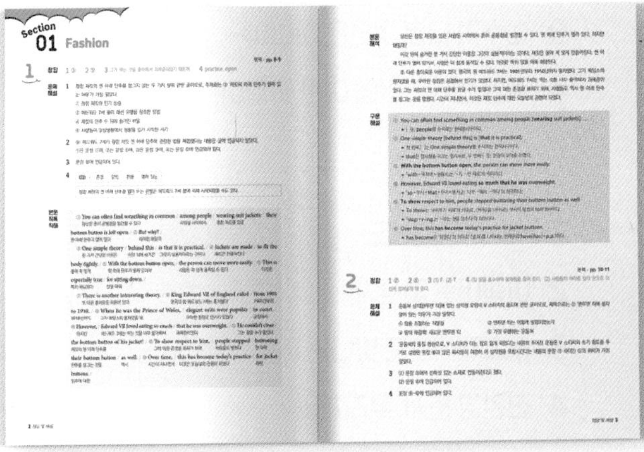

정답 및 해설

정답의 이유를 알려주는 문제 해설, 빠르게 해석할 수 있는 방법을 보여주는 직독직해, 한눈에 보는 본문 해석, 해석이 안 되는 부분이 없도록 도와주는 구문 해설로 알차게 구성했습니다.

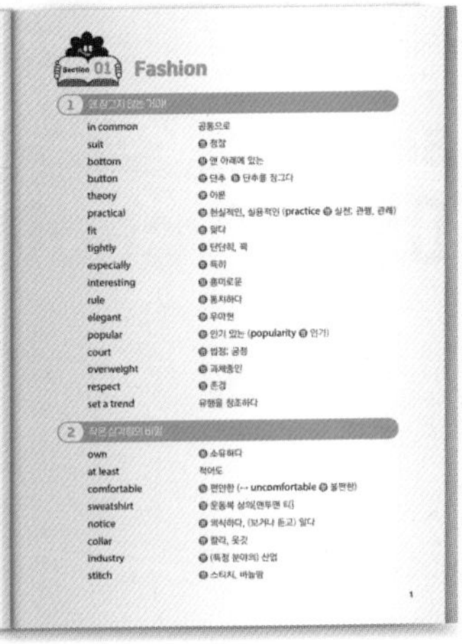

어휘 암기장

본문에 나온 단어와 숙어를 한눈에 볼 수 있도록 정리했습니다. 간단한 확인 문제도 있으니, 가지고 다니며 암기하고 확인해 볼 수 있어요.

Contents

Section

01

Fashion

1 왜 잠그지 않는 거야!

2 작은 삼각형의 비밀

3 이 단추의 용도가 뭐야?

4 수염을 기르려면 세금을~

Section 01

1

Think!
옷의 단추를
꼼꼼히 잠그나요?

127 words

You can often find something in common among people wearing suit jackets: their bottom button is left open. But why?

One simple theory behind this is that it is practical. Jackets are made to fit the body tightly. With the bottom button open, the person can move more easily. This is especially true for sitting down.

There is another interesting theory. King Edward VII of England ruled from 1901 to 1910. When he was the Prince of Wales, elegant suits were popular in court. However, Edward VII loved eating so much that he was overweight. He couldn't close the bottom button of his jacket! To show respect to him, people stopped buttoning their bottom button as well. Over time, this has become today's practice for jacket buttons.

Knowledge Bank

에드워드 7세(Edward VII)

에드워드 7세는 1901년부터 1910년까지 영국의 국왕이었다. 그는 자유분방하고 호탕한 성격으로, 외교에 능통했던 왕으로 평가받는다. 그는 대식가로도 유명한데, 하루 식사로 코스 요리를 10번이나 먹었다는 이야기가 전해지기도 한다. 그의 허리둘레는 48인치 가까이 되었다고 전해진다.

1 글의 주제로 가장 알맞은 것은?

① the rise in the popularity of suit jackets
② how King Edward VII set a fashion trend
③ why the bottom button of jackets is left open
④ the secret behind the number of buttons on a jacket
⑤ when people started wearing suits in their daily lives

2 글의 내용과 일치하지 않는 것은?

① 오늘날 정장 재킷의 맨 아래 단추를 잠그지 않는 것은 흔한 일이다.
② 정장 재킷의 맨 아래 단추가 열려 있으면 몸을 움직이기 쉽다.
③ 우아한 정장은 에드워드 7세가 웨일스의 왕자였을 때 인기가 있었다.
④ 사람들은 에드워드 7세를 따라 정장 재킷의 맨 아래 단추를 잠그지 않았다.
⑤ 에드워드 7세는 정장 재킷의 맨 아래 단추와 관련한 법을 제정하였다.

고난도 서술형

3 에드워드 7세가 재킷 맨 아래 단추를 잠그지 못한 이유를 우리말로 쓰시오.

____

서술형

4 다음 빈칸에 알맞은 단어를 보기에서 골라 쓰시오.

보기			
respect	closed	practice	open

The __________ of leaving the bottom button of a suit jacket __________ may have been started by King Edward VII.

Words in common 공통으로 suit 명 정장 bottom 형 맨 아래에 있는 button 명 단추 동 단추를 잠그다 theory 명 이론 practical 형 현실적인, 실용적인 (practice 명 실천; *관행, 관례) fit 동 맞다 tightly 부 단단히, 꽉 especially 부 특히 interesting 형 흥미로운 rule 동 통치하다 elegant 형 우아한 popular 형 인기 있는 (popularity 명 인기) court 명 법정; *궁정 overweight 형 과체중인 respect 명 존경 [문제] set a trend 유행을 창조하다

Section 01

2

Think!
맨투맨 티를 즐겨 입나요?

119 words

Most people own at least one comfortable sweatshirt. However, few people notice the triangle shape just below the collar. This shape was on the very first sweatshirts. In the fashion industry, it is sometimes called the "V-stitch." It is made from stretchable material, like the waistband on a pair of shorts. At first, this extra piece of cloth had a practical purpose. (①) Sweatshirts were exercise clothing. (②) People sweat a lot when they exercise, and the sweat makes clothing wet and uncomfortable. (③) The V-stitch had extra material that soaked up sweat and reduced discomfort. (④) In addition, it allowed people to put their head through the collar more easily. (⑤) But many companies still include the triangle as a classic design feature.

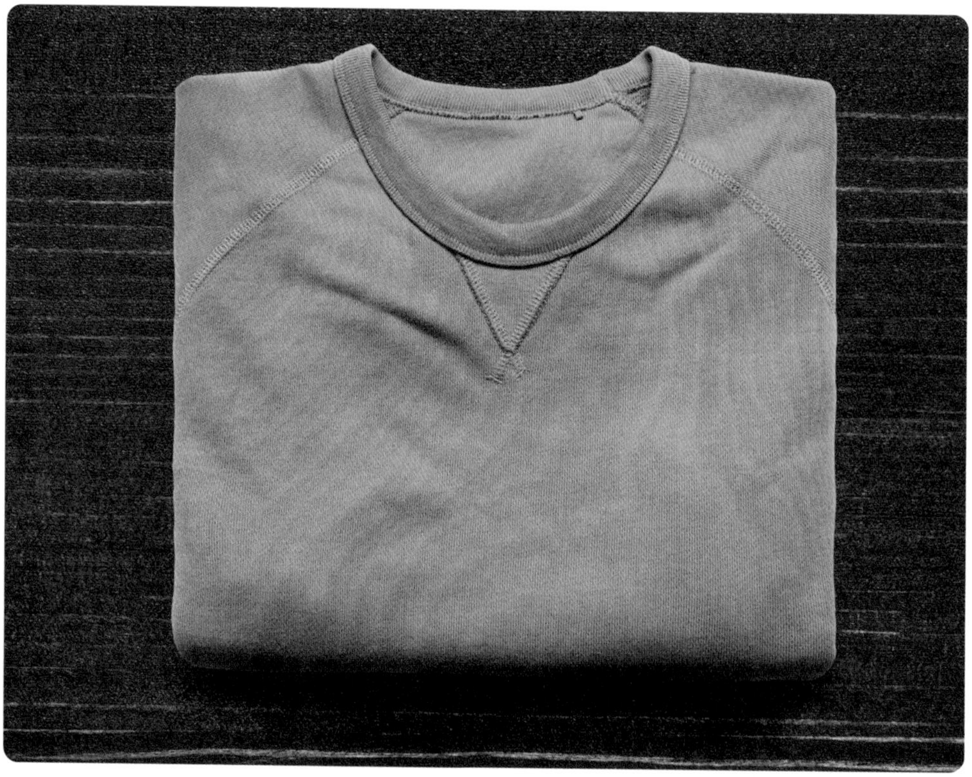

1 글의 제목으로 가장 알맞은 것은?

① Materials That Control Sweat
② Why Sweatshirts Have Triangles
③ How the Sweatshirt Was Invented
④ Sweat Solution: A New Sweatshirt
⑤ The Most Fashionable Exercise Clothes

2 다음 문장이 들어갈 위치로 가장 알맞은 곳은?

> Due to improvements in the quality of sportswear, the V-stitch is no longer necessary.

① ② ③ ④ ⑤

3 V 스티치에 관한 글의 내용과 일치하면 T, 그렇지 않으면 F를 쓰시오.

(1) 신축성이 없는 소재로 만들어져 옷의 형태를 유지시킨다. ________
(2) 처음에는 실용적인 용도를 가지고 있었다. ________

서술형

4 글에서 언급된 V 스티치의 기능 두 가지를 우리말로 쓰시오.

(1) ____
(2) ____

Words **own** ⓢ 소유하다 **at least** 적어도 **comfortable** ⓗ 편안한 (↔ **uncomfortable** ⓗ 불편한) **sweatshirt** ⓜ 운동복 상의 [맨투맨 티] **notice** ⓢ 의식하다, (보거나 듣고) 알다 **collar** ⓜ 칼라, 옷깃 **industry** ⓜ (특정 분야의) 산업 **stitch** ⓜ 스티치, 바늘땀 **stretchable** ⓗ 신축성이 있는 **material** ⓜ 직물, 옷감 **waistband** ⓜ (치마·바지의) 허리 밴드 **a pair of** 한 벌의, 한 쌍의 **shorts** ⓜ 반바지 **extra** ⓗ 여분의 **cloth** ⓜ 천, 옷감 (**clothing** ⓜ 의류 **clothes** ⓜ 옷, 의복) **purpose** ⓜ 목적, 용도 **sweat** ⓢ 땀을 흘리다 ⓜ 땀 **soak up** ~을 빨아들이다, 흡수하다 **discomfort** ⓜ 불편, 불쾌 [문제] **control** ⓢ 통제하다, 조절하다 **fashionable** ⓗ 유행하는 **due to** ~ 덕분에, ~로 인해 **improvement** ⓜ 향상 **sportswear** ⓜ 운동복 **necessary** ⓗ 필요한

Section 01

3

Think!

용도를 알 수 없는 패션 아이템은 무엇이 있을까요?

129 words

Have you ever wondered why there are buttons on jacket sleeves? The origin is unclear, but there may be a painful story behind it.

The idea may have come from Napoleon. His soldiers often wiped their noses on the sleeves of their jackets. Napoleon didn't like this dirty habit. He wanted a way to stop it. So he came up with a clever but rather cruel solution. He had metal buttons sewn onto the sleeves.

(a) Whenever the soldiers tried to wipe their noses with their sleeves, the rough metal scratched their faces. (b) It was very painful. (c) So they started to use handkerchiefs instead of their sleeves. (d) In the past, soldiers had to carry lots of heavy equipment. (e) However, jacket sleeves with buttons later became fashionable even among non-military people.

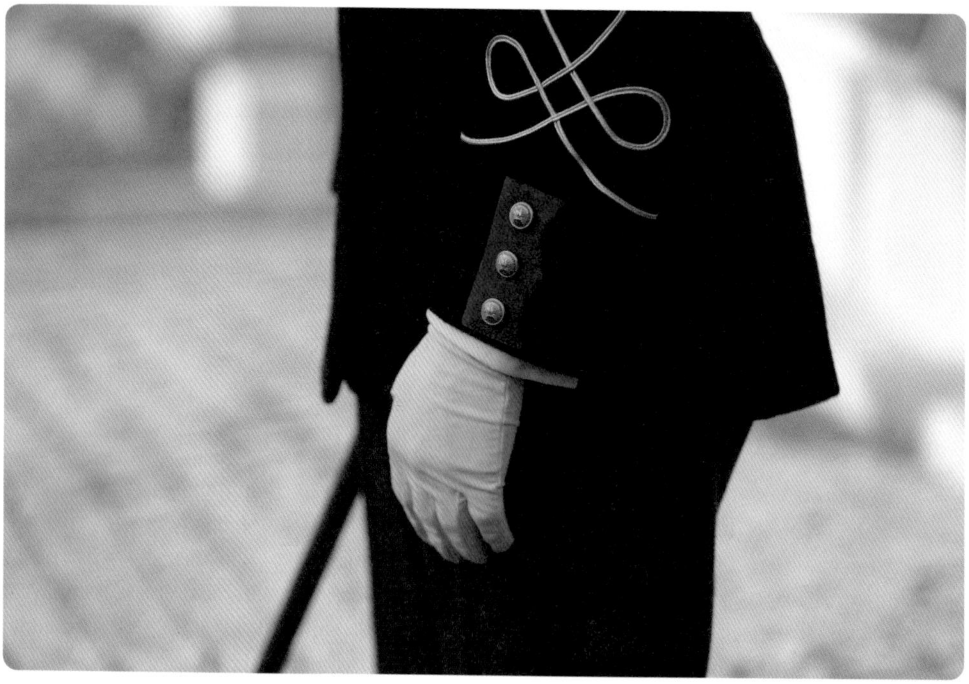

1 글의 제목으로 가장 알맞은 것은?

① The Best Material for Buttons
② Napoleon's Battle Against Buttons
③ Fashion from an Unexpected Place
④ The Trouble with Soldiers' Equipment
⑤ Why People Liked to Dress Like Napoleon

2 글의 (a)~(e) 중, 전체 흐름과 관계없는 문장은?

① (a) ② (b) ③ (c) ④ (d) ⑤ (e)

서술형

3 글의 밑줄 친 this dirty habit이 의미하는 내용을 우리말로 쓰시오.

____

서술형

4 다음 빈칸에 알맞은 표현을 글에서 찾아 쓰시오.

Napolean wanted to break a bad habit of his soldiers, so he added __________ __________ that would scratch them to their jacket sleeves.

Words wonder (동) 궁금해하다 sleeve (명) 소매 origin (명) 기원, 출신 unclear (형) 불분명한 painful (형) 고통스러운 wipe one's nose ~의 콧물을 닦다 habit (명) 습관 come up with 찾아내다, 생각해 내다 clever (형) 영리한 rather (부) 다소 cruel (형) 잔인한 solution (명) 해결책 metal (형) 금속의 sew (동) 바느질하다 (sew-sewed-sewn/sewed) rough (형) 거친 scratch (동) 긁다 handkerchief (명) 손수건 equipment (명) 장비, 용품 [문제] material (명) 재료 battle (명) 전투, 투쟁 unexpected (형) 예상 밖의 trouble (명) 문제

Section 01

4

Think!

What unique taxes have you heard of?

131 words

Many men around the world have beards. Interestingly, Russian men had to pay money to have beards under the rule of Peter the Great, a powerful Russian *czar.

Peter the Great wanted to make the country ____________. (A) So Peter the Great tried to make all Russian men shave. (B) He introduced many things from Western Europe, such as laws, a military system, and even fashion. (C) At that time, many Western European men shaved, but Russian men grew long beards. If a man wanted to grow a beard, he had to pay a tax. And he had to carry a token which showed that he had already paid the tax. Peter the Great even hired beard police to collect the beard tax. If a man refused to pay, the police shaved his beard off!

*czar 황제, 군주

Knowledge Bank

러시아의 표트르 대제 (Peter the Great)

강력한 개혁을 이끈 러시아 군주이다. 그는 서유럽 유학을 통해 자국인 러시아도 서유럽처럼 변해야 한다는 믿음을 갖게 되었고, 황제의 권력을 절대적으로 만들고 각종 개혁과 전쟁을 이끌었다. 그는 군대를 근대화하고 러시아 최초의 함대를 건설하는 등, 러시아를 유럽 열강에 편입시키는 데 기여했다. 그러나 군사력과 행정 제도의 모방에만 치우친 채 국민의 정치·사상의 자유를 외면했다는 점에서 그의 개혁은 불완전했다고 평가받고 있다.

1 What is the passage mainly about?

① an unusual tax in Russia
② modern men's beard styles
③ the most powerful czar in history
④ interesting jobs around the world
⑤ the influence of Western Europe on the world

고난도

2 Which is the best choice for the blank?

① better for men
② bigger than before
③ more like Western Europe
④ more beautiful and famous
⑤ richer than other countries

3 Which is the best order of the sentences (A)~(C)?

① (A) – (B) – (C)　　② (A) – (C) – (B)
③ (B) – (A) – (C)　　④ (B) – (C) – (A)
⑤ (C) – (B) – (A)

4 Write T if the statement is true or F if it is false.

(1) When a man paid the beard tax, he got a token. ________
(2) Police collected the tax and shaved anyone who did not pay. ________

Words beard ⓜ (턱)수염　pay ⓢ 지불하다　rule ⓜ 규칙; *통치, 지배　powerful ⓗ 강력한　shave ⓢ 면도하다　introduce ⓢ 소개하다; *도입하다　law ⓜ 법, 법률　military ⓗ 군사의　system ⓜ 제도, 체제　tax ⓜ 세금　token ⓜ 표시, 징표　hire ⓢ 고용하다　collect ⓢ 모으다; *징수하다　refuse ⓢ 거부하다　[문제] unusual ⓗ 특이한　influence ⓜ 영향

Review Test

1 단어의 뜻이 바르게 연결되지 않은 것을 고르시오.

① powerful: 강력한 ② military: 군사의 ③ tax: 세금
④ wonder: 궁금해하다 ⑤ sew: 보다

2 다음 단어에 해당하는 영영풀이를 찾아 연결하시오.

1) beard · · ⓐ being pleasant to wear
2) comfortable · · ⓑ hair that grows on a man's face
3) clever · · ⓒ smart and quick at learning

3-4 다음 글을 읽고, 물음에 답하시오.

There is another interesting theory. King Edward VII of England ruled from 1901 to 1910. When he was the Prince of Wales, elegant suits were popular in court. However, 에드워드 7세는 먹는 것을 너무 좋아해서 과체중이었다. He couldn't close the bottom button of his jacket! To show respect to him, people stopped buttoning their bottom button as well. Over time, this has become today's practice for jacket buttons.

3 밑줄 친 buttoning과 쓰임이 다른 것을 고르시오.

① Playing basketball is enjoyable. ② Jane likes reading novels.
③ Dancing makes her feel alive. ④ Andy is cooking in the kitchen.
⑤ My job is teaching English.

서술형 **4** 밑줄 친 우리말과 같은 뜻이 되도록 상자 안의 말을 바르게 배열하시오.

overweight, was, eating, loved, that, he, so much

Edward VII ________________________________

5-6 다음 글을 읽고, 물음에 답하시오.

In the fashion industry, it is sometimes called the "V-stitch." It is made from stretchable material, like the waistband on a pair of shorts. At first, this extra piece of cloth had a practical purpose. Sweatshirts were exercise clothing. People sweat a lot when they exercise, and the sweat makes clothing wet and uncomfortable. The V-stitch had extra material that soaked up sweat and reduced discomfort. In addition, it allowed people to put their head through the collar more easily. Due to improvements in the quality of sportswear, the V-stitch is no longer necessary. But many companies still include the triangle as a classic design feature.

수능유형 **5** V-stitch에 관한 내용과 일치하지 않는 것을 고르시오.

① 신축성 있는 소재로 만들었다.
② 실용적인 목적을 가지고 있었다.
③ 땀을 흡수하여 불쾌함을 줄여주는 역할을 했다.
④ 머리를 칼라 안으로 더 쉽게 집어넣게 해 주었다.
⑤ 현재에는 어느 회사도 쓰지 않는다.

서술형 **6** 다음 질문에 우리말로 답하시오.

Q. Why is the V-stitch no longer necessary?

____

7-8 다음 글을 읽고, 물음에 답하시오.

Have you ever wondered why there are buttons on jacket sleeves? The origin is unclear, but there may be a painful story behind it. The idea may have come from Napoleon. His soldiers often wiped their noses on the sleeves of their jackets. Napoleon didn't like this dirty habit. (A) So he came up with a clever but rather cruel solution. (B) He had metal buttons sewn onto the sleeves. (C) He wanted a way to stop it. Whenever the soldiers tried to wipe their noses with their sleeves, the rough metal scratched their faces.

7 문장 (A)~(C)를 글의 흐름에 알맞게 배열한 것을 고르시오.

① (A) – (B) – (C)
② (B) – (A) – (C)
③ (B) – (C) – (A)
④ (C) – (A) – (B)
⑤ (C) – (B) – (A)

8 다음 영영풀이가 나타내는 단어를 글에서 찾아 쓰시오.

something that a person does regularly and repeatedly

____

환경도 지키고, 스타일도 멋있게!

'친환경'이라는 단어는 다양한 분야에서 사용됩니다. 하지만 빠르게 변화하는 유행과 소비를 부추기는 문화가 자리 잡으면서, 패션 산업은 친환경과 공존하기 어려워 보입니다. 유행이 지난 옷들이 너무 많이 버려지고, 팔리지 않은 제품을 소각하는 관행은 비판을 받아왔습니다. 그러나 최근 패션 업계에도 친환경 바람이 불고 있습니다.

슬로 패션 (Slow Fashion)

'패스트 패션(fast fashion)'이라는 말을 들어본 적이 있나요? 주문을 하면 바로 완성되는 패스트푸드와 마찬가지로, 유행하는 옷을 빠르게 생산하여 저렴하게 판매하는 방식을 가리키는 말이에요. 최첨단 트렌드에 맞는 옷을 빠르게 공급하지만, 그만큼 버려지는 옷이 많아 환경에 문제가 되고 있어요. 이러한 패스트 패션의 반대 개념이 바로 슬로 패션(slow fashion)이에요. 유행을 쫓아가지 않고 오래 입을 수 있는 옷을 지향하며, 환경과 사회에 미치는 악영향을 최소한으로 하는 패션을 의미해요. 슬로 패션은 유행을 따르지 않는 것에 그치지 않고 재활용 소재로 옷을 만들고, 공정 거래를 통해 노동자들의 권익을 보호하는 데에도 노력하고 있습니다.

비건 패션 (Vegan Fashion)

동물성 식재료를 사용하지 않는 비건(vegan) 식단이 있는 것처럼, 패션에도 비건이 존재합니다. 비건 패션은 모피, 가죽, 울 등의 동물성 소재를 사용하지 않고 옷을 만드는 것을 의미하지요. 비건 패션은 동물도 인간과 마찬가지로 감정과 고통을 느끼며, 생명체로서 존중받아야 마땅하다는 가치를 강조합니다. 동물 학대에 대한 인식이 높아지면서, 유명 패션 브랜드들도 모피나 동물의 가죽을 사용하지 않는 제품을 늘리고 있습니다. 세계 4대 패션쇼 중 하나인 런던 패션위크는 2018년부터 패션쇼에서 모피로 만든 옷을 금지했으며, 많은 나라에서 모피 생산을 위한 동물 사육을 금지하고 있습니다.

업사이클링 (Upcycling)

옷은 만드는 과정뿐만 아니라 버려지는 과정에서도 많은 환경오염을 발생시켜요. 티셔츠 한 장을 만드는 과정을 생각해 볼까요? 면화를 재배하려면 많은 물과 살충제가 필요하고, 제작 과정에서는 염료와 표백제가 사용됩니다. 전 세계 폐수의 약 20%는 옷을 만드는 과정에서 발생한다고 해요. 이러한 환경 문제를 해결하기 위해 패션 업계에서도 여러 노력을 기울이고 있어요. 업사이클링 패션은 업그레이드와 리사이클링(재활용)의 합성어로 버려진 제품을 재활용하는 것에 그치지 않고 새로운 제품으로 다시 생산하는 것을 의미해요. 대표적인 예로, 자동차의 방수천과 안전벨트로 가방을 만드는 독일의 프라이탁이라는 브랜드가 있어요.

Section

02

Culture

1 파인애플은 맛있기만 한 게 아니야

2 무시무시한 음력 7월!

3 빗자루를 왜 뛰어넘지?

4 태국 원숭이는 복도 많네!

Section 02

1

Think!
손님을 환영할 때 무엇을 대접하나요?

126 words

In some cultures, the pineapple is considered a symbol of welcoming others. But how did this idea get started?

Europeans first learned about pineapples in 1493. Christopher Columbus was taking his second trip to the Caribbean. His crew found an unusual fruit. The outside was rough like a pinecone. However, the inside was like an apple. They brought the unique fruit back to Europe.

Later, European farmers tried to grow pineapples. However, the environment was not good for growing them. It took almost two hundred years to successfully cultivate pineapples. For this reason, pineapples were very rare, and they became the perfect gift for guests. Hosts used pineapples as decorations or in dishes when guests visited them. This showed how much the hosts valued their guests.

1 글의 제목으로 가장 알맞은 것은?

① The Top Rules for Hosting Guests
② The Tragic History of Pineapples
③ Growing the First Pineapples in Europe
④ Why Europeans Love to Eat Pineapples
⑤ Welcome Your Guests with Pineapples

2 글의 내용과 일치하지 않는 것은?

① 유럽인들은 1493년에 처음으로 파인애플을 알게 되었다.
② 콜럼버스는 카리브해로의 첫 번째 여행에서 파인애플을 발견했다.
③ 콜럼버스와 그의 선원들은 파인애플을 유럽으로 가져왔다.
④ 한때 파인애플은 유럽에서 매우 희귀한 과일이었다.
⑤ 파인애플을 장식으로 사용하기도 했다.

서술형

3 다음 질문에 우리말로 답하시오.

Q: Why did it take two hundred years to successfully grow pineapples?

____

서술형

4 다음 빈칸에 알맞은 단어를 글에서 찾아 쓰시오.

Pineapples became a symbol of __________ others because they were __________ in Europe for a long time.

Words culture 명 문화 consider 동 고려하다; 여기다 symbol 명 상징 European 명 유럽인 형 유럽의 trip 명 여행 unusual 형 특이한 outside 명 겉(면) (↔ inside 명 안(쪽)) pinecone 명 솔방울 unique 형 특이한 environment 명 환경 successfully 부 성공적으로 cultivate 동 경작하다, 재배하다 rare 형 드문 guest 명 손님 host 명 주인, 주최자 동 주최하다 decoration 명 장식 dish 명 요리 value 동 소중하게 생각하다 [문제] tragic 형 비극적인

Section 02

2

Think!
특별히 믿는 미신이나 징크스가 있나요?

120 words

Some Chinese people are superstitious about the seventh month of the *lunar calendar. They believe the gate to the world of the dead opens at that time. That means the spirits of the dead can return to earth. So they call the seventh month the "ghost month."

During this time, Chinese people worry that bad things will happen. (①) So they do not move into a new house or get married. (②) Some people make lots of food for the ghosts. (③) Others burn paper money to give the ghosts comfort. (④) They even have a special "ghost festival" on the fifteenth day of the month. (⑤) On that day, people put paper lights on rivers to help the ghosts find their way back home.

*lunar calendar 음력

1 글의 제목으로 가장 알맞은 것은?

① The Gate to the New World
② Why People Believe in Ghosts
③ A Monthly Tradition in China
④ Be Careful during the Ghost Month
⑤ A Lesson from Chinese Superstition

2 다음 문장이 들어갈 위치로 가장 알맞은 곳은?

Instead, they try to make the ghosts happy.

① ② ③ ④ ⑤

고난도

3 글에 따르면, 중국인들이 음력 7월을 귀신의 달이라고 부르는 이유는?

① 중국에서 숫자 7은 불행을 상징하기 때문에
② 불행한 사고가 가장 많이 발생하는 달이기 때문에
③ 귀신을 목격하는 사람들이 가장 많은 달이기 때문에
④ 귀신이 이승으로 돌아올 수 있는 기간이라고 믿기 때문에
⑤ 귀신들이 각자의 집으로 돌아가는 기간이라고 믿기 때문에

서술형

4 중국인들이 ghost festival에서 강에 종이등을 띄우는 이유를 우리말로 쓰시오.

____

Words

superstitious 형 미신을 믿는 (superstition 명 미신) gate 명 출입문 spirit 명 영혼 return 동 돌아오다[가다] earth 명 지구; *세상, 이승 ghost 명 귀신, 유령 get married 결혼하다 burn 동 (불이) 타오르다; *태우다 paper money 지폐 comfort 명 안락; *위로, 위안 light 명 빛; *등 [문제] monthly 형 매월의 tradition 명 전통 careful 형 주의 깊은 lesson 명 교훈

Section 02

3

Think!
결혼식에서
특별한 이벤트를
본 적이 있나요?

138 words

My friends John and Olivia had a beautiful wedding. They gave rings to each other. That is ⓐ a typical custom. But something surprising happened at the party.

"Let's jump the broom!" the MC said. I had to ask a woman next to me what ⓑ this meant. "They are going to jump over a broom," she said. "It shows that they are husband and wife now!" She said that jumping the broom came from an African American tradition. During the 1800s, marriage was banned among African American slaves. To secretly show their love, slaves jumped over a broom. ⓒ This symbolized sweeping the past away and linking families.

Times have changed, but John and Olivia wanted to keep ⓓ this tradition in their wedding. They even let guests try ⓔ it! I thought that was the best part of their wedding.

Knowledge Bank 미국의 '쌀 던지기(Rice Throwing)' 풍습

할리우드 영화를 보면, 결혼식을 치르고 나오는 신랑과 신부에게 쌀을 뿌리는 모습을 종종 볼 수 있다. 이러한 풍습을 '쌀 던지기'라고 하는데, 이는 이탈리아의 결혼식에서도 볼 수 있다. '쌀 던지기'는 우리나라의 결혼식에서 다산과 행복을 기원하며 신부에게 대추나 밤을 던지는 폐백 풍습과 비슷하다. 하객들은 신랑, 신부에게 쌀을 뿌리며 수많은 쌀알처럼 자식을 많이 낳고 번창하라고 기원해 준다

1 글의 주제로 가장 알맞은 것은?

① a modern wedding custom
② the origin of wedding rings
③ a unique wedding tradition
④ the problems with marriage
⑤ the importance of keeping traditions

2 글의 밑줄 친 ⓐ~ⓔ 중, 가리키는 대상이 나머지 넷과 다른 것은?

① ⓐ ② ⓑ ③ ⓒ ④ ⓓ ⑤ ⓔ

고난도

3 글에 드러난 필자의 태도로 가장 알맞은 것은?

① 비판적인 ② 호의적인
③ 훈계하는 ④ 무관심한
⑤ 부러워하는

4 글의 내용과 일치하면 T, 그렇지 않으면 F를 쓰시오.

(1) 1800년대 아프리카계 미국인 노예들은 결혼할 수 없었다. ________
(2) 빗자루를 넘는 행동은 새집을 깨끗이 하고 가족을 이룬다는 의미이다. ________

Words wedding 명 결혼(식) typical 형 전형적인 custom 명 관습, 풍습 broom 명 빗자루 MC 명 사회자 (master of ceremonies) mean 동 뜻하다, 의미하다 (mean-meant-meant) African American 형 아프리카계 미국인의 marriage 명 결혼 ban 동 금지하다 slave 명 노예 secretly 부 비밀스럽게, 몰래 symbolize 동 상징하다 sweep 동 (빗자루 등으로) 쓸다, 털다 link 동 연결하다, 잇다 [문제] modern 형 현대의 origin 명 기원, 유래 importance 명 중요성

Section 02

4

Think!
Do you know any festivals celebrating animals?

121 words

On the last Sunday of November, there is a big party in Lopburi, Thailand. (a) Chefs prepare fresh fruit, vegetables, and ice cream in front of a temple. (b) The food is served for free. (c) It is difficult to keep food fresh in hot weather. (d) Would you like to join this party? (e) Unfortunately, it is only for the more than 4,000 long-tailed monkeys living in Lopburi!

The people of Lopburi hold the festival to thank the monkeys. The monkeys made Lopburi ______________________. Thousands of people visit the city each year to see the monkeys. The local people also believe that giving food to the monkeys can bring good luck to the town. For these reasons, people set up the buffet for the monkeys.

Knowledge Bank 태국 롭부리(Lopburi)의 원숭이 축제

롭부리는 태국의 수도 방콕에서 약 150km 떨어진 도시이다. 과거에는 긴 역사와 더불어 유서 깊은 사원들로 유명했지만, 오늘날에는 그곳에 살고 있는 수많은 원숭이로 더 유명하다. 이 지역에서 성공한 한 호텔 사업가가 마을에 관광객들을 끌어모아 준 원숭이들에게 감사하는 마음으로 1989년에 이 축제를 시작했다. 원숭이 축제는 이제 롭부리를 대표하는 지역 축제가 되었다.

1 Which sentence does NOT fit in the context among (a)~(e)?

① (a) ② (b) ③ (c) ④ (d) ⑤ (e)

2 Which is the best choice for the blank?

① a famous tourist spot
② a safe area for monkeys
③ a city with many festivals
④ a good place to make a wish
⑤ the cleanest city in the world

고난도

3 Which is NOT true about the monkey festival according to the passage?

① It is held on the last Sunday of November.
② It is held in Lopburi, Thailand.
③ Free food is served in front of the temple.
④ About 4,000 monkeys come from all over the world.
⑤ A buffet is prepared for the monkeys.

서술형

4 Fill in the blanks with the words from the passage.

People of Lopburi give food to monkeys to thank them and to bring __________ __________ to the town.

Words prepare ⓢ(음식을) 준비하다, 마련하다 vegetable ⓜ채소, 야채 in front of ~ 앞에 temple ⓜ사찰, 신전 for free 무료로 join ⓢ참여하다 unfortunately ⓟ불행하게도, 유감스럽게도 thank ⓢ감사하다, 감사를 표하다 local ⓗ지역의, 현지의 good luck 행운 set up ~을 마련하다 buffet ⓜ뷔페 [문제] make a wish 소원을 빌다

Review Test

1 단어의 뜻이 바르게 연결되지 않은 것을 고르시오.

① spirit: 영혼 ② local: 가까운 ③ custom: 관습
④ modern: 현대의 ⑤ unfortunately: 불행하게도

2 다음 밑줄 친 단어와 반대 의미의 단어를 고르시오.

Chewing gum is banned in Singapore.

① meant ② allowed ③ prepared ④ valued ⑤ joined

3-4 다음 글을 읽고, 물음에 답하시오.

Europeans first learned about pineapples in 1493. Christopher Columbus was taking his second trip to the Caribbean. His crew found an unusual fruit. The outside was rough like a pinecone. However, the inside was like an apple. They brought the unique fruit back to Europe. Later, European farmers tried to grow pineapples. However, the environment was not good for growing them. It took almost two hundred years to successfully cultivate pineapples. For this reason, pineapples were very __________, and they became the perfect gift for guests. Hosts used pineapples as decorations or in dishes when guests visited them. 이것은 그 주인이 얼마나 손님을 소중하게 생각하는지 보여줄 수 있었다.

수능유형 **3** 빈칸에 들어갈 말로 가장 적절한 것을 고르시오.

① big ② common ③ rare ④ sour ⑤ colorful

서술형 **4** 밑줄 친 우리말과 같은 뜻이 되도록 상자 안의 말을 바르게 배열하시오.

their guests, how much, valued, the hosts

This showed ______________________________.

5-6 다음 글을 읽고, 물음에 답하시오.

Some Chinese people are superstitious about the seventh month of the *lunar calendar. ⓐ They believe the gate to the world of the dead opens at that time. That means the spirits of the dead can return to earth. So they call the seventh month the "ghost month." During this time, Chinese people worry that bad things will happen. So ⓑ they do not move into a new house or get married. Instead, ⓒ they try to make the ghosts happy. Some people make lots of food for the ghosts. Others burn paper money to give the ghosts comfort. ⓓ They even have a special "ghost festival" on the fifteenth day of the month. On that day, people put paper lights on rivers to help the ghosts find ⓔ their way back home.

*lunar calendar 음력

수능유형 **5** 밑줄 친 ⓐ~ⓔ 중, 가리키는 대상이 나머지 넷과 다른 것을 고르시오.

① ⓐ ② ⓑ ③ ⓒ ④ ⓓ ⑤ ⓔ

서술형 **6** 다음 질문에 우리말로 답하시오.

Q. Why do Chinese people burn paper money?

____

7-8 다음 글을 읽고, 물음에 답하시오.

My friends John and Olivia had a beautiful wedding. They gave rings to each other. That is a typical custom. But something surprising happened at the party. "Let's jump the broom!" the MC said. I had to ask a woman next to me what this meant. "They are going to jump over a broom," she said. (a) "It shows that they are husband and wife now!" (b) She said that jumping the broom came from an African American tradition. (c) John and Olivia's wedding cake was chocolate with vanilla icing, and it tasted amazing. (d) During the 1800s, marriage was banned among African American slaves. (e) To secretly show their love, slaves jumped over a broom. This symbolized sweeping the past away and linking families.

수능유형 **7** (a)~(e) 중, 전체 흐름과 관계없는 문장을 고르시오.

① (a) ② (b) ③ (c) ④ (d) ⑤ (e)

서술형 **8** 다음 빈칸에 알맞은 단어를 글에서 찾아 쓰시오.

At John and Olivia's wedding, they jumped over a(n) ____________. This tradition symbolizes sweeping the past away and linking ____________.

동물에 의한, 동물을 위한 축제

세계 여러 나라에서 우리가 상상도 할 수 없었던 동물 축제가 열립니다. 과거의 악습을 반성하는 축제부터 동물의 경주를 응원하는 축제까지, 세계의 독특한 동물 축제들을 소개합니다.

고양이 축제 카텐스투트(Kattenstoet)

과거 벨기에에서는 고양이가 전염병을 옮기는 주된 원인이라고 믿었습니다. 그래서 사람들은 종탑에서 고양이를 던지는 끔찍한 짓을 저질렀죠. 이후, 고양이에 대한 잘못된 인식이 개선되면서 과거를 반성하기 위해 고양이 축제가 만들어졌어요. 3년 주기로 벨기에의 서부 지역에서 열리는 이 축제에서, 고양이 분장을 한 사람들이 퍼레이드를 하고, 희생된 고양이들을 기리기 위한 행사가 열린다고 합니다.

귀사찬 개더링(Guisachan Gathering)

골든 리트리버는 스코틀랜드의 귀사찬(Guisachan) 지역에서 탄생했어요. 이를 기념하기 위해 스코틀랜드의 한 골든 리트리버 단체가 2000년대 초부터 5년 주기로 행사를 개최하고 있어요. 전 세계 수백 마리의 골든 리트리버와 그의 반려 가족이 귀사찬에 모여 그들의 탄생을 기념합니다. 골든 리트리버와의 산책, 훈련 세미나 등 매년 다양한 행사들이 열려요.

울리 웜 페스티벌(Woolly Worm Festival)

이 축제는 1978년부터 미국의 노스캐롤라이나주에서 매년 10월에 개최되어 왔어요. 과거부터 사람들은 "woolly worm"이라고 불리는 이사벨라 불나방 애벌레의 몸통 색깔을 통해 겨울 날씨를 예측해 왔어요. 이 축제는 그들의 능력을 기념하기 위한 행사들로 구성되어 있는데, 그중 애벌레의 달리기 시합이 가장 큰 주목을 받아요. 승리한 애벌레의 주인은 상금을 받고, 우승한 애벌레에게는 그해의 겨울 날씨를 예측할 수 있는 자격이 주어지지요!

Section

03

Food

1 바나나보다 중요해질지도 몰라!

2 버터가 다 떨어졌다고요? 걱정 마세요!

3 실수가 나쁜 것만은 아니야~

4 식당 인테리어에 이런 비밀이!

Section 03

1

Think!
바나나 나무를 닮은 식물을 본 적 있나요?

138 words

The food crisis around the world is getting worse due to the climate change. Up to 783 million people regularly go hungry. The good news is that there could be a solution. It is a plant called enset.

Enset is a staple food in Ethiopia. It looks like a banana tree and can grow to a height of about 4 to 13 meters. Unlike the fruits of other plants, the fruit of the enset cannot be eaten, but its roots and stems can. They are used to make *porridge and bread.

There are several benefits of enset as ______________________. It grows quickly and can be harvested in any season. The plant does not catch diseases easily. It can also live up to seven years without water! It is possible that enset will feed many people despite worsening climate change.

*porridge 포리지(오트밀 등에 물이나 우유를 부어 걸쭉하게 죽처럼 끓인 음식)

Knowledge Bank 식용 곤충

최근 제시되는 미래 식량으로는 곤충이 있다. 곤충을 사육할 때 소모되는 물과 곡류의 양은 소나 돼지를 사육할 때보다 현저히 적게 들어 매우 효율적이다. 사육 과정에서 배출되는 이산화탄소의 양 또한 훨씬 적기 때문에 환경오염을 줄일 수 있다는 장점이 있다. 단백질 함량이 고기와 비슷해 영양적으로도 미래 식량으로서 손색이 없다. 현재 허가된 국내 식용 곤충으로는 메뚜기, 누에 번데기, 쌍별귀뚜라미 등이 있다.

1 글의 제목으로 가장 알맞은 것은?

① The Dangers of Eating Too Much Enset
② Why Do Some Plants Catch Diseases Easily?
③ Fruits That Look and Taste Similar to Bananas
④ The Main Causes of Hunger Around the World
⑤ Could This Ethiopian Plant Solve World Hunger?

고난도

2 글의 빈칸에 들어갈 말로 가장 알맞은 것은?

① a locally grown crop
② a plant going extinct
③ the food of the future
④ Ethiopia's national dish
⑤ a product sold worldwide

서술형

3 다음 질문에 우리말로 답하시오.

Q: Which part of enset can be eaten?

____

서술형

4 다음 빈칸에 알맞은 단어를 글에서 찾아 쓰시오.

> Enset could stop people from going ________ because it grows quickly, does not catch ________ easily, and can live a long time without ________.

Words crisis (명) 위기 worse (형) 더 나쁜 (worsen (동) 악화되다) climate (명) 기후 up to ~까지 regularly (부) 정기적으로 solution (명) 해결책 plant (명) 식물 staple food 주식 unlike (전) ~와 달리 root (명) 뿌리 stem (명) 줄기 benefit (명) 혜택 quickly (부) 빨리 harvest (동) 수확하다 season (명) 계절 disease (명) 질병 easily (부) 쉽게 despite (전) ~에도 불구하고
[문제] danger (명) 위험 cause (명) 원인 hunger (명) 굶주림, 기아 locally (부) 생산지에서 crop (명) 작물 extinct (형) 멸종된 national (형) 국가의, 전국적인 dish (명) 요리 product (명) 상품, 제품 worldwide (부) 전 세계에

Section 03

2

Think!
버터를 좋아하나요?

125 words

Here is how you can easily make your own butter. First, fill half a jar with heavy cream and shake it for a long time. The cream will start to thicken. Why does this happen? It's because cream is a mixture of milk fat and water. When you shake it, the fat molecules stick together. Eventually, they will form yellow lumps. These lumps are butter. Now place the lumps of butter in a bowl of cold water. Rinse the butter at least two times in this way. Finally, take out the butter and squeeze it until there is no more water. If you don't get all the water out, your butter will quickly go bad. Once you finish squeezing, your homemade butter will be ready!

Knowledge Bank 리코타 치즈 만들기

집에서 손쉽게 치즈를 만들 수도 있다. 우유는 물, 지방, 단백질, 탄수화물 등으로 구성된다. 이 우유에서 단백질을 분리하면 치즈가 된다. 우유가 가진 단백질은 산을 만나면 젤리처럼 탄탄하게 굳는 성질이 있다. 따라서 식초나 레몬즙을 넣고 천천히 저어주면 단백질들이 응고되어 서로 뭉친다. 이것을 거즈에 걸러주면 리코타 치즈가 된다.

1 글의 제목으로 가장 알맞은 것은?

① The Origins of Heavy Cream
② A New Trend in Butter Making
③ The Science Behind Making Cream
④ Why Butter Is Bad for Your Health
⑤ Homemade Butter from Heavy Cream

고난도 서술형

2 글의 밑줄 친 this가 의미하는 내용을 우리말로 쓰시오.

____

3 글의 내용과 일치하면 T, 그렇지 않으면 F를 쓰시오.

(1) You must put the yellow lumps into warm water to make butter. ________
(2) Homemade butter will go bad if you don't squeeze it well. ________

서술형

4 다음 빈칸에 알맞은 단어를 글에서 찾아 쓰시오.

After you __________ the cream, you will have lumps, which are __________.

Words fill (동) 채우다 jar (명) 병 heavy cream 유지가 많은 크림 shake (동) 흔들다 thicken (동) 걸쭉해지다, 짙어지다 mixture (명) 혼합물 fat (명) 지방 molecule (명) 분자 stick together 함께 뭉치다 eventually (부) 결국 form (동) 형성되다 lump (명) 덩어리 place (동) 놓다[두다] bowl (명) 그릇 rinse (동) 씻다 at least 적어도 finally (부) 마침내 take out 꺼내다 squeeze (동) 짜다[쥐다] go bad 썩다, 나빠지다 homemade (형) 집에서 만든, 손수 만든 [문제] origin (명) 기원, 근원

Section 03

3

Think!
요리하다가 실수했던 적이 있나요?

139 words

Some popular foods may have been invented by accident. According to one story, brownies were invented accidentally by a woman in the United States. She was trying to bake a chocolate cake, but she forgot to add baking powder. Baking powder is the ingredient that makes cakes rise. So her cake was __________. She served it to her guests anyway, and they loved it!

Some people say tofu was also invented by mistake. A Chinese man was cooking for his elderly parents. They had trouble chewing their food and could only eat soft food. He made soybean soup, but they complained it was tasteless. So he added salt and cooked the soup for a few more minutes. When it cooled down, it turned into a delicious soybean jelly. His parents loved it, and now tofu is enjoyed around the world.

1 글의 제목으로 가장 알맞은 것은?

① Two Cultures, One Recipe
② Brownies Made from Tofu
③ Chefs Injured in Accidents
④ Best Foods for Old People
⑤ A Pair of Delicious Mistakes

2 글의 빈칸에 들어갈 말로 가장 알맞은 것은?

① dry ② flat ③ soft
④ chewy ⑤ sweet

3 글의 내용과 일치하면 T, 그렇지 않으면 F를 쓰시오.

(1) 손님들은 여자가 만든 초콜릿 케이크를 싫어했다. ________
(2) 남자가 만든 콩 수프가 식자 맛있는 콩 젤리가 되었다. ________

서술형

4 다음 빈칸에 알맞은 단어를 보기에서 골라 쓰시오.

보기	tried	forgot	soft	hard

Brownies were invented when an American woman __________ to add baking powder to a cake. Tofu was invented by a Chinese man trying to make __________ food for his elderly parents.

Words popular 형 인기 있는 invent 동 발명하다 by accident 우연히 (= accidentally) bake 동 굽다 forget 동 잊어버리다 ingredient 명 재료 rise 동 오르다; *(빵·케이크 등이) 부풀다 serve 동 (음식을) 제공하다, 대접하다 tofu 명 두부 by mistake 실수로 elderly 형 나이가 지긋한, 연로한 chew 동 씹다 (chewy 형 쫄깃쫄깃한) soybean 명 콩, 대두 complain 동 불평하다 tasteless 형 맛없는 cool down 식다 [문제] recipe 명 조리법 injure 동 (사고로) 부상을 입히다 a pair of 한 쌍의

Section 03

4

Think!
Which colors make you feel happy?

132 words

Did you know that there are secrets behind the colors used in restaurants?

Red and yellow

Think about the colors inside fast-food restaurants. There are two common colors. (a) Almost all fast-food restaurants use red and yellow. (b) Both are warm colors. (c) Studies show that warm colors make people excited and cause them to eat more! (d) Eating too much fast food can be bad for your health. (e) So fast-food restaurants use these colors to make people eat a lot.

Green

People think that cool colors, such as blue and green, reduce their appetite by making them calm. ___________, green is actually linked to food. People think of green as the color of nature and freshness. This makes it the color of healthy, clean food. So green is used in restaurants that sell fresh, healthy food.

1 Which sentence does NOT fit in the context among (a)~(e)?

① (a) ② (b) ③ (c) ④ (d) ⑤ (e)

2 Which is NOT true according to the passage?

① Fast-food restaurants use a lot of red and yellow.
② Warm colors can make people excited.
③ Cool colors can make people eat more.
④ Green is considered a color of nature.
⑤ Restaurants that serve healthy food use green a lot.

3 Which is the best choice for the blank?

① In short ② Similarly
③ However ④ Moreover
⑤ For example

서술형

4 Fill in the blanks with the words from the passage.

Many fast-food restaurants use __________ __________ because they cause people to eat __________ food.

Words secret 명 비밀 common 형 흔한; *공통의 study 명 공부; *연구 excited 형 들뜬, 흥분한 cause 동 야기하다 reduce 동 줄이다 appetite 명 식욕 calm 형 차분한 actually 부 실제로는, 사실은 link 동 연결하다 think of A as B A를 B로 생각하다[여기다] nature 명 자연 freshness 명 신선함 (fresh 형 신선한) healthy 형 건강한; *건강에 좋은

Review Test

1 단어의 뜻이 바르게 연결되지 않은 것을 고르시오.

① fill: 인지하다 ② invent: 발명하다 ③ place: 놓다 ④ origin: 기원 ⑤ squeeze: 짜다

2 다음 영영풀이에 해당하는 단어를 보기에서 골라 쓰시오.

보기 | shake serve calm popular

1) to give food or drink to someone ____________

2) not upset, disturbed, or excited ____________

3-4 다음 글을 읽고, 물음에 답하시오.

Unlike the fruits of other plants, the fruit of the enset cannot be eaten, but its roots and stems can. They are used to make *porridge and bread. There are several benefits of enset as the food of the future. It grows quickly and can be harvested in any season. The plant does not catch diseases easily. It can also live up to seven years without water! <u>악화되고 있는 기후 변화에도 불구하고 엔셋은 많은 사람들을 먹여 살릴 가능성이 있다.</u>

*porridge 포리지(오트밀 등에 물이나 우유를 부어 걸쭉하게 죽처럼 끓인 음식)

수능유형 **3** 미래 식량으로서 엔셋의 이점에 관한 내용과 일치하지 않는 것을 고르시오.

① 빨리 자란다.
② 어떤 계절에도 수확할 수 있다.
③ 어느 지역에서나 쉽게 재배할 수 있다.
④ 쉽게 병에 걸리지 않는다.
⑤ 물 없이도 7년까지 살 수 있다.

서술형 **4** 밑줄 친 우리말과 같은 뜻이 되도록 상자 안의 말을 바르게 배열하시오.

many people, is, that, feed, it, possible, enset, will

______________________________ despite worsening climate change.

5-6 다음 글을 읽고, 물음에 답하시오.

According to one story, brownies were invented accidentally by a woman in the United States. She was trying to bake a chocolate cake, but she forgot to add baking powder. Baking powder is the ingredient that makes cakes rise. So her cake was flat. She served it to her guests anyway, and they loved it!

Some people say tofu was also invented by mistake. A Chinese man was cooking for his elderly parents. They had trouble chewing their food and could only eat soft food. He made soybean soup, but they complained ⓐ it was tasteless. So he added salt and cooked ⓑ the soup for a few more minutes. When ⓒ it cooled down, ⓓ it turned into a delicious soybean jelly. His parents loved ⓔ it, and now tofu is enjoyed around the world.

수능유형 **5** 밑줄 친 ⓐ~ⓔ 중, 가리키는 대상이 나머지 넷과 다른 것을 고르시오.

① ⓐ ② ⓑ ③ ⓒ ④ ⓓ ⑤ ⓔ

6 다음 영영풀이가 나타내는 단어를 글에서 찾아 쓰시오.

one of the items that are used to make a food, product, etc.

____

7-8 다음 글을 읽고, 물음에 답하시오.

Red and yellow

Think about the colors inside fast-food restaurants. There are two common colors. Almost all fast-food restaurants use red and yellow. Both are warm colors. Studies show that warm colors make people excited and cause them to eat more! So fast-food restaurants use these colors to make people eat a lot.

Green

(①) People think that cool colors, such as blue and green, reduce their appetite by making them calm. (②) However, green is actually linked to food. (③) People think of green as the color of nature and freshness. (④) So green is used in restaurants that sell fresh, healthy food. (⑤)

서술형 **7** 다음 질문에 우리말로 답하시오.

Q. Why do fast-food restaurants use warm colors?

____

수능유형 **8** 다음 문장이 들어갈 위치로 가장 알맞은 곳을 고르시오.

This makes it the color of healthy, clean food.

① ② ③ ④ ⑤

아주 맛있는 실수

여러분이 좋아하는 음식이 실수로 만들어진 음식이라면 믿으실 건가요? 우연히 탄생한 음식들을 알아봅시다.

쫄면

여름철 냉면과 함께 별미로 손꼽히는 쫄면! 이 쫄면이 냉면 제조 과정에서 우연히 탄생했다는 사실을 아시나요? 1970년, 인천에 냉면용 면을 판매하는 한 가게가 있었습니다. 어느 날 직원의 실수로 두꺼운 틀로 면을 뽑게 되었는데, 만들어진 면은 칼국수 면처럼 두툼했고 식감은 질겼지요. 그 직원은 면을 버리기가 아까워 가까운 분식집에 가져다가 비빔국수를 만들어 달라고 했어요. 그런데 이게 웬걸! 그 국수는 의외로 맛이 좋고 면발도 매우 쫄깃했어요. 이를 본 분식집 주인은 두꺼운 면을 매운 양념에 버무려서 '쫄면'이라는 이름으로 팔기 시작했다네요.

떡볶이

떡볶이의 역사는 조선시대까지 거슬러 올라가지만, 우리가 흔히 먹는 매콤한 고추장 떡볶이는 비교적 그 역사가 짧아요. 고추장 떡볶이에 관한 유래는 여러 가지가 있는데 한 이야기는 1950년대로 거슬러 올라갑니다. 한 할머니가 짜장면을 먹다가 실수로 떡을 짜장면 그릇에 빠뜨렸어요. 할머니는 그 떡을 먹어 보았는데, 생각보다 그 맛이 좋았다고 해요. 여기에 칼칼한 고추장을 첨가하면 더 맛있을 것 같아 개발했고 그것이 지금 우리가 먹는 고추장 떡볶이가 되었다고 합니다.

대패 삼겹살

대패 삼겹살은 우리에게 너무도 유명한 요리 연구가인 백종원 씨에 의해 탄생했습니다. 어느 날 그는 고기를 썰기 위한 기계를 사러 갔다가 실수로 햄을 써는 기계를 사오게 됩니다. 어쩔 수 없이 햄 써는 기계로 삼겹살을 썰어 팔았는데, 손님들의 반응이 의외로 아주 좋았던 것이지요. 손님들이 고기의 모양이 마치 대팻밥처럼 생겼다고 하여 '대패' 삼겹살이라는 이름이 탄생하게 되었습니다.

Section

04

Nature & Environment

1 4초면 충분해요
2 어질어질 꽃 냄새
3 무지개색으로 빛나는 해변
4 친환경 도시, 쿠리치바

Section 04

1

Think!
펭귄은 잠을 어떻게 잘까요?

135 words

Chinstrap penguins live in Antarctica. Their name comes from the thin black line that runs under their chin. These animals survive in Antarctica's difficult conditions with an unusual sleep pattern. They sleep for very short periods, about four seconds. This is called microsleep. Chinstraps have more than 10,000 microsleeps each day. These add up to around 11 hours of sleep. The penguins do this because a long, deep sleep could be ____________.

After the chinstrap penguins lay their eggs, one parent goes hunting for food. The other parent must protect the eggs or babies at all times. This is because birds called brown *skuas want to eat them. However, it is not easy to be awake for 24 hours a day. So, chinstrap penguins need microsleep. They use it to keep their eggs and babies safe.

*skua 도둑갈매기

Knowledge Bank
도둑갈매기
'스쿠아(Skua)'라고 불리는 도둑갈매기는 남극의 포식자다. 천적이 없기 때문에 번식력이 뛰어나다. 먹이로 펭귄의 알을 훔치거나 갓 태어난 새끼 펭귄을 사냥한다. 겁이 없기 때문에 사람을 무서워하지 않으며 매우 영리해 사람의 얼굴도 구별할 줄 안다고 한다.

1 글의 제목으로 가장 알맞은 것은?

① How Animals Get Their Names
② Do Penguins Sleep in the Daytime?
③ The Dangers of Living in Antarctica
④ Why Animals Sleep Longer in Winter
⑤ A Strange Sleep Pattern for Species Survival

2 글의 빈칸에 들어갈 말로 가장 알맞은 것은?

① secure ② healthy ③ important
④ dangerous ⑤ uncomfortable

✧✩✧
고난도

3 글의 내용과 일치하지 않는 것은?

① 턱끈펭귄의 이름은 그들의 생김새로부터 유래되었다.
② 턱끈펭귄의 마이크로 수면은 약 4초간 지속된다.
③ 턱끈펭귄의 총 수면시간은 약 11시간이다.
④ 턱끈펭귄의 부모는 함께 먹이를 사냥하러 간다.
⑤ 갈색 도둑갈매기는 턱끈펭귄의 알을 잡아먹을 수 있다.

서술형

4 다음 빈칸에 알맞은 단어를 글에서 찾아 쓰시오.

Chinstrap penguins sleep for very ________ periods so that they can ________ their eggs from other birds.

Words Antarctica (명) 남극 대륙 run (동) 달리다; *이어지다 chin (명) 턱 survive (동) 살아남다 (survival (명) 생존) condition (명) 상태; *((복수형)) 환경 unusual (형) 특이한, 드문 period (명) 기간 second (명) (시간 단위인) 초 each day 날마다 add up to 결국 ~되다 lay (동) 놓다; *(알을) 낳다 (lay-laid-laid) protect (동) 보호하다 at all times 항상 awake (형) 깨어 있는 [문제] daytime (명) 낮 (시간) danger (명) 위험 (dangerous (형) 위험한) species (명) (생물 분류의 기본 단위) 종(種) secure (형) 안심하는; *안전한 uncomfortable (형) 불편한

Section 04

2

Think!
꽃을 생각하면 어떤 이미지가 떠오르나요?

134 words

Most people think that flowers are small and pretty, have bright colors, and smell nice. But the titan arum is __________! We can find the titan arum in Indonesia. It is one of the tallest flowers in the world. It can grow up to 10 centimeters in one day! When the titan arum finishes growing, it is usually around 3 meters tall. (a) It does not bloom as often as other flowers. (b) And when it does, it does not have a sweet smell. (c) Some perfumes use sweet flower scents. (d) Actually, it smells terrible! (e) People say that it smells like rotting meat. This is why it is sometimes called the "*corpse flower." To make matters worse, its bad smell can draw some insects like beetles and flies. The insects even lay their eggs in the flower.

*corpse 시체

1 글의 빈칸에 들어갈 말로 가장 알맞은 것은?

① strong ② colorful ③ beautiful
④ common ⑤ different

2 글을 통해 titan arum에 관해 알 수 있는 내용을 모두 고르시오.

① 서식지 ② 꽃말
③ 크기 ④ 색깔
⑤ 개화 시기

3 글의 (a)~(e) 중, 전체 흐름과 관계없는 문장은?

① (a) ② (b) ③ (c) ④ (d) ⑤ (e)

서술형

4 titan arum이 '시체꽃'이라고 불리는 이유를 우리말로 쓰시오.

____

Words bright ⓗ 밝은 grow ⓓ 자라다, 성장하다 up to ~까지 finish ⓓ 끝내다 bloom ⓓ (꽃이) 피다, 꽃을 피우다 sweet ⓗ 달콤한 perfume ⓜ 향수 scent ⓜ 향기 terrible ⓗ 끔찍한 rot ⓓ 썩다 meat ⓜ 고기 to make matters worse 설상가상으로 beetle ⓜ 딱정벌레 fly ⓓ 날다 ⓜ *파리 [문제] colorful ⓗ 형형색색의, 알록달록한 common ⓗ 흔한

Section 04

3

Think!
자연이 만들어 낸
멋진 장소를
알고 있나요?

135 words

Once there was a beach in California that was full of trash. People threw garbage, including cans, plastic, and a lot of glass, onto ⓐ it.

(A) Today, ⓑ this place is known as Glass Beach. Unlike in the past, it is now a beautiful place that many people want to visit!

(B) Surprisingly, *Mother Nature took care of the problem by herself. Over the years, the ocean's waves broke down the glass and made ⓒ it into tiny smooth pieces that look like jewelry. They made the beach sparkle with all the colors of the rainbow!

(C) In 1967, the government stopped people from throwing their trash ⓓ there. Projects were started to clean up ⓔ the area. Most of the trash was removed. However, one big problem remained: how to get rid of the small pieces of glass covering the beach.

*Mother Nature (만물의 어머니 같은) 대자연

1 글의 주제로 가장 알맞은 것은?

① a beach that is in trouble
② how Glass Beach was created
③ famous beaches around the world
④ the government's efforts to clean a beach
⑤ the process of removing garbage from a beach

✦✧✦
고난도

2 단락 (A)~(C)를 글의 흐름에 알맞게 배열한 것은?

① (A) – (B) – (C)
② (A) – (C) – (B)
③ (B) – (A) – (C)
④ (C) – (A) – (B)
⑤ (C) – (B) – (A)

3 글의 밑줄 친 ⓐ~ⓔ 중, 가리키는 대상이 나머지 넷과 다른 것은?

① ⓐ ② ⓑ ③ ⓒ ④ ⓓ ⑤ ⓔ

4 Glass Beach에 관한 글의 내용과 일치하면 T, 그렇지 않으면 F를 쓰시오.

(1) 한때 쓰레기로 가득 차 있었다. ________
(2) 정부에 의해 모든 유리 조각들이 제거되었다. ________

Words be full of ~로 가득 차다 throw ⓢ 던지다, 버리다(throw–threw–thrown) garbage ⓝ 쓰레기 (= trash) including ⓟ ~을 포함하여 be known as ~로 알려져 있다 take care of ~을 돌보다; *~을 처리하다 by oneself 혼자 wave ⓝ 파도 break down ~을 부수다 tiny ⓐ 아주 작은 smooth ⓐ 매끄러운 jewelry ⓝ 보석류 sparkle ⓢ 반짝이다 government ⓝ 정부 clean up ~을 치우다[청소하다] area ⓝ 지역 remove ⓢ 제거하다, 치우다 remain ⓢ 남아 있다 get rid of ~을 처리하다[없애다] cover ⓢ 가리다, 덮다 [문제] process ⓝ 과정

Section 04

4

Think!
How can we make our cities more eco-friendly?

132 words

Curitiba, Brazil, was once a city that was full of poor people and pollution. In 1970, however, everything changed. A team of city workers came together to make Curitiba ________________ in the world. (①) They thought of an idea that could help both poor families and the environment. (②) So, they called this the Green Exchange Program. (③) Poor people gave their trash to the local centers and got food or bus tickets. (④) Children could bring in cans and bottles and receive school supplies in return. (⑤) Through this program, people could get what they needed and clean up the city at the same time. The people also worked together to plant flowers, trees, and grass.

Now Curitiba is cleaner and safer, with 16 parks, 14 forests, and over 1,000 public green spaces for people to enjoy!

Knowledge Bank 쿠리치바의 환경 정책

브라질 남부 파라나(Parana) 주의 수도인 쿠리치바(Curitiba)는 도시 계획을 통해 친환경적인 도시를 조성하고자 했다. 도시를 바람직한 방향으로 발전시키는 동시에, 사회 · 문화 · 교육 · 환경 문제까지도 해결하려고 노력했다. 그 결과 현재 '지구에서 환경적으로 가장 올바르게 사는 도시', '세계에서 가장 혁신적인 도시' 등으로 평가받고 있다. 쿠리치바의 도시 계획은 세계의 여러 도시에 영향을 미쳤으며, 우리나라의 버스 전용 차선과 광역 버스 정책 등도 쿠리치바의 교통 정책을 모델로 했다.

1 Which is the best title for the passage?

① The Features of Curitiba, Brazil
② Many Tourist Attractions to Visit in Curitiba
③ Why the People of Curitiba Suffer from Poverty
④ Recycling: The Best Way to Protect the Environment
⑤ How Curitiba's People Overcame the City's Problems

2 Which is the best choice for the blank?

① the safest city
② the most exciting city
③ one of the richest cities
④ one of the greenest cities
⑤ the most popular tourist destination

3 Where would the following sentence best fit in?

The idea was to exchange trash for food.

① ② ③ ④ ⑤

서술형

4 Fill in the blanks with the words from the box.

trash	pollution	space	environment

Curitiba
was a city full of poor people and (1) __________

↓

Efforts to become environmentally friendly
– started the Green Exchange Program
– helped both poor people and the (2) __________
– gave people food in exchange for (3) __________
– planted flowers, trees, and grass

↓

became a cleaner and safer city

Words pollution (명) 오염 come together (하나로) 합치다, (함께) 모이다 environment (명) 환경 exchange (명) 교환 (동) 교환하다, 주고받다 bring (동) 가져오다 receive (동) 받다 school supplies 학용품 in return 보상으로, 답례로 plant (동) 심다 grass (명) 풀, 잔디 green (형) 녹색의; 친환경적인 [문제] feature (명) 특징 attraction (명) 끌림; *명소 suffer from ~로 고통받다 poverty (명) 빈곤 overcome (동) 극복하다 destination (명) 목적지 in exchange for ~와 교환으로, ~ 대신에

Review Test

1 단어의 뜻이 바르게 연결되지 않은 것을 고르시오.

① remain: 남아 있다 ② bloom: (꽃이) 피다 ③ overcome: 극복하다
④ common: 독특한 ⑤ smooth: 매끄러운

2 다음 밑줄 친 말과 비슷한 의미의 단어를 고르시오.

Please get rid of the bug on my back.

① remove ② throw ③ cover ④ receive ⑤ exchange

3-4 다음 글을 읽고, 물음에 답하시오.

Chinstrap penguins live in Antarctica. Their name comes from the thin black line that runs under their chin. (①) These animals survive in Antarctica's difficult conditions with an unusual sleep pattern. (②) They sleep for very short periods, about four seconds. (③) Chinstraps have more than 10,000 microsleeps each day. (④) These add up to around 11 hours of sleep. (⑤) The penguins do this because a long, deep sleep could be dangerous. After the chinstrap penguins lay their eggs, one parent goes hunting for food. The other parent must protect the eggs or babies at all times. This is because birds called brown *skuas want to eat them. However, it is not easy to be awake for 24 hours a day. So, chinstrap penguins need microsleep. They use it to keep their eggs and babies safe.

*skua 도둑갈매기

수능유형 **3** 다음 문장이 들어갈 위치로 가장 알맞은 곳을 고르시오.

This is called microsleep.

① ② ③ ④ ⑤

서술형 **4** 밑줄 친 it이 가리키는 것을 글에서 찾아 쓰시오.

____

5-6 다음 글을 읽고, 물음에 답하시오.

We can find the titan arum in Indonesia. 그것은 세계에서 가장 키가 큰 꽃들 중 하나이다. It can grow up to 10 centimeters in one day! When the titan arum finishes growing, it is usually around 3 meters tall. It does not bloom as often as other flowers. And when it does, it does not have a sweet smell. Actually, it smells terrible! People say that it smells like rotting meat. This is why it is sometimes called the "*corpse flower." ____________, its bad smell can draw some insects like beetles and flies. The insects even lay their eggs in the flower.

*corpse 시체

서술형 **5** 밑줄 친 우리말과 같은 뜻이 되도록 상자 안의 말을 바르게 배열하시오.

one, the world, flowers, of, the tallest, in

It is ______________________________________.

6 빈칸에 들어갈 말로 가장 알맞은 것을 고르시오.

① In short ② Therefore ③ Instead
④ On the other hand ⑤ To make matters worse

7-8 다음 글을 읽고, 물음에 답하시오.

A team of city workers came together to make Curitiba one of the greenest cities in the world. (A) The idea was to exchange trash for food. (B) They thought of an idea that could help both poor families and the environment. (C) So, they called this the Green Exchange Program. Poor people gave their trash to the local centers and got food or bus tickets. Children could bring in cans and bottles and receive school supplies in return. Through this program, people could get what they needed and clean up the city at the same time. The people also worked together to plant flowers, trees, and grass. Now Curitiba is cleaner and safer!

7 문장 (A)~(C)를 글의 흐름에 알맞게 배열한 것을 고르시오.

① (A) – (C) – (B) ② (B) – (A) – (C) ③ (B) – (C) – (A)
④ (C) – (A) – (B) ⑤ (C) – (B) – (A)

서술형 **8** 다음 빈칸에 알맞은 표현을 글에서 찾아 쓰시오.

In the Green Exchange Program, children gave cans and bottles and received ____________ ____________.

독특한 자세로 잠을 자는 동물들

여러분은 어떤 자세로 잠을 자나요? 독특한 자세로 자는 동물들을 소개합니다.

큰 군함조

최대 길이가 2.3m에 이르고, 시속 400km의 속도를 자랑하며 날아다니는 큰 새는 무엇일까요? 그것은 바로 큰군함조입니다. 큰군함조는 열흘이 넘는 기간 동안 쉬지 않고 수천 킬로미터를 날 수 있어요. 그 비결은 바로 그들의 수면 방법에 있답니다! 큰군함조의 뇌는 한쪽만 잠을 자고 나머지 한쪽은 깨어 있을 수 있어요. 그래서 잠을 자면서 비행을 할 수 있습니다. 그들은 한 번에 약 10초씩, 하루에 약 42분을 잡니다.

해달

해달은 인간만큼 센스가 넘치는 동물입니다. 그들은 물에 등을 대고 누워 둥둥 떠서 잠을 자는데, 자는 동안 조류에 떠내려가지 않기 위한 그들만의 특별한 습관이 있어요. 바로 수면 위에 있는 해초를 몸에 두르고 자는 것이죠. 또 하나의 기발하고 귀여운 해달만의 수면법이 있는데요. 다른 해달과 손을 잡고 자는 것이에요. 특히 새끼 해달은 엄마, 아빠의 배 위에 누워서 잠을 청하기도 한답니다!

홍학

홍학은 보통 한 쪽 다리로만 서 있습니다. 그런데 잘 때도 한 쪽 다리로 서 있는다는 사실, 알고 있나요? 우리가 보기엔 불편해 보일지라도, 홍학은 이 자세가 오히려 편하답니다! 홍학은 두 발을 땅에 딛고 있을 때보다 한 쪽 다리로 잠을 잘 때 더 안정적인 자세를 취할 수 있어요. 근육도 더 적게 사용한다고 하네요. 또한, 홍학의 허벅지는 다리와 수평적인 구조로 되어 있기 때문에, 허벅지가 의자의 역할을 한답니다!

Section

05

Psychology

Section 05

1

Think!
항상 정확한 일정을 세우나요?

129 words

According to Hofstadter's law, a project always takes a longer time than planned. Maybe you have experience with this. For example, you have homework that you think will be easy. You leave a short amount of time to complete it. In the end, you almost miss the deadline. Things like this happen because we believe too strongly in our abilities. We usually think we can work faster than we really can. Also, unexpected events often cause delays.

Of course, this is a problem. However, there are some tips that help you avoid Hofstadter's law. Compare your current plan with past ones to make sure that it is realistic. Also, consider giving yourself extra time to finish your project. This will help you meet your deadline despite any unexpected delays.

1 글의 제목으로 가장 알맞은 것은?

① Better Late Than Never
② Hofstadter's Law: Why Your Plans Fail
③ The Interesting History of Hofstadter's Law
④ Why Hofstadter's Law Might Not Be Useful
⑤ The Benefits of Comparing Yourself to Others

서술형

2 글의 밑줄 친 this가 가리키는 내용을 우리말로 쓰시오.

____

3 글의 내용과 일치하면 T, 그렇지 않으면 F를 쓰시오.

(1) Hofstadter의 법칙은 계획보다 더 빨리 일을 끝내는 것을 말한다. ________
(2) 사람들은 자신의 능력을 믿지 않는 경향이 있다. ________
(3) 현재와 과거의 계획을 비교하는 것은 현실적인 계획 수립에 도움이 된다. ________

서술형

4 다음 빈칸에 알맞은 단어를 보기에서 골라 쓰시오.

보기	project	less	plan	more

Hofstadter's law says that we always need ________ time to finish a ________ than we expect.

Words law 명 법; *법칙 complete 동 완료하다 miss 동 놓치다 deadline 명 기한, 마감 기한 happen 동 발생하다 ability 명 능력 unexpected 형 예기치 않은 event 명 사건, 일 delay 명 지연, 지체 avoid 동 피하다 compare A with B A와 B를 비교하다 current 형 현재의 past 형 지난 realistic 형 현실적인 extra 형 추가의 meet 동 만나다; *(기한 등을) 지키다
[문제] useful 형 유용한 benefit 명 혜택, 이득

Section 05

2

Think!
과소비를 해본 적이 있나요?

127 words

Getting something new can sometimes have an unexpected effect. Suddenly you feel unhappy with your old stuff and want to buy more new things. This is called the Diderot effect. It was named after a French philosopher who was poor for most of his life. (A) When he brought it home, it made his other things look ugly in comparison. (B) One day he was given a beautiful red robe. (C) So he started replacing all his furniture and clothes with new items. This is how the Diderot effect ______________________. One new thing causes you to buy more new things. As a result, you end up with items you don't need. To prevent the Diderot effect, try to purchase things that fit your current style and match what you already have.

Knowledge Bank 드니 디드로(Denis Diderot, 1713~1784)

드니 디드로는 프랑스의 철학가이자 예술비평가, 출판 편집자였다. 계몽주의 철학가였던 그는 1745년 이후 백과사전 집필과 편집을 맡았다. 이 백과사전은 지구 곳곳에 흩어져 있는 지식을 검토하고 모으는 것이 목표였다. 이는 지식 체계를 재정립하였고 이후 프랑스 혁명을 촉발하는 계기가 되었다.

1 글의 주제로 가장 알맞은 것은?

① 유행에 민감한 사람들의 특징
② 한 프랑스 철학자의 검소한 삶
③ 사람들이 선물을 주고받는 이유
④ 오래된 가구의 수명을 늘리는 방법
⑤ 계획에 없었던 소비를 하게 되는 이유

2 문장 (A)~(C)를 글의 흐름에 알맞게 배열한 것은?

① (A) – (B) – (C)　② (A) – (C) – (B)　③ (B) – (A) – (C)
④ (B) – (C) – (A)　⑤ (C) – (A) – (B)

고난도

3 글의 빈칸에 들어갈 말로 가장 알맞은 것은?

① reveals the true reason for giving gifts
② helps you organize all your possessions
③ prevents you from wasting your money
④ makes your current style much trendier
⑤ leads you to a series of unplanned purchases

서술형

4 다음 빈칸에 알맞은 단어를 보기에서 골라 쓰시오.

보기				
	look	replace	buy	fit

When people get something new, they sometimes want to ________ their older stuff. We can prevent this by choosing items that ________ what we already have.

Words stuff 명 것, 물건　French 형 프랑스의　philosopher 명 철학자　in comparison ~와 비교하여　robe 명 예복[가운]　replace 동 대신하다; *바꾸다　end up with 결국 ~하게 되다　prevent 동 막다, 방지하다　purchase 동 구매하다 명 구매　fit 동 (모양·크기가 어떤 사람·사물에) 맞다　match 동 어울리다, (색깔·무늬·스타일이 서로) 맞다　[문제] reveal 동 드러내다[밝히다]　organize 동 준비하다; *정리하다　possession 명 (주로 복수로) 소유물　trendy 형 최신 유행의　lead 동 이끌다　a series of 일련의

Section 05

3

Think!
많은 정보를
한 번에 분석해야
했던 적이 있나요?

155 words

Say the colors of the words in the box below as fast as you can!

REDGREENBLUEPINKYELLOW

Wasn't it easy? Now try this. Again, say the color that each word is written in.

REDGREENBLUEPINKYELLOW

Did you find that more difficult? Did it take longer? Did you say the word instead of the color? If so, you experienced the Stroop Effect. It happens because the brain needs extra time to work when it handles *conflicting information. In this experiment, the word *red* is written in yellow. The word's meaning and its color are conflicting. When there is conflicting information, the brain generally does the more familiar job first. The brain is more familiar with reading words than with naming colors. So words are recognized more quickly than colors. However, the experiment asks you to say the color, not the word. So your brain has to hold on to the wrong answer until the right answer comes. This __________ your brain!

*conflicting 상충되는

1 글에 따르면, 스트룹 효과가 발생하는 이유는?

① 정보의 양과 뇌의 용량 차이 때문에
② 뇌의 반응 속도가 사람마다 다르기 때문에
③ 뇌에 충분한 양의 정보가 전달되지 않았기 때문에
④ 뇌가 새로운 정보를 기존의 정보와 대조하기 때문에
⑤ 뇌가 상충되는 정보를 다룰 때 시간이 더 필요하기 때문에

2 글의 빈칸에 들어갈 말로 가장 알맞은 것은?

① calms ② wakes up
③ speeds up ④ stimulates
⑤ slows down

3 글의 내용과 일치하면 T, 그렇지 않으면 F를 쓰시오.

(1) 뇌는 상충되는 정보 중에 익숙하지 않은 작업을 먼저 수행한다. ________
(2) 뇌는 색 이름을 말하는 것보다는 단어를 읽는 것에 더 익숙하다. ________

고난도

4 다음 중, 스트룹 효과를 일으킬 수 있는 것으로 가장 알맞은 것은?

①

② 빨강 파랑 노랑 보라

③

④

⑤ 빨강 파랑 노랑 보라
파랑 노랑 보라 빨강

Words find ⓓ 찾다; *~라고 생각하다 experience ⓓ 경험하다 handle ⓓ 다루다 experiment ⓜ 실험 meaning ⓜ 의미 generally ⓟ 일반적으로 familiar ⓐ 익숙한, 친숙한 name ⓓ 이름을 지어 주다; *이름을 대다 recognize ⓓ 인식하다 hold on to ~을 고수하다, 계속 보유하다 [문제] calm ⓓ 진정시키다 stimulate ⓓ 자극하다 slow down ~을 늦추다

Section 05

4

Think!
Can you refuse a favor from your friend?

124 words

Your friend asks you to walk to the playground with her. You say you're busy, so she asks you to walk to the corner instead. It's not far, so you agree. When you get there, she asks you to go a little farther. The pattern repeats until you arrive at the playground.

This is the "foot-in-the-door" technique. (①) It is a classic strategy in sales. (②) A long time ago, salespeople went from house to house. (③) To prevent this, salespeople would sometimes put their foot in the way of the door so it couldn't be closed. (④)

The foot-in-the-door technique uses small requests. (⑤) Each new request is not that big. By focusing on getting one small yes after another, this technique often leads to a big yes.

Knowledge Bank 면전에서 문 닫기(door-in-the-face) 기법

본문에서 설명한 문간에 발 들여놓기(foot-in-the-door) 기법과 상반된 것이다. 상대가 수락하기 어려운 요구를 먼저 제시하여 거절을 당한 후, 실제로 원하는 것을 요구하는 것이다. 처음의 요구보다 부담이 적은 요구를 하면, 상대방이 이를 들어줄 가능성이 커진다. 부탁을 한 번 거절했다는 미안함 때문에 상대방이 두 번째 요구에 너그러운 태도를 보이는 경향이 있기 때문이다.

1 Which is the best title for the passage?

① Small Acts Make a Difference
② One Way to Ask for a Big Favor
③ Do Sales Techniques Really Work?
④ Tricks of the Trade: How to Sell Anything
⑤ Avoiding the Foot-in-the-Door Technique

2 Where would the following sentence best fit in?

The people in the homes could simply close the door if they didn't want to buy anything.

① ② ③ ④ ⑤

고난도

3 Which is the best example of the "foot-in-the-door" technique?

① "This is limited edition. There is only one left."
② "If you buy this cake, I'll give you two cookies for free!"
③ "If you find $100 expensive, I can offer this product for $90."
④ "I'm going to be honest with you. I'm so busy now. Please do it for me."
⑤ "Thank you for solving question number one. Would you do the next one?"

서술형

4 Fill in the blanks with one word from the passage.

The "foot-in-the-door" technique can be used to make requests. First you ask for a ________ favor. Then you continue asking for more ________ favors until you get what you want.

Words ask ⑧ 부탁하다, 요청하다 playground ⑲ 운동장, 놀이터 corner ⑲ (길)모퉁이 far ⑱ 먼 ⑨ 멀리 (far-farther-farthest) pattern ⑲ (정형화된) 양식, 패턴 repeat ⑧ 반복되다 arrive ⑧ 도착하다 technique ⑲ 기법 classic ⑱ 전형적인, 대표적인 strategy ⑲ 전략 sale ⑲ ((복수형)) 영업(부) salesperson ⑲ 판매원 prevent ⑧ 막다 request ⑲ 요청 focus on ~에 집중하다 lead to ~로 이어지다 [문제] difference ⑲ 차이 favor ⑲ 부탁 work ⑧ 일하다; *효과가 있다 trick ⑲ 비결, 요령 trade ⑲ 영업, 장사 limited ⑱ 제한된, 한정된 edition ⑲ 판 product ⑲ 상품, 제품 honest ⑱ 정직한, *솔직한 continue ⑧ 계속하다

Review Test

1 단어의 뜻이 바르게 연결되지 않은 것을 고르시오.

① generally: 일반적으로 ② handle: 다루다 ③ experiment: 실험
④ familiar: 익숙한 ⑤ replace: 드러내다

2 다음 밑줄 친 단어와 반대 의미의 단어를 고르시오.

The train arrives in 10 minutes.

① misses ② leaves ③ avoids ④ compares ⑤ matches

3-4 다음 글을 읽고, 물음에 답하시오.

According to Hofstadter's law, a project always takes a longer time than planned. Maybe you have experience with this. ____________, you have homework that you think will be easy. You leave a short amount of time to complete ⓐ it. In the end, you almost miss the deadline. Things like this happen because we believe too strongly in our abilities. We usually think we can work faster than we really can. Also, unexpected events often cause delays. Of course, this is a problem. However, there are some tips that help you avoid Hofstadter's law. Compare your current plan with past ones to make sure that ⓑ it is realistic.

3 빈칸에 들어갈 말로 가장 알맞은 것을 고르시오.

① Instead ② Thus ③ Moreover ④ Therefore ⑤ For example

서술형 **4** 밑줄 친 ⓐ와 ⓑ가 가리키는 것을 글에서 찾아 쓰시오.

ⓐ: ____________________ ⓑ: ____________________

5-6 다음 글을 읽고, 물음에 답하시오.

Getting something new can sometimes have an unexpected effect. (①) Suddenly you feel unhappy with your old stuff and want to buy more new things. (②) This is called the Diderot effect. (③) One day he was given a beautiful red robe. (④) When he brought it home, it made his other things look ugly in comparison. (⑤) So he started replacing all his furniture and clothes with new items. This is how the Diderot effect leads you to a series of unplanned purchases. You end up with items you don't need. To prevent the Diderot effect, <u>당신의 현재 스타일에 맞는 물건들을 구매하려고 노력해라</u> and match what you already have.

수능유형 **5** 다음 문장이 들어갈 위치로 가장 알맞은 곳을 고르시오.

It was named after a French philosopher who was poor for most of his life.

① ② ③ ④ ⑤

서술형 **6** 밑줄 친 우리말과 같은 뜻이 되도록 상자 안의 말을 바르게 배열하시오.

try, style, things, that, your, current, purchase, fit, to

____

7-8 다음 글을 읽고, 물음에 답하시오.

Your friend asks you to walk to the playground with her. You say you're busy, so she asks you to walk to the corner instead. It's not far, so you agree. When you get there, she asks you to go a little farther. The pattern repeats until you arrive at the playground. This is the "foot-in-the-door" technique. It is a classic strategy in sales. A long time ago, salespeople went from house to house. The people in the homes could simply close the door if they didn't want to buy anything. To prevent this, salespeople would sometimes put their foot in the way of the door so it couldn't be closed. The foot-in-the-door technique uses ____________. Each new request is not that big. By focusing on getting one small yes after another, this technique often leads to a big yes.

수능유형 **7** 빈칸에 들어갈 말로 가장 알맞은 것을 고르시오.

① direct orders ② complex tasks ③ large demands
④ small requests ⑤ immediate actions

8 다음 영영풀이가 나타내는 단어를 글에서 원형으로 찾아 쓰시오.

to happen again and again

____

더 좋은 선택은 무엇일까?

우리는 매일매일 선택을 하면서 살아갑니다. 어떤 선택은 너무 어려워서 우리를 큰 고민에 빠뜨립니다. 이러한 고민 중, 선택할 길은 하나로 정해져 있지만 어느 쪽을 선택해도 좋지 못한 결과가 나오는 곤란한 문제를 딜레마(dilemma)라고 하는데요. 심리학에는 흥미로운 딜레마 사례가 있어요. 함께 그 딜레마를 살펴보고 여러분이라면 어떤 결정을 할지 고민해 봅시다.

고슴도치 딜레마

독일의 철학자 쇼펜하우어는 고슴도치가 추운 겨울을 견디기 위해 서로 모여 체온을 유지하려고 할 때의 딜레마를 설명합니다. 고슴도치들은 서로 가까이 다가가면 가시 때문에 서로에게 상처를 내게 되어요. 그렇지만 멀리 떨어져 있으면 추위를 겪게 되지요. 이는 우리 인간관계와도 비슷해요. 사람들은 다른 사람들과 친해지고 싶으면서도 혹시나 다른 사람에게 상처를 받아 갈등을 겪지 않을까 염려하게 됩니다. 우리는 어떻게 해야 남들과 가까이하면서도 상처받지 않을 수 있을까요?

죄수의 딜레마

한 마을에서 함께 도둑질을 한 두 명의 범인이 잡혔습니다. 경찰은 이 죄수들을 각각 다른 방에서 심문하면서 이렇게 말해요. "당신이 범인이라는 증거를 가지고 있다. 범죄에 대해 말하지 않더라도 1년간 감옥에 있어야 한다. 하지만 저지른 죄를 모두 밝히면 당신을 풀어줄 것이고, 공범 혼자 10년 동안 감옥에 있을 것이다. 대신 둘 다 자백하면 5년을 감옥에서 보내게 된다." 결과는 어떻게 될까요?

두 죄수는 각자 자백하는 것이 자신에게 유리한 선택이라고 생각하게 됩니다. 자백하지 않아도 1년을 감옥에서 보내야 하고, 자백하면 바로 풀려나니까요. 결국 두 죄수 모두 자백을 선택하고, 감옥에서 5년을 살게 됩니다. 1년씩만 살고 풀려날 수 있었지만요. 이처럼 나에게는 가장 좋은 선택이 결국은 나뿐만 아니라 상대방에게도 불리한 결과를 가져오는 것을 죄수의 딜레마라고 합니다. 여러분은 어떤 선택을 할 것 같나요?

Section

06

Body & Health

Section 06

1

Think!
종이에 손가락을
베인 적이 있나요?

133 words

Have you ever cut your finger on paper? Paper cuts are usually small. However, the pain they cause is __________. Why do these minor injuries hurt so much?

(a) One reason is that our fingers are very sensitive. (b) There are more pain *receptors in your fingers than in most other parts of your body. (c) So, when you get a paper cut, a lot of pain signals are sent to the brain. (d) The brain is the organ that uses the most energy. (e) As a result, we feel a strong pain. Also, the edge of a piece of paper is uneven. It's hard to see this without a microscope. However, the rough edge will damage your finger more than a sharp knife would.

No matter how small a paper cut is, it will make you say, "Ouch!"

*receptor (인체의) 수용기[감각기]

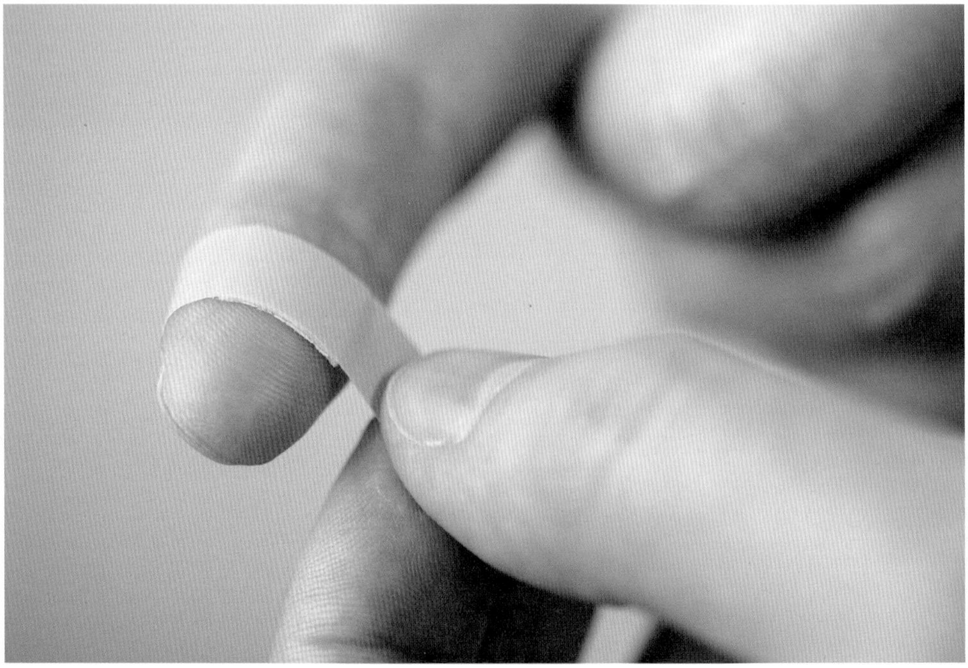

1 글의 제목으로 가장 알맞은 것은?

① How to Avoid Getting Paper Cuts
② The Best Way to Treat a Paper Cut
③ Paper Cuts: More Painful Than They Look!
④ The Surprising Way That the Brain Senses Pain
⑤ Why Children Get More Paper Cuts Than Adults

2 글의 빈칸에 들어갈 말로 가장 알맞은 것은?

① mild ② intense ③ expected
④ dangerous ⑤ preventable

3 글의 (a)~(e) 중, 전체 흐름과 관계없는 문장은?

① (a) ② (b) ③ (c) ④ (d) ⑤ (e)

서술형

4 다음 빈칸에 알맞은 단어를 글에서 찾아 쓰시오.

Problem	Paper cuts (1) __________ a lot.
Reasons	• Our fingers are very (2) __________ because they have many pain receptors. • The edge of a piece of paper is uneven and (3) __________.

Words cut ⑧ 베다 (cut-cut-cut) ⑲ (베인) 상처 pain ⑲ 아픔, 통증 (painful ⑱ 아픈) cause ⑧ ~을 야기하다[초래하다] minor ⑱ 작은[가벼운] injury ⑲ 부상 hurt ⑧ 다치게[아프게]하다 sensitive ⑱ 세심한; *민감한 signal ⑲ 신호 organ ⑲ 기관 edge ⑲ 끝, 가장자리 uneven ⑱ 평평하지 않은; *고르지 않은 microscope ⑲ 현미경 rough ⑱ 고르지 않은, 거친 damage ⑧ 손상을 주다 [문제] treat ⑧ 대하다; *치료하다 sense ⑧ 감지하다 mild ⑱ 가벼운, 순한 intense ⑱ 극심한, 강렬한 expected ⑱ 예상되는 preventable ⑱ 예방할 수 있는

Section 06

2

Think!
녹음된 자신의 목소리를 들어 본 적이 있나요?

119 words

Do you remember the first time you heard a recording of your own voice? You were probably surprised by how it sounded. (①) The reason is that sound travels in waves. (②)

When another person speaks, the sound waves travel through the air. (③) When they reach your ears, you hear them. (④) But when you speak, the sound waves also move through the bones of your head. (⑤) So they reach your ears in two different ways, which makes your voice sound lower and stronger.

_____________, when you hear a recording of your voice, the sound waves are traveling only through the air. So your voice sounds higher and weaker. For this reason, many people don't like to hear recordings of their own voice.

Knowledge Bank 나이가 들면 목소리가 변하는 이유

나이가 들면 피부에 주름이 생기고 근육이 노화하듯 목소리에도 변화가 생긴다. 팔다리의 근육이 가늘어지는 것처럼 성대 근육도 가늘어져 기능이 약해진다. 성대는 하루에 수만 번 열렸다 닫히며 소리를 낸다. 하지만 나이가 들면 성대 근육이 탄력을 잃게 되고, 성대가 제대로 닫히지 않아 목소리가 변하는 것이다.

1 글의 제목으로 가장 알맞은 것은?

① The Real Sound of Your Voice
② How Sound Waves Are Formed
③ Methods for Improving Your Voice
④ The Problem with Recording Sound
⑤ The Amazing Design of the Human Ear

2 다음 문장이 들어갈 위치로 가장 알맞은 곳은?

But that's how your voice sounds to other people.

① ② ③ ④ ⑤

3 글의 빈칸에 들어갈 말로 가장 알맞은 것은?

① In short ② In addition ③ For example
④ As a result ⑤ On the other hand

고난도 서술형

4 다음 빈칸에 알맞은 단어를 글에서 찾아 쓰시오.

How Your Voice Sounds to You

When You Speak to Others	When You Hear a Recording of Your Own Voice
Sound waves travel through the air and your (1) ___________.	Sound waves travel only through the air.
So your voice sounds (2) ___________ and stronger.	So your voice sounds (3) ___________ and weaker.

Words recording 명 녹음(된 것) (record 동 녹음하다) sound 동 (소리가) 들리다 명 소리, 음 travel 동 (빛·소리 등이) 이동하다, 나아가다 wave 명 파동 reach 동 도달하다 bone 명 뼈 strong 형 (목소리가) 강한, 선명한 weak 형 (빛·소리 등이) 약한 [문제] form 동 형성하다 method 명 방법 improve 동 개선하다 design 명 디자인; 설계; *구조

Section 06

3

Think!
하루에 키를 여러 번 재 본 적이 있나요?

120 words

How tall are you? (A) This is because your spine contains 33 small bones that are connected by discs. (B) It may sound strange, but you're actually taller in the morning than you are in the evening. (C) Surprisingly, your answer depends on what time of day you measure yourself. These discs are soft and contain liquid. They allow your spine to easily move in many directions.

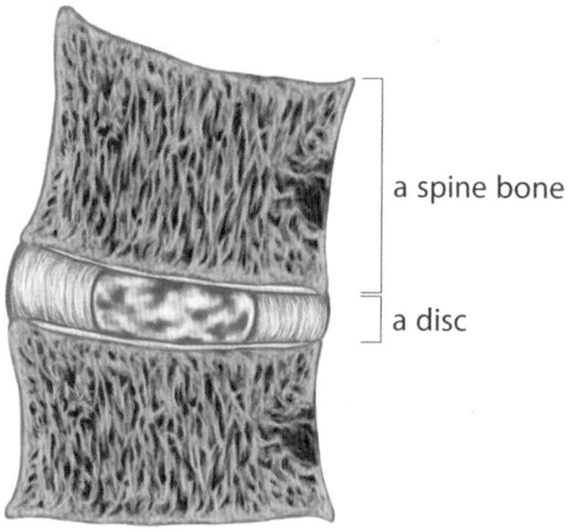

▲ a spine

During the day, gravity pulls the bones of your spine downward. They squeeze the discs and make them flatter. As a result, you become up to one centimeter shorter. When you lie down to sleep, however, gravity no longer causes the bones to squeeze the discs. The discs get __________, and you gain back your lost height.

1 글의 제목으로 가장 알맞은 것은?

① Keeping Your Spine Healthy
② Gravity Can Make Us Shorter
③ Can We Live without Gravity?
④ Important Functions of the Spine
⑤ Why Your Spine Has Many Bones

2 문장 (A)~(C)를 글의 흐름에 알맞게 배열한 것은?

① (A) – (B) – (C)
② (A) – (C) – (B)
③ (B) – (A) – (C)
④ (B) – (C) – (A)
⑤ (C) – (B) – (A)

고난도

3 글의 빈칸에 들어갈 말로 가장 알맞은 것은?

① softer
② harder
③ thicker
④ shorter
⑤ stronger

서술형

4 다음 빈칸에 알맞은 단어를 글에서 찾아 쓰시오.

Discs allow your spine to __________ in many directions. This is because they are soft and contain __________.

Words spine ⓜ 척추 contain ⓓ 포함하다, 함유하다 connect ⓓ 연결하다 disc ⓜ 원반; *(등뼈나 목뼈의) 디스크 depend on ~에 의존하다; *~에 달려 있다 measure ⓓ 측정하다, 재다 soft ⓗ 부드러운; *무른 liquid ⓜ 액체 allow ⓓ 허락하다, 가능하게 하다 direction ⓜ 방향 gravity ⓜ 중력 downward ⓟ 아래쪽으로 squeeze ⓓ 짜내다; *짓누르다 flat ⓗ 납작한 (flat-flatter-flattest) gain ⓓ 얻다 lost ⓗ 잃어버린 height ⓜ 키, 높이 [문제] function ⓜ 기능 thick ⓗ 두꺼운 (thick-thicker-thickest)

Section 06

4

Think!
How do we taste food?

120 words

When you have a stuffed nose, you cannot taste well. Why is this? It is because your nose helps you taste. (①) The *taste buds on your tongue only recognize basic tastes, such as sweet, sour, bitter, and salty. (②) When you eat something, the scent of the food goes into your nose and stimulates the **nerve cells in it. (③) Then these send information about the taste to the brain. (④) However, when your nose is stuffed, the scent cannot __________ the nerve cells because of the ***mucus. (⑤) So you cannot taste the food well.

Then, does holding your nose work when you want to avoid tasting bitter medicine? It does not because we don't use our sense of smell when tasting bitter flavors!

*taste bud 미뢰　**nerve cell 신경 세포
***mucus (코 등에서 나오는) 점액

1 What is the passage mainly about?

① how to cure a stuffed nose
② senses used in tasting food
③ different types of basic tastes
④ the functions of the nerve cells
⑤ the relationship between brain and nose

2 Where would the following sentence best fit in?

The rest of the taste comes from smelling.

① ② ③ ④ ⑤

고난도

3 Which is the best choice for the blank?

① feel ② create
③ reach ④ rebuild
⑤ satisfy

4 Write T if the statement is true or F if it is false.

(1) Taste buds on the tongue cannot recognize a sour taste. ________
(2) You can avoid a bitter taste if you hold your nose. ________

Words stuffed 형 (코가) 막힌 taste 동 맛을 느끼다 명 맛 tongue 명 혀 recognize 동 알아보다, 인식하다 basic 형 기본적인 sweet 형 달콤한 sour 형 신, 시큼한 bitter 형 맛이 쓴 salty 형 짠 scent 명 향기, 냄새 stimulate 동 자극하다 work 동 효과가 있다; 기능하다 avoid 동 피하다 medicine 명 약 flavor 명 맛, 풍미 [문제] rest 명 나머지 rebuild 동 다시 세우다 satisfy 동 만족시키다

Review Test

1 단어의 뜻이 바르게 연결되지 않은 것을 고르시오.

① intense: 극심한 ② organ: 기관 ③ satisfy: 만족시키다
④ flat: 작은 ⑤ edge: 끝, 가장자리

2 다음 영영 뜻풀이에 해당하는 단어를 보기에서 골라 쓰시오.

보기 | connect measure stimulate avoid

1) to find the exact size of something ____________
2) to create a reaction in a body ____________

3-4 다음 글을 읽고, 물음에 답하시오.

Have you ever cut your finger on paper? Paper cuts are usually small. However, the pain they cause is intense. Why do these minor injuries hurt so much? One reason is that our fingers are very sensitive. There are more pain *receptors in your fingers than in most other parts of your body. So, when you get a paper cut, a lot of pain signals are sent to the brain. ____________, we feel a strong pain. Also, the edge of a piece of paper is uneven. It's hard to see this without a microscope. However, the rough edge will damage your finger more than a sharp knife would. *receptor (인체의) 수용기[감각기]

3 빈칸에 들어갈 말로 가장 알맞은 것을 고르시오.

① However ② In addition ③ For example
④ As a result ⑤ On the other hand

서술형 **4** 종이에 베인 손가락의 상처가 많이 아픈 이유 두 가지를 우리말로 쓰시오.

1) ________________________________
2) ________________________________

5-6 다음 글을 읽고, 물음에 답하시오.

Do you remember the first time you heard a recording of your own voice? You were probably surprised by how it sounded. But that's how your voice sounds to other people. The reason is that sound travels in waves. When another person speaks, the sound waves travel through the air. When they reach your ears, you hear them. But when you speak, the sound waves also move through the bones of your head. So they reach your ears in two different ways, 그리고 이것은 당신의 목소리를 더 낮고 더 선명하게 들리게 만든다. On the other hand, when you hear a recording of your voice, the sound waves are traveling only through the air. So your voice sounds higher and weaker.

수능유형 **5** 글의 내용과 일치하지 않는 것을 고르시오.

① 소리는 파동을 통해 이동한다.
② 다른 사람이 말할 때 음파는 공기를 통해 이동한다.
③ 자신이 말할 때 음파는 머리뼈를 통과해 이동한다.
④ 녹음된 자신의 목소리에 대한 음파는 공기를 통해 이동한다.
⑤ 녹음된 자신의 목소리는 더 낮고 더 선명하게 들린다.

서술형 **6** 밑줄 친 우리말과 같은 뜻이 되도록 상자 안의 말을 바르게 배열하시오.

stronger, sound, makes, which, lower, and, your voice

____

7-8 다음 글을 읽고, 물음에 답하시오.

You're actually taller in the morning than you are in the evening. This is because your spine contains 33 small bones that are connected by discs. These discs are soft and contain liquid. They allow your spine to easily move in many directions.

(①) During the day, gravity pulls the bones of your spine downward. (②) They squeeze the discs and make them flatter. (③) When you lie down to sleep, however, gravity no longer causes the bones to squeeze the discs. (④) The discs get thicker, and you gain back your lost height. (⑤)

수능유형 **7** 다음 문장이 들어갈 위치로 가장 알맞은 곳을 고르시오.

As a result, you become up to one centimeter shorter.

① ② ③ ④ ⑤

8 다음 영영풀이가 나타내는 단어를 글에서 찾아 쓰시오.

the distance from the bottom to the top of someone or something

____

신기한 인체 이야기

거짓말을 하면 코가 변한다고?

거짓말을 할 때마다 코가 길어지는 피노키오. 우리는 동화 속의 이야기로만 알고 있는데요. 알고 보면 전혀 불가능한 이야기도 아니라는 사실!

미국의 연구진은 사람이 거짓말을 할 때 카테콜아민이라는 화학 물질이 분비되어 콧속 조직이 팽창하게 된다는 사실을 발견했습니다. 스페인 연구진도 비슷한 연구를 통해 사람들이 거짓말을 할 때 코와 눈 주변의 온도가 올라간다는 사실을 알아냈습니다. 연구진들은 이러한 현상이 체온을 조절하는 두뇌의 뇌섬엽과 관련이 있는 것으로 보고 있습니다. 코 주변의 온도가 올라가면 코가 팽창하고 가려움을 느낄 수 있다고 하네요.

누군가와 얘기하는 도중에 상대방이 자꾸 코를 만지고 있다면, 다시 한번 물어보세요! 혹시 거짓말을 하고 있을지도 모르니까요.

목소리에도 지문이 있대요!

사람의 손가락에 지문이 있듯이 목소리에도 지문이 있다는 사실을 알고 있었나요? 이것을 '성문(소리 지문)'이라고 합니다. 사람마다 성대의 길이, 입안 구조 등이 다르기 때문에 서로 다른 고유의 소리를 갖게 되는 것이죠. 유전자가 같은 일란성 쌍둥이조차도 지문과 마찬가지로 성문이 다르다고 하네요.

이처럼 성문은 사람마다 고유하여 범인을 잡는 데도 활용되고 있습니다. 성문을 분석하면 그 사람의 나이, 성별, 키, 몸무게, 출신 지역 등을 알 수 있기 때문이죠. 또한, 범인이 목소리를 변조한다고 해도 컴퓨터를 통해 원래 목소리로 복원할 수 있다고 합니다. 마음이 한결 든든해지는 것 같지 않나요?

Section

07

Marketing

Section 07

1

Think!
물건을 살 때
가격을 많이
고려하나요?

124 words

Imagine seeing an expensive item in a store. Then you see an item that is similar but cheaper. The cheaper item is still over your budget. But it seems like ________________. This is called the anchoring effect.

The anchoring effect happens because of the way people process information. They usually rely the most on the information that they find first—the "anchor." Once they have an anchor, they compare other things to it.

The anchoring effect can be a powerful tool for selling products. That is because it can change the way customers think. For example, many restaurants place a few expensive dishes at the top of their menu. Customers see these items first. So, the other dishes seem cheap, even if they really aren't.

1 글의 제목으로 가장 알맞은 것은?

① Why People Bargain for a Lower Price
② Why Buying Decisions Are So Difficult
③ The History Behind a Famous Product
④ How Companies Invented a New Product
⑤ How First Experiences Shape Our Opinions of Products

2 글의 빈칸에 들어갈 말로 가장 알맞은 것은?

① a good deal
② a bad choice
③ an entire plan
④ an interesting object
⑤ a higher quality product

3 글의 내용과 일치하면 T, 그렇지 않으면 F를 쓰시오.

(1) 닻 내림 효과에서 나중에 발견한 정보가 닻에 해당된다. ________
(2) 닻 내림 효과는 소비자의 생각을 바꾸는 것에 효과적이다. ________
(3) 비싼 음식이 메뉴판의 가장 밑에 위치하는 것은 닻 내림 효과의 예시이다. ________

서술형

4 다음 빈칸에 알맞은 단어를 글에서 찾아 쓰시오.

People heavily __________ on the information they see __________.
This information is called the __________.

Knowledge Bank 왼쪽 자릿수 효과(Left Digit Effect)

제품 가격에 관한 소비자의 심리 경향 중 하나는 왼쪽 자릿수 효과다. 대부분의 사람들이 숫자를 왼쪽에서 오른쪽으로 읽는 습관이 있다는 점에서 시작된 심리학 용어이다. 숫자가 길어지면 기억하기 힘들어지므로 처음에 읽은 왼쪽 숫자만 기억하게 되는 현상을 뜻한다. 상점에 가면 1,000원보다는 990원, 10,000보다는 9,900원에 판매되는 상품들은 모두 이 효과를 적용한 것이라고 볼 수 있다.

Words imagine ⓢ 상상하다 budget ⓜ 예산, 비용 anchor ⓢ 닻을 내리다 ⓜ 닻 effect ⓜ 효과 process ⓢ 처리하다 information ⓜ 정보 rely on ~에 의존하다 compare A to B A를 B와 비교하다 powerful ⓗ 강력한 tool ⓜ 도구 product ⓜ 상품, 제품 customer ⓜ 고객 dish ⓜ 요리 even if (비록) ~일지라도 [문제] bargain ⓢ 협상[흥정]하다 invent ⓢ 발명하다 experience ⓜ 경험 shape ⓢ (어떤) 모양으로 만들다; *형성하다 choice ⓜ 선택 entire ⓗ 전체의 object ⓜ 물건

Section 07

2

Think!
유행에 민감한 편인가요?

125 words

When a product becomes popular, do you buy it even if you do not need it? If so, you are experiencing the "*bandwagon effect."

The term comes from American parades. (①) In the past, bandwagons would carry a band. (②) When people heard the music, they followed the bandwagon. (③) But most of them did not know why they had joined the crowd. (④)

These days, the term "bandwagon effect" is used to describe the act of people doing something just because others are doing it. (⑤) We can see this in our daily lives. Advertisements that say things like "Ten bottles are sold every second" also use this effect. But you should not buy things just because others do. Make sure you buy items only when you need them!

*bandwagon 퍼레이드의 선두에 서는 악대차

Knowledge Bank **반대되는 개념인 스놉 효과**

다른 사람들의 행동이나 의견을 주관 없이 따르는 편승 효과(bandwagon effect)와 반대되는 속물 효과(snob effect)도 있다. 속물 효과는 많은 사람들이 구매하는 제품이 아닌 차별화된 제품을 구매하려는 심리로, 고가의 제품이나 명품을 선호하는 경향 등이 이에 해당된다.

1 글의 요지로 가장 알맞은 것은?

① 광고에 나온 제품을 사야 한다.
② 대중의 행동을 따르는 것이 현명하다.
③ 많이 팔리는 제품의 품질은 믿을 만하다.
④ 유행을 따라 불필요한 구매를 하면 안 된다.
⑤ 물건을 살 때 다른 사람의 조언이 도움이 된다.

2 다음 문장이 들어갈 위치로 가장 알맞은 곳은?

Soon, more and more people gathered, and they formed a big crowd.

① ② ③ ④ ⑤

고난도

3 다음 중, 편승 효과(bandwagon effect)를 이용한 광고 문구로 가장 알맞은 것은?

① "이 제품의 효과는 과학적으로 입증되었습니다."
② "이 제품으로 당신의 증상은 곧 개선될 것입니다."
③ "열 명 중 아홉 명이 이 제품을 사용하고 있습니다."
④ "이 제품을 쓰면 유명 배우처럼 아름다워질 것입니다."
⑤ "이 제품은 당신에게 특별한 품격을 선물할 것입니다."

서술형

4 다음 빈칸에 알맞은 단어를 보기에서 골라 쓰시오.

보기	situation	crowd	parade	reason

In the past, bandwagons were used in ________s. They carried bands, and people followed them. As the ________ grew bigger, more people often joined it without knowing the ________. Today the term "bandwagon effect" is used when people do something just because other people are doing it.

Words term 명 용어 parade 명 행렬, 거리 행진 carry 동 나르다, 옮기다 band 명 악단, 악대 follow 동 따라가다 join 동 함께 하다[합류하다] crowd 명 군중, 무리 describe 동 묘사하다 daily 형 매일의 advertisement 명 광고 sell 동 팔다 (sell-sold-sold) second 명 초 [문제] gather 동 모이다 form 동 형성[구성]하다 situation 명 상황 reason 명 이유

Section 07

3

Think!

광고를 따라 해보고 싶은 적이 있나요?

143 words

Have you ever seen a TV advertisement that really grabbed your attention? Did it make you feel like the person in it? If so, you might have been influenced by mirror neurons in the brain. When you see someone doing something, your brain's mirror neurons react ______________________. This can even cause you to copy what you have seen. Marketing experts try to use this effect.

For example, imagine there is a TV advertisement for a hamburger. (a) The advertisement may show the model taking a bite of the hamburger. (b) Due to mirror neurons, people who watch the advertisement may start to copy the model. (c) Without even noticing it, they might imitate the model's emotions and facial expressions. (d) People put lots of different things on hamburgers. (e) Viewers may feel like they have bitten the hamburger. As a result, the advertisement makes them want the real thing!

1 글의 제목으로 가장 알맞은 것은?

① The Worst Tricks of Food Brands
② See It, Feel It: How Mirror Neurons Function
③ The Ways Marketing Experts Make Money
④ How Mirror Neurons Can Help Your Memory
⑤ Watching Too Much TV Is Bad for Your Neurons

2 글의 (a)~(e) 중, 전체 흐름과 관계없는 문장은?

① (a) ② (b) ③ (c) ④ (d) ⑤ (e)

고난도

3 글의 빈칸에 들어갈 말로 가장 알맞은 것은?

① as if you were in danger
② like it is a familiar image
③ by focusing on something else
④ as if you were actually doing it yourself
⑤ by figuring out the reason for the action

4 글의 내용과 일치하면 T, 그렇지 않으면 F를 쓰시오.

(1) Mirror neurons only work when you perform an action yourself. ______
(2) Advertisements can use mirror neurons to make viewers want what they see. ______

Knowledge Bank 자이언스 효과

자이언스 효과는 미국의 심리학자 Robert Zajonc(로버트 자이언스)가 정립한 것으로, 처음에는 호감을 느끼지 못했던 대상일지라도 노출이 반복되면 호감도가 증가하는 현상이다. 대체로 사람들은 낯선 대상에 대해 공격적이고 비판적이지만, 대상과의 접촉이 거듭될수록 호의를 갖게 된다고 한다.

Words advertisement 명 광고 grab 동 붙잡다 attention 명 주의, 주목 influence 동 영향을 주다 mirror 명 거울 neuron 명 뉴런 brain 명 뇌 react 동 반응하다 copy 동 복사하다; *따라 하다 expert 명 전문가 take a bite 한 입을 베어 물다 notice 동 알아채다 imitate 동 모방하다 emotion 명 감정 facial expression 얼굴 표정 viewer 명 시청자 bite 동 물다 (bite-bit-bitten) as a result 그 결과 [문제] trick 명 속임수 function 동 기능하다[작용하다]

Section 07

4

Think!

What things do you consider when you choose a restaurant?

128 words

It is Friday night. You enter your favorite steak restaurant. You can smell the delicious food. There is an open kitchen, so you can see the chef cooking. He puts a piece of meat on the hot grill. It makes a sizzling sound and turns brown. All of these things make your mouth water.

Many restaurants know that tasty food is not enough to attract customers. The sights, smells, and sounds of the food all affect a customer's experience. So restaurants use these to get more customers. If the entire experience is good, customers ______________________!

So when you visit your favorite restaurant, do not just taste the food. Pay attention to how the restaurant satisfies your other senses. Keep your eyes, ears, and nose open for a sizzling experience!

1 Which is the best title for the passage?

① How to Be a Good Chef
② The New Trend of Eating Out
③ Some Tips for Opening a Restaurant
④ What Attracts Customers: Delicious Food Isn't Enough
⑤ Tasty Food: The Most Important Thing for Restaurants

고난도

2 Which is the best choice for the blank?

① don't focus on the food
② enjoy the food even more
③ respect the quality of the food
④ know the importance of their senses
⑤ don't think that the taste of the food is important

3 Find the word in the passage which has the given meaning.

the ways our body gets information about the things around us

____

서술형

4 What does the underlined these refer to in the passage? Write it in Korean.

____

Words favorite ⓗ 마음에 드는, 매우 좋아하는 steak ⓜ 스테이크 piece ⓜ 조각; *점 grill ⓜ 그릴, 석쇠 sizzle ⓢ (음식이) 지글거리는 소리를 내다 water ⓢ 물을 주다; *군침이 돌다 tasty ⓗ 맛있는 (= delicious) attract ⓢ 끌다, 유인하다 sight ⓜ 시력; *모습 affect ⓢ 영향을 미치다 satisfy ⓢ 만족시키다 sense ⓜ 감각 [문제] trend ⓜ 동향, 추세 eat out 외식하다 focus on ~에 집중하다 respect ⓢ 존중하다 quality ⓜ 질 importance ⓜ 중요성

Review Test

1 단어의 뜻이 바르게 연결되지 않은 것을 고르시오.

① budget: 예산 ② dish: 요리 ③ customer: 고객
④ describe: 함께 하다 ⑤ situation: 상황

2 다음 단어에 해당하는 영영풀이를 찾아 연결하시오.

1) sizzle · · ⓐ to cause a change in something or someone
2) affect · · ⓑ a specific word or phrase
3) term · · ⓒ to make the sound of frying food

3-4 다음 글을 읽고, 물음에 답하시오.

When a product becomes popular, do you buy it even if you do not need it? If so, you are experiencing the "*bandwagon effect." The term comes from American parades. In the past, bandwagons would carry a band. When people heard the music, they followed the bandwagon. Soon, more and more people gathered, and they formed a big crowd. But most of them did not know why they had joined the crowd. These days, the term "bandwagon effect" is used to describe the act of people doing something just because others are doing it. We can see this in our daily lives. Advertisements that say things <u>like</u> "Ten bottles are sold every second" also use this effect.

*bandwagon 퍼레이드의 선두에 서는 악대차

3 밑줄 친 like와 쓰임이 다른 것을 고르시오.

① He runs <u>like</u> the wind. ② This tastes <u>like</u> chocolate.
③ She looks <u>like</u> her mother. ④ He fought <u>like</u> a lion.
⑤ They <u>like</u> to go hiking on the weekends.

4 글의 내용과 일치하면 T, 그렇지 않으면 F를 쓰시오.

1) 악대차의 악단 소리를 듣고 따라가는 무리의 대부분은 이유도 모른 채 따라다녔다. ______
2) 편승효과는 다른 사람들이 어떤 일을 하기 때문에 자신도 그 일을 하는 현상이다. ______

5-6 다음 글을 읽고, 물음에 답하시오.

Did a TV advertisement make you feel like the person in it? If so, you might have been influenced by mirror neurons in the brain. When you see someone doing something, your brain's mirror neurons react as if you were actually doing it yourself. This can even cause you to copy what you have seen. Marketing experts try to use this effect. For example, imagine there is a TV advertisement for a hamburger. The advertisement may show the model taking a bite of the hamburger. ____________ mirror neurons, people who watch the advertisement may start to copy the model.

5 빈칸에 들어갈 말로 가장 알맞은 것을 고르시오.

① Despite ② Except for ③ Due to ④ Instead of ⑤ Unlike

6 다음 영영풀이가 나타내는 단어를 글에서 찾아 쓰시오.

something that is introduced to the public to help sell a product

____

7-8 다음 글을 읽고, 물음에 답하시오.

It is Friday night. You enter your favorite steak restaurant. (①) You can smell the delicious food. (②) There is an open kitchen, so you can see the chef cooking. (③) He puts a piece of meat on the hot grill. (④) All of these things make your mouth water. (⑤) Many restaurants know that tasty food is not enough to attract customers. The sights, smells, and sounds of the food all affect a customer's experience. So restaurants use these to get more customers. If the entire experience is good, customers enjoy the food even more! So when you visit your favorite restaurant, do not just taste the food. Pay attention to <u>그 식당이 당신의 다른 감각들을 만족시키는 방법</u>. Keep your eyes, ears, and nose open for a sizzling experience!

수능유형 **7** 다음 문장이 들어갈 위치로 가장 알맞은 곳을 고르시오.

It makes a sizzling sound and turns brown.

① ② ③ ④ ⑤

서술형 **8** 밑줄 친 우리말과 같은 뜻이 되도록 상자 안의 말을 바르게 배열하시오.

your other senses, how, satisfies, the restaurant

____

감각을 홀리는 마케팅!

우리는 무언가를 느끼고 기억할 때 감각을 이용해요. 그래서 이 감각은 마케팅에 아주 유용하게 쓰이고 있어요. 우리의 감각을 자극하는 마케팅에는 무엇이 있는지 살펴봅시다.

향기 마케팅

길을 지나가다 어딘가 익숙한 향기를 맡고 과거의 기억이나 경험이 떠오른 적이 있지 않나요? 이것을 프루스트 효과라고 합니다. 향기 마케팅은 바로 이 프루스트 효과에서 발전했어요. 향기를 통해 소비자의 경험과 기억을 브랜드와 연결 짓는 것이죠. 예를 들면, 과거 던킨도너츠는 사람들이 커피의 맛뿐만 아니라 향을 좋아한다는 점을 파악하고 '향기 라디오' 마케팅을 선보였어요. 버스 라디오에서 던킨도너츠 광고가 나오면 버스에 설치된 방향제에서 커피 향기가 분사되도록 말이에요! 사람들은 커피 향을 맡으면서 던킨도너츠를 자연스럽게 떠올리게 되었답니다. 이 캠페인이 진행된 기간 동안 매출이 늘었다고 해요. 여러분은 냄새로 기억하는 브랜드나 상품이 있나요?

징글 마케팅

광고에 나온 음악이나 효과음을 따라 한 적이 있지 않나요? 이 또한 마케팅이 될 수 있습니다! 효과음이나 짧은 멜로디를 통해서 특정 상품 혹은 브랜드를 떠올리도록 하는 것을 징글(jingle) 마케팅이라고 해요. jingle은 '딸랑'이라는 의성어의 의미도 있고 비슷한 소리를 반복하는 것을 의미하기도 하는데요. 라디오, 텔레비전의 CM송을 징글이라고 하기도 합니다. 징글 마케팅은 우리의 청각을 이용해요. 반복되는 특정 소리나 멜로디를 통해 사람들의 기억에 해당 브랜드를 각인시키는 효과를 노렸답니다. OTT 서비스인 넷플릭스를 틀면 '두둥'하는 소리가 나오죠. 우리는 아무런 영상을 보지 않아도 '두둥'하면 자동적으로 넷플릭스를 떠올리게 됩니다. 바로 이러한 경우를 징글 마케팅의 예시로 볼 수 있어요!

Section

08

Origins

1 스카치테이프가 자동차와 관계가 있다고?

2 날씨 아래에 있다는 것은?

3 달을 닮은 빵

4 오른손 좀 확인해 보겠습니다~

Section 08

1

Think!
스카치테이프를
자주 사용하나요?

127 words

In the 1920s, cars with two different colors of paint were popular. Unfortunately, this made life difficult for car painters.

First, they painted the car one color. (①) Next, they glued paper over the parts of the car that had to stay the original color. (②) Finally, they painted the car a second color. (③) When the paper was removed, the car was two colors. (④) So a man named Richard Gurley Drew decided to find a solution. (⑤) Two years later, he invented paper tape that could be removed cleanly and easily.

It was a great success, but Drew wasn't satisfied. He began experimenting with cellophane, a new thin, clear plastic material used for packaging. In 1930, he invented the first clear tape. Today we know his invention as "Scotch tape."

Knowledge Bank 스카치테이프(Scotch tape) 이름의 유래

Richard Drew가 테이프를 개발하는 과정에서 접착제를 얼마나 넣어야 할지 알아보기 위해 실험을 했다. 한 도장공이 Drew가 만든 샘플 테이프를 사용했는데 접착력이 약해 잘 붙지 않자, Drew가 접착제를 아껴 발랐다고 생각해서 Drew를 '인색한 사람(scotch)'이라고 불렀다. 1920-30년대에는 scotch가 '인색한 사람이나 부족한 물건'을 뜻하는 속어로 사용되고 있었다. 이에 영감을 받아 scotch라는 단어를 테이프의 이름으로 쓰게 되었다.

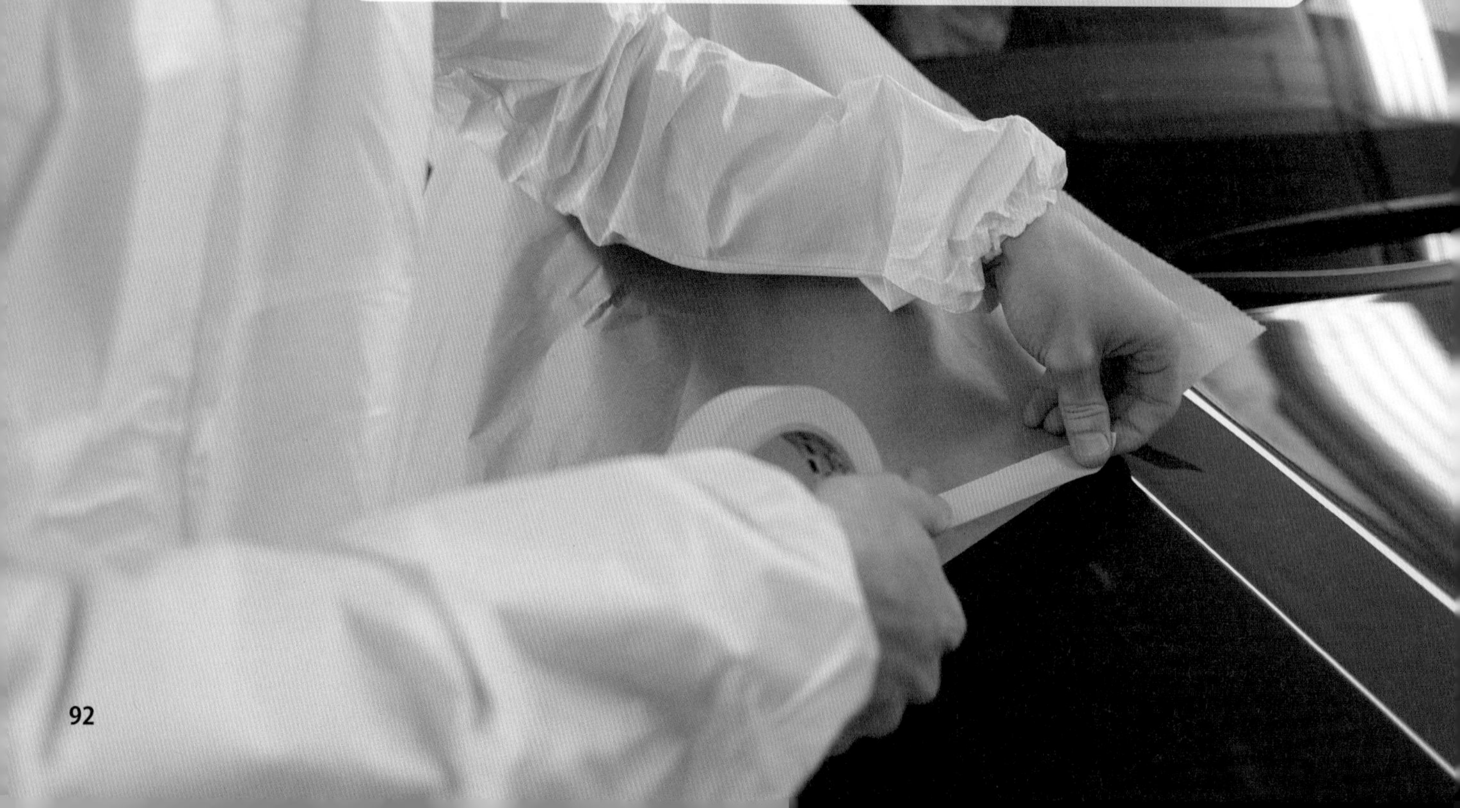

1 글의 주제로 가장 알맞은 것은?

① why cars are usually only one color
② the many different uses of cellophane
③ how Scotch tape came to be invented
④ why glue is so much stronger than tape
⑤ the invention of a new kind of car paint

고난도

2 다음 문장이 들어갈 위치로 가장 알맞은 곳은?

> However, it was nearly impossible to completely remove the glue from the cars.

① ② ③ ④ ⑤

3 글의 내용과 일치하면 T, 그렇지 않으면 F를 쓰시오.

(1) 1920년대에 두 가지 색을 가진 차가 유행했다. ________
(2) Richard Gurley Drew가 발명한 종이테이프는 실패로 돌아갔다. ________

서술형

4 다음 빈칸에 알맞은 단어를 보기에서 골라 쓰시오.

보기	remove	glue	colored	clear

> In the past, it was difficult to paint cars two different colors. So a man invented paper tape that was easy to ________. Later, he also invented ________ tape by experimenting with cellophane.

Words popular 형 인기 있는 unfortunately 부 불행하게도 glue 동 (접착제로) 붙이다 명 접착제 stay 동 유지하다, ~인 채로 있다 original 형 원래의 remove 동 없애다, 제거하다 decide 동 결심하다 solution 명 해결책 success 명 성공 satisfied 형 만족하는 experiment 동 실험하다 cellophane 명 셀로판 clear 형 분명한; *투명한 material 명 재료, 물질 packaging 명 포장, 포장재 invent 동 발명하다 (invention 명 발명품) [문제] use 명 용도 nearly 부 거의 impossible 형 불가능한 completely 부 완전히

Section 08

2

Think!
몸이 좋지 않음을 영어로 어떻게 표현할 수 있을까요?

126 words

If you are feeling a bit unwell, you may say that you're "under the weather." What does our health have to do with the weather? There are several common theories about the origin of this idiom.

One popular theory suggests that it came from the language of sailors. When the weather was bad, the sea would be rough. This made the boat move a lot, which often made sailors ill. They had to go below deck to rest and get better. That meant they were literally under the bad weather taking place above deck.

At first, the idiom was only used to talk about seasickness. As time went on, it took on a __________ meaning. Today, "under the weather" can be used for any type of illness.

✧✧✧ 고난도

1 글의 주제로 가장 알맞은 것은?

① the reason that sailors often get ill
② how bad weather inspired an idiom
③ why it is difficult to learn new idioms
④ the theory behind the trend away from sailing
⑤ how to make yourself feel better when you are sick

2 글의 빈칸에 들어갈 말로 가장 알맞은 것은?

① wider ② narrow ③ hidden
④ strange ⑤ traditional

3 글의 내용과 일치하면 T, 그렇지 않으면 F를 쓰시오.

(1) 배가 움직여 아픈 선원들은 주로 갑판 위에 머물렀다. ________
(2) 오늘날 'under the weather'는 모든 종류의 질병에 쓰일 수 있다. ________

서술형

4 다음 빈칸에 알맞은 단어를 글에서 찾아 쓰시오.

One theory about the origin of the idiom "under the weather" is that it came from __________ who went under the deck of the boat when they were __________.

Words unwell ⓗ 몸이 편치 않은, 아픈 have to do with ~와 관계가 있다 several ⓗ 몇몇의 common ⓗ 흔한 theory ⓜ 이론 origin ⓜ 기원, 유래 idiom ⓜ 관용어 come from ~에서 비롯되다 language ⓜ 언어 sailor ⓜ 선원 (sailing ⓜ 배 타기) ill ⓗ 아픈 (illness ⓜ 병) below ⓟ 아래에 deck ⓜ (배의) 갑판 rest ⓓ 쉬다 get better 좋아지다, 호전되다 mean ⓓ 의미하다 (mean–meant–meant) literally ⓑ 문자 그대로 take place 일어나다 above ⓟ 위에 seasickness ⓜ 뱃멀미 [문제] inspire ⓓ 영감을 주다

Section 08

3

Think!
크루아상을 보면
무엇이 떠오르나요?

152 words

Many people assume that the croissant comes from France. __________, it is actually based on a type of Austrian bread, the kipfel. (a) Both the croissant and the kipfel are shaped like a *crescent moon. (b) When it is viewed from Earth, the moon changes shape night after night.

(c) According to legend, the kipfel was created in 1683 after Austria defeated the **Ottoman Empire in a battle. (d) The Ottomans had surrounded the city of Vienna. (e) Luckily, the city was protected by tall walls. One night, an Austrian baker heard strange sounds beneath his bakery. He realized the Ottomans were digging a tunnel under the city walls! He quickly alerted the Austrian soldiers. The tunnel was destroyed, and the city was saved!

To celebrate, he made some special bread. It was shaped like the moon on the Ottoman Empire's flag. Nearly 100 years later, the kipfel was brought to France, where it became the croissant.

▲ 튀르키예의 국기

*crescent 초승달 모양 **Ottoman Empire 오스만 제국(오늘날의 튀르키예)

Knowledge Bank 도넛의 유래

도넛은 미국인 선장 핸슨 그레고리(Hanson Gregory)가 발명했다. 그가 빵 가운데에 구멍을 뚫은 이유에 대해서는 몇 가지 설이 있다. 배를 운전하는 중에도 빵을 먹을 수 있도록 빵에 구멍을 뚫어 조타석의 키 손잡이에 꽂아 놓고 먹었다는 이야기가 가장 대표적이다. 또한, 빵의 가운데가 잘 익지 않아 동그란 후추통 뚜껑을 사용해 반죽을 잘라냈다는 설도 있고, 구두쇠였던 핸슨이 선원들에게 나눠 줄 빵의 재료를 아끼기 위해 가운데를 뚫었다는 이야기도 전해진다.

1 글의 제목으로 가장 알맞은 것은?

① The Bakers of the Ottoman Empire
② The Origin of Moon-Shaped Bread
③ Why Austrians Won't Eat Croissants
④ Croissants: One Bread, Many Shapes
⑤ A Battle between Two Kinds of Bread

2 글의 빈칸에 들어갈 말로 가장 알맞은 것은?

① However
② Therefore
③ In addition
④ For example
⑤ In other words

3 글의 (a)~(e) 중, 전체 흐름과 관계없는 문장은?

① (a) ② (b) ③ (c) ④ (d) ⑤ (e)

4 글의 내용과 일치하지 않는 것은?

① 비엔나는 높은 벽들로 보호됐다.
② 오스만 제국은 벽을 넘어 침입하려고 했다.
③ 오스트리아는 제빵사 덕분에 오스만 제국을 물리쳤다.
④ 제빵사는 승리를 기념하기 위해 특별한 빵을 만들었다.
⑤ kipfel은 오스만 제국의 국기에 있는 달처럼 생겼다.

Words
assume ⓢ (당연한 것으로) 여기다, 생각하다 **croissant** ⓜ 크루아상 **be based on** ~에 기반을 두다 **shaped** ⓗ ~ 모양[형태]의, 생긴 (**shape** ⓜ 형태, 모양) **view** ⓢ 보다 **legend** ⓜ 전설 **create** ⓢ 만들다 **defeat** ⓢ 패배시키다 **empire** ⓜ 제국 **battle** ⓜ 싸움, 전투 **surround** ⓢ 둘러싸다 **protect** ⓢ 보호하다 **beneath** ⓙ ~ 아래에 **realize** ⓢ 알아채다 **dig** ⓢ 파다 **alert** ⓢ 알리다 **soldier** ⓜ 병사 **destroy** ⓢ 파괴하다 **save** ⓢ 구하다 **celebrate** ⓢ 기념하다 **flag** ⓜ 기, 깃발 **bring** ⓢ 가져오다 (**bring-brought-brought**)

Section 08

4

Think!
Why do you think people shake hands when they meet?

142 words

When two people meet, they often shake hands. Today this seems perfectly normal. But why did people start grabbing each other's hands and shaking them in the first place?

It is believed that it started in ancient times. (A) Many of these paintings show soldiers. (B) Paintings from as early as the fifth century BC show people shaking hands. (C) So some experts think shaking hands was a way of checking for weapons. A person with a weapon in his or her hand couldn't grab another person's hand.

Also, people sometimes hid weapons in their sleeves. If someone did this, moving the person's hand up and down would reveal the weapon. Since people usually carried weapons in their right hands, it was common to always use the right hand in a handshake. Eventually, this became a gesture of peace between two people who were meeting.

1 Which is the best title for the passage?

① The Origin of the Handshake
② Greetings from around the World
③ Finding Weapons in Ancient Times
④ Communicating with Hand Gestures
⑤ Why Do People Use Their Right Hands?

2 Which is the best order of the sentences (A)~(C)?

① (A) – (B) – (C) ② (A) – (C) – (B)
③ (B) – (A) – (C) ④ (B) – (C) – (A)
⑤ (C) – (A) – (B)

서술형

3 Why did people usually shake hands with their right hands? Write it in Korean.

____

서술형

4 Fill in the blanks with the words from the box.

selling	carrying	hidden	powerful

In the past, people shook hands to show that they weren't __________ weapons. The shaking motion was used to reveal __________ weapons.

Words shake hands 악수하다 (shake-shook-shaken) perfectly ㊇ 완전히, 지극히 normal ㊉ 평범한, 정상적인 grab ㊍ 붙잡다 in the first place 우선[먼저]; *처음에 ancient ㊉ 고대의 expert ㊔ 전문가 weapon ㊔ 무기 hide ㊍ 숨기다 (hide-hid-hidden) sleeve ㊔ 소매 reveal ㊍ 밝히다; *드러내 보이다 carry ㊍ 들고 다니다, 지니고 있다 handshake ㊔ 악수 eventually ㊇ 결국 gesture ㊔ 몸짓, 제스처 peace ㊔ 평화 [문제] greeting ㊔ 안부 인사 communicate ㊍ 의사소통을 하다 motion ㊔ 동작

Review Test

1 단어의 뜻이 바르게 연결되지 않은 것을 고르시오.

① original: 원래의 ② invention: 혁신 ③ impossible: 불가능한
④ completely: 완전히 ⑤ alert: 알리다

2 다음 밑줄 친 단어와 반대 의미의 단어를 고르시오.

The dog revealed its teeth and growled at me.

① showed ② used ③ hid ④ protected ⑤ realized

3-4 다음 글을 읽고, 물음에 답하시오.

If you are feeling a bit unwell, you may say that you're "under the weather." What does our health have to do with the weather? There are several common theories about the origin of this idiom. One popular theory suggests that it came from the language of sailors. (A) This made the boat move a lot, which often made sailors ill. (B) When the weather was bad, the sea would be rough. (C) They had to go below deck to rest and get better. That meant they were literally under the bad weather taking place above deck. At first, the idiom was only used to talk about seasickness. As time went on, it took on a wider meaning. Today, "under the weather" can be used for any type of illness.

3 문장 (A)~(C)를 글의 흐름에 알맞게 배열한 것을 고르시오.

① (A) – (B) – (C) ② (A) – (C) – (B) ③ (B) – (A) – (C)
④ (B) – (C) – (A) ⑤ (C) – (B) – (A)

서술형 **4** 다음 질문에 대해 우리말로 답하시오.

Q. Nowadays, what is "under the weather" used to talk about?

____

5-6 다음 글을 읽고, 물음에 답하시오.

According to legend, the kipfel was created in 1683 after Austria defeated the *Ottoman Empire in a battle. The Ottomans had surrounded the city of

Vienna. Luckily, 그 도시는 높은 벽으로 보호되고 있었다. One night, an Austrian baker heard strange sounds beneath his bakery. He realized the Ottomans were digging a tunnel under the city walls! He quickly alerted the Austrian soldiers. The tunnel was destroyed, and the city was saved! __________, he made some special bread. It was shaped like the moon on the Ottoman Empire's flag. Nearly 100 years later, the kipfel was brought to France, where it became the croissant.

*Ottoman Empire 오스만 제국(오늘날의 튀르키예)

서술형 **5** 밑줄 친 우리말과 같은 뜻이 되도록 상자 안의 말을 바르게 배열하시오.

was, tall walls, protected, the city, by

____

수능유형 **6** 빈칸에 들어갈 말로 가장 알맞은 것을 고르시오.

① By accident ② To celebrate ③ By mistake
④ As a punishment ⑤ Out of anger

7-8 다음 글을 읽고, 물음에 답하시오.

Why did people start grabbing each other's hands and shaking them in the first place? (a) It is believed that it started in ancient times. (b) Paintings from as early as the fifth century BC show people shaking hands. (c) Many of these paintings show soldiers. (d) In some cultures, soldiers were paid with salt as their salary. (e) So some experts think shaking hands was a way of checking for weapons. A person with a weapon in his or her hand couldn't grab another person's hand. Also, people sometimes hid weapons in their sleeves. If someone did this, moving the person's hand up and down would reveal the weapon. Since people usually carried weapons in their right hands, it was common to always use the right hand in a handshake. Eventually, this became a gesture of peace between two people who were meeting.

수능유형 **7** (a)~(e) 중, 전체 흐름과 관계없는 문장을 고르시오.

① (a) ② (b) ③ (c) ④ (d) ⑤ (e)

서술형 **8** 밑줄 친 this가 의미하는 것을 우리말로 쓰시오.

____

영화관 삼총사! 어디에서 왔니?

영화관에 들어서면 어디선가 고소~한 냄새가 납니다. 밥을 먹고 왔더라도, 영화관에 그냥 들어가기가 섭섭해 스낵 코너로 향하게 되죠. 영화관 간식의 대표 주자들로는 팝콘과 콜라와 나초가 있는데요. 이 음식들을 언제부터 먹게 된 걸까요?

평화의 상징 팝콘!

팝콘은 원래 인디언의 음식이었습니다. 인디언들이 살고 있던 아메리카 대륙은 날씨가 매우 따뜻해 옥수수가 잘 자랐다고 합니다. 인디언들은 이 옥수수를 가지고 다양한 요리를 해 먹었는데요. 그중 하나가 바로 튀긴 옥수수인 '팝콘'이었습니다. 이후 영국인들이 아메리카 대륙으로 이주해 오면서 팝콘을 알게 됩니다. 인디언들은 영국 이주민들이 팝콘을 좋아하는 것을 보고, 만날 때마다 팝콘을 선물했고 팝콘은 점차 인디언과 영국 이주민 사이의 평화의 징표가 되었다고 하네요.

속이 답답할 땐 콜라로 치료하세요!

속이 더부룩할 때 콜라를 찾게 되지 않나요? 사실 콜라는 음료수가 아니라 약이었다는 사실! 코카콜라를 처음 만든 사람은 약사입니다. 1886년 미국 애틀랜타주에 살던 약사 존 펨버턴(John Pemberton) 은 콜라 열매와 설탕, 카페인을 섞어 코카콜라를 만듭니다. 코카콜라는 소화 불량이나 두통을 치료하는 약으로 판매되었다고 해요. 2년 후, 존은 콜라에 대한 모든 권리를 사업가 아사 캔들러(Asa Candler) 에게 팔게 됩니다. 이후 미국에서 술을 금지하는 금주령이 시행되면서 술 대용으로 콜라가 큰 인기를 끌게 되었다고 하네요.

바삭바삭 나초~

나초 역시 팝콘처럼 옥수수를 이용해 만든 음식입니다. 아메리카 대륙에는 옥수수 가루를 반죽해 납작하게 구운 토르티야 빵이 있었습니다. 1943년 어느 날, 장사를 마친 멕시코의 한 식당에 손님들이 찾아왔습니다. 식당에서 일하던 이그나시오 나초 아나야 (Ignacio Nacho Anaya)는 손님들을 위해 부엌에 남은 재료로 스낵을 만들었습니다. 그는 토르티야를 튀겨 치즈와 함께 손님들에게 대접했어요. 이 튀긴 토르티야가 바로 우리가 알고 있는 바삭바삭한 나초랍니다.

Section

09

Sports & Entertainment

1 세상에 이런 규칙이!

2 환상의 쇼에 당신을 초대합니다

3 럭비 선수들의 댄스 타임~

4 아무나 가질 수 없어요

Section 09

1

Think!
야구 규칙을 잘 알고 있나요?

122 words

The game of baseball is played by two teams of nine players. A player from one team throws a small ball. Then a player from the other team tries to hit it with a bat. Baseball has been popular for more than 150 years. However, some of the rules in the 19th century ____________________.

For example, batters could request the kind of pitch they wanted. They would ask the pitchers to throw the ball either high or low. (A) But in the past they would sometimes ask spectators for help in making decisions. (B) Another difference was the role of the *umpires. (C) Today, they play a **neutral role by enforcing the rules. That doesn't sound very fair, does it? Fortunately, these rules were later changed.

*umpire 심판 **neutral 중립적인

Knowledge Bank 야구 방망이에 관한 과거의 규칙

야구 방망이에도 특별한 규칙이 있었다. 과거 미국의 내셔널 리그에서는 경기 중 득점이 많지 않을 것을 염려해서 야구 방망이의 한쪽 면이 납작한 모양을 갖도록 규칙을 변경했다. 이 덕분에 공은 멀리 날아갔고 점수를 많이 내기 시작했다. 그러나 이 야구 방망이는 잘 쪼개졌고, 그 규칙은 1893년에 폐지되었다.

1 글의 제목으로 가장 알맞은 것은?

① The Rules of Modern Baseball
② Strange Rules from Baseball's Past
③ Baseball: The Most Difficult Game
④ Why Does Baseball Have Umpires?
⑤ Finding a New Way to Play Baseball

고난도

2 글의 빈칸에 들어갈 말로 가장 알맞은 것은?

① were too complex to understand
② were helpful for playing the game fairly
③ were much stricter than the current rules
④ were very different from the rules of today
⑤ were similar to the rules of most other sports

3 문장 (A)~(C)를 글의 흐름에 알맞게 배열한 것은?

① (A) – (C) – (B)　② (B) – (A) – (C)　③ (B) – (C) – (A)
④ (C) – (A) – (B)　⑤ (C) – (B) – (A)

서술형

4 다음 빈칸에 알맞은 단어를 글에서 찾아 쓰시오.

Baseball rules in the 19th century

Who	What they could do
Batters	They could request a low or high (1) ________.
Umpires	They could ask (2) ________ to help them make (3) ________.

Words player 명 선수　throw 동 던지다　hit 동 치다　bat 명 방망이 (batter 명 타자)　request 동 요구하다　pitch 명 경기장; *투구 (pitcher 명 투수)　spectator 명 관중　make a decision 결정하다　difference 명 차이점　role 명 역할　enforce 동 집행[시행]하다　fair 형 공평한 (fairly 부 공평하게)　fortunately 부 운 좋게도　[문제] complex 형 복잡한　helpful 형 도움이 되는　strict 형 엄격한　current 형 현재의　similar 형 유사한

Section 09

2

Think!
지금까지 본 공연 중 가장 환상적인 공연은 무엇이었나요?

138 words

Did you know that there is a theater in Las Vegas that has a giant pool? This is where the show *O* is performed. It was created by a Canadian circus. *O* sounds like *eau*, the French word for water. This name is fitting because the show takes place in and around water.

Eighty-five world-class acrobats, swimmers, and divers use the giant pool in their performances. Gymnasts leap through the air on floating stages. Divers jump into the pool from breathtaking heights. Teams of swimmers move gracefully together underwater. They dance to the music that plays through underwater speakers. There are also many scuba divers in the water at all times. They help the performers use air hoses to breathe beneath the surface of the pool.

If you visit Las Vegas someday, how about seeing this amazing show?

1 글의 제목으로 가장 알맞은 것은?

① French Words Used in English
② An Aquatic Show in Las Vegas
③ How to Communicate Underwater
④ The Most Popular Show in Canada
⑤ Las Vegas: The Wettest Place in the World

고난도

2 *O* 쇼 관한 글의 내용과 일치하지 않는 것은?

① 캐나다 서커스단이 만들었다.
② 세계적인 수준의 곡예사들도 참여한다.
③ 다이버들이 높은 곳에서 물속으로 점프한다.
④ 수중 스피커를 통해서 음악이 재생된다.
⑤ 연기자들은 수중에서는 호흡을 참는다.

3 다음 영영 뜻풀이에 해당하는 단어를 글에서 찾아 쓰시오.

the top layer of an area of water or land

____

서술형

4 쇼에 '*O*'라는 이름이 잘 어울리는 이유를 우리말로 쓰시오.

____

Words giant (형) 거대한 perform (동) 공연하다 (performance (명) 공연 performer (명) 연기자) circus (명) 서커스단, 곡예단 fitting (형) 잘 어울리는, 적합한 take place 개최되다, 일어나다 world-class (형) 세계적 수준의 acrobat (명) 곡예사 gymnast (명) 체조 선수 leap (동) 뛰어오르다 floating (형) 떠 있는 stage (명) 무대 breathtaking (형) 숨이 막히는, 숨이 멎는 듯한 height (명) 높이 gracefully (부) 우아하게 underwater (부) 물속에서 (형) 수중의 hose (명) 호스 breathe (동) 호흡하다 beneath (전) ~ 아래에 surface (명) 표면, 수면 [문제] aquatic (형) 물과 관련된 wet (형) 젖은; *습한

Section 09

3

Think!
스포츠 경기에서 춤을 추는 모습을 본 적이 있나요?

135 words

The All Blacks are New Zealand's national rugby team. Before every international match, they perform a famous war dance. It is known as the *haka*. The *haka* is a tradition of the Maori. The Maori lived in New Zealand before the Europeans arrived. *Haka* dancers chant and slap their bodies while opening their eyes wide and sticking out their tongues.

In the past, the dance was performed to scare the enemy before a battle. It was also used to ask the war god for help. Over time, however, it became more of a social event. Performing the *haka* brought people together. It showed their spirit and strength. Today you can see the *haka* at many events, including weddings and funerals. But the best place to see the *haka* is at an All Blacks rugby match!

1 글의 제목으로 가장 알맞은 것은?

① Traditional Maori-Style Rugby
② A Dance That Became a Sport
③ A War in Ancient New Zealand
④ New Zealand's Traditional Dance
⑤ A Rugby Team's Funny Celebration

2 글에서 하카 춤의 동작으로 언급되지 않은 것은?

① 구호 외치기
② 몸 찰싹 때리기
③ 눈 크게 뜨기
④ 발 구르기
⑤ 혀 내밀기

3 글에서 과거에 하카 춤을 춘 목적으로 언급된 것을 모두 고르시오.

① 적에게 겁을 주기 위해
② 건강과 행복을 기원하기 위해
③ 전쟁의 희생자들을 기리기 위해
④ 럭비 경기의 시작을 알리기 위해
⑤ 전쟁의 신에게 도움을 구하기 위해

서술형

4 다음 빈칸에 알맞은 단어나 표현을 글에서 찾아 쓰시오.

The haka is a traditional Maori ________ ________. Today it is a symbol of their ________ and strength. It is performed by New Zealand's national rugby team.

Words national ⓗ 국가의, 국가적인 international ⓗ 국제적인 match ⓜ 경기 war dance (전쟁 전에 추는) 출전의 춤 chant ⓓ 구호를 외치다 slap ⓓ 철썩 때리다 wide ⓑ 크게 열어[뜨고] stick out ~을 내밀다 tongue ⓜ 혀 scare ⓓ 겁주다 battle ⓜ 전투 more of ~에 더 가까운 것, 오히려 ~ bring together ~을 연합[결속]시키다 spirit ⓜ 정신, 영혼 strength ⓜ 힘 funeral ⓜ 장례식 [문제] ancient ⓗ 고대의, 먼 옛날의 celebration ⓜ 축하 행사 symbol ⓜ 상징

Section 09

4

Think!

Have you ever seen a winning team receiving a trophy?

127 words

The most famous sports trophy in the world is given to the winner of the World Cup soccer tournament every four years. (①)

The first is the Jules Rimet Trophy. (②) It was awarded to the World Cup winner from 1930 to 1970. (③) Each winning team kept the trophy for four years before giving it to the next winner. (④) However, there was a special rule—if a team won the World Cup three times, they could keep the trophy forever. (⑤) In 1970, Brazil won the World Cup for the third time and ______________________.

After this, a new trophy—the *FIFA World Cup Trophy—was designed, and the special rule was changed. Now, no team can keep the FIFA World Cup Trophy. Instead, they get a copy of the trophy.

*FIFA (Federation Internationale de Football Association) 국제축구연맹

Knowledge Bank FIFA컵(FIFA 월드컵 트로피)

FIFA의 공모를 통해 선정된 FIFA컵은 이탈리아의 조각가인 실비오 가자니가(Silvio Gazzaniga)가 디자인했다. 트로피에는 두 명의 선수가 팔로 지구를 떠받치고 있는 모습이 조각되어 있는데, 이는 감격스러운 승리의 순간을 상징한다. 트로피의 밑 부분에는 우승국의 이름을 새길 수 있는 명판이 있다. 이 명판에 우승국의 이름이 그 나라의 언어로 새겨진다. 현재의 FIFA컵에는 총 17개의 칸이 있어 2038년 월드컵 우승국의 이름까지 새겨질 예정이다.

1 Which is the best title for the passage?

① Jules Rimet: Trophy Designer
② The Rule That Defeated Brazil
③ The Two Trophies of a Tournament
④ How Sports Trophies Are Designed
⑤ The Greatest World Cup Champions

2 Where would the following sentence best fit in?

However, there are two different World Cup trophies.

① ② ③ ④ ⑤

고난도

3 Which is the best choice for the blank?

① was given the Jules Rimet Trophy
② was told to change the special rule
③ was unable to win the trophy again
④ was able to get a copy of the trophy
⑤ was given the FIFA World Cup Trophy

4 Write T if the statement is true or F if it is false.

(1) The Jules Rimet Trophy was first awarded in 1930. ________
(2) The FIFA World Cup Trophy belongs to Brazil now. ________

Words trophy ⑲ 트로피 tournament ⑲ 토너먼트 award ⑤ 수여하다 keep ⑤ 가지고 있다, 보유하다 design ⑤ 만들다, 고안하다 copy ⑲ 복제품 [문제] defeat ⑤ 패배시키다 champion ⑲ 챔피언, 우승자 unable ⑱ ~할 수 없는 belong to ~에게 속하다, ~의 소유이다

Review Test

1 다음 밑줄 친 단어와 비슷한 의미의 단어를 고르시오.

I saw a cat <u>leap</u> from a second-floor window.

① slap ② hit ③ request ④ perform ⑤ jump

2 다음 밑줄 친 단어와 반대 의미의 단어를 고르시오.

Let's take a picture in front of that <u>giant</u> statue.

① ancient ② tiny ③ helpful ④ similar ⑤ wet

3-4 다음 글을 읽고, 물음에 답하시오.

The show *O* was created by a Canadian circus. *O* sounds like eau, the French word for water. This name is fitting because the show takes place in and around water. Eighty-five world-class acrobats, swimmers, and divers use a giant pool in their performances. Gymnasts leap through the air on floating stages. Divers jump into the pool from breathtaking heights. Teams of swimmers move gracefully together underwater. They dance to the music that plays through underwater speakers. There are also many scuba divers in the water at all times. <u>그들은 연기자들이 수영장의 수면 아래에서 호흡하기 위해 공기 호스를 사용하는 것을 돕는다.</u>

3 다음 영영풀이가 나타내는 단어를 글에서 찾아 쓰시오.

correct for the situation or purpose

____

서술형 **4** 밑줄 친 우리말과 같은 뜻이 되도록 상자 안의 말을 바르게 배열하시오.

help, the performers, use, they, air hoses

________________________________ to breathe beneath the surface of the pool.

5-6 다음 글을 읽고, 물음에 답하시오.

The *haka* is a tradition of the Maori. The Maori lived in New Zealand before the Europeans arrived. *Haka* dancers chant and slap their bodies while opening their eyes wide and sticking out their tongues. In the past, the dance was performed to scare the enemy before a battle. It was also used to ask the war god for help. Over time, ___________, it became more of a social event. Performing the *haka* brought people together. It showed their spirit and strength.

5 빈칸에 들어갈 말로 가장 알맞은 것을 고르시오.

① thus ② as a result ③ however
④ for example ⑤ in other words

서술형 **6** 다음 질문에 우리말로 답하시오.

Q. What are the two things that the *haka* shows in a social event?

____

7-8 다음 글을 읽고, 물음에 답하시오.

There are two different World Cup trophies. The first is the Jules Rimet Trophy. It was awarded to the World Cup winner from 1930 to 1970. Each winning team kept the trophy for four years before giving it to the next winner. However, there was a special rule—if a team won the World Cup three times, they could keep the trophy forever. In 1970, Brazil won the World Cup for the third time and was given the Jules Rimet Trophy. After this, a new trophy—the *FIFA World Cup Trophy—was designed, and the special rule was changed. Now, no team can keep the FIFA World Cup Trophy. Instead, they get a copy of the trophy.

*FIFA (Federation Internationale de Football Association) 국제축구연맹

수능유형 **7** Jules Rimet Trophy에 관한 글의 내용과 일치하지 않는 것을 고르시오.

① 1930년부터 1970년까지 월드컵 우승팀에게 주어졌다.
② 우승팀은 다음 우승팀에게 넘겨주기 전 4년 동안 가지고 있을 수 있었다.
③ 한 팀이 세 번 우승할 경우, 그 팀이 영원히 보유할 수 있었다.
④ 1970년에 세 번 우승한 브라질 팀이 받았다.
⑤ 새로운 FIFA World Cup Trophy와 디자인이 같다.

서술형 **8** 다음 빈칸에 알맞은 표현을 글에서 찾아 쓰시오.

From 1930 to 1970, the Jules Rimet Trophy was used, and Brazil kept it after they won three times. Now, the FIFA World Cup Trophy is used, and no team can keep it forever. Winners get __________ __________ of the trophy instead.

세계의 이색 축제

축제는 그 나라의 문화와 역사를 고스란히 담고 있는데요. 수많은 나라들만큼 다양하고 흥미로운 축제들이 많이 있습니다. 세계의 이색 축제에는 어떤 것들이 있는지 함께 살펴볼까요?

터키의 메시르 마주누 축제(Mesir Macunu Festival)

터키에는 하늘에서 떨어지는 조청을 잡으면 소원이 이루어진다고 하는 축제가 있다고 하는데요. 바로 터키의 도시 마니사(Manisa)에서 매년 3월에 열리는 '메시르 마주누' 축제입니다. '메시르 마주누'는 41가지 향신료와 허브를 달여서 만든 것으로 우리나라의 조청과 비슷한데요. 500년 전 술탄의 병든 어머니를 낫게 한 신비의 묘약으로 알려져 있습니다. 병에서 나은 술탄의 어머니가 메시르 마주누의 효과에 탄복하여 백성들에게 나누어 주었고, 이를 기념하여 축제가 열리기 시작했습니다. 이 축제는 2012년에 유네스코 인류무형문화유산으로 등재되기도 하였는데요. 하늘에서 떨어지는 메시르 마주누를 손으로 잡으면 1년 안에 원하는 바를 이룰 수 있다고 하니, 기회가 되면 이 축제에 꼭 참여해 보세요!

영국 노팅힐 카니발(Nottinghill Carnival)

노팅힐은 런던의 유명한 관광지로, 영화 <노팅힐>의 주 무대가 된 지역이기도 합니다. 이곳에서 1966년부터 약 50년 넘게 매년 8월에 개최되는 대규모 축제가 있다고 하는데요. 바로 노팅힐 카니발입니다.

노팅힐 카니발은 노팅힐 지역으로 이주한 아프리카계 카리브해인(Afro-Caribbean) 이민자들이 자신들의 문화와 전통을 알리기 위해 시작한 거리 축제입니다. 카리브해 국가의 전통 의상을 입은 참가자들이 하이드파크에서 노팅힐까지 생동감 넘치는 화려한 퍼레이드를 진행한다고 하네요. 춤과 악기 연주, 노래까지 다양한 볼거리들로 가득하다고 하니, 8월에 런던을 방문하게 되면 노팅힐 카니발을 놓치지 마세요!

Section 10
Art

1 비슷하지만 다른 둘
2 모두 진품이 맞아요
3 제가 아는 그 악기가 맞나요?!
4 왜 이런 별명이?

Section 10

1

Think!
바이올린이나
비올라를 연주해
본 적 있나요?

138 words

The violin and the viola are both orchestral *stringed instruments. However, there are a few differences between them. Most violins are around 35 centimeters long. On the other hand, the viola can be 45 centimeters long.

The sounds of the two instruments are also different. The violin has a very high pitch. The viola produces a deeper sound than the violin, but not as deep as the cello. <u>That</u> places the viola in the middle of the stringed instrument family.

The instruments' bows are also different. (a) Violin bows are lighter than bows for violas. (b) Furthermore, the part of the bow that is held in the hand, known as the "frog," is also different. (c) On a violin bow, the frog is pointy. (d) Basically, a violin is made of wood. (e) However, on a viola bow, it has a round shape.

*stringed instruments 현악기

Knowledge Bank 플루트와 클라리넷

바이올린과 비올라처럼 생김새가 비슷한 악기가 있다. 바로 서양의 대표적인 관악기인 플루트와 클라리넷이다. 플루트는 부드러운 고음이 나고, 중간 음역에서는 온화한 소리가 나는 것이 특징이다. 클라리넷은 넓은 음역의 연주가 가능하고 다양한 장르의 음악에 사용되는 것이 특징이다. 두 악기의 가장 큰 차이점은 연주 자세로, 플루트는 가로로 눕혀, 클라리넷은 세로로 세워 연주를 해야 한다.

1 글의 주제로 가장 알맞은 것은?

① 세계에서 가장 큰 악기
② 좋은 악기를 고르는 방법
③ 바이올린과 비올라의 차이점
④ 현악기의 활을 만드는 데 쓰이는 재료
⑤ 오케스트라에서 연주되는 현악기의 종류

서술형

2 글의 밑줄 친 That이 의미하는 것을 우리말로 쓰시오.

____

3 글의 (a)~(e) 중, 전체 흐름과 관계없는 문장은?

① (a) ② (b) ③ (c) ④ (d) ⑤ (e)

4 비올라에 관한 글의 내용과 일치하지 않는 것은?

① 오케스트라에서 연주된다.
② 길이가 45cm에 이르는 것도 있다.
③ 현악기군 중에서도 매우 높은 소리를 낸다.
④ 바이올린 활보다 무거운 활로 연주한다.
⑤ 손에 잡히는 활 부분의 모양이 둥글다.

Words **orchestral** (형) 오케스트라[관현악단]의 **pitch** (명) 경기장; *음의 높이 **family** (명) 가족; *(같은 종류의) 집단, 군 **bow** (명) (바이올린 등을 켜는) 활 **furthermore** (부) 더욱이 **hold** (동) 잡다 (hold-held-held) **known as** ~로 알려진 **pointy** (형) 끝이 뾰족한 **basically** (부) 근본적으로, 기본적으로

Section 10

2

Think!
아래에 있는
모네의 그림들의
특징은 무엇일까요?

123 words

Claude Monet was a famous French painter. Here is an interesting story about his paintings. One day, several people brought paintings to court. Each of them said their painting had been painted by Monet. All of the paintings showed the same scene, but each one was a little different. They wanted the judge to decide which one was really painted by Monet. The judge knew a lot about art. After he looked at the paintings, he said, "They all were!"

Monet painted ______________ at different times of the day to capture the change of light. For example, his most famous works of art show *water lilies in his garden at different times of the day. He made about 250 of these water lily paintings!

*water lily (식물) 수련

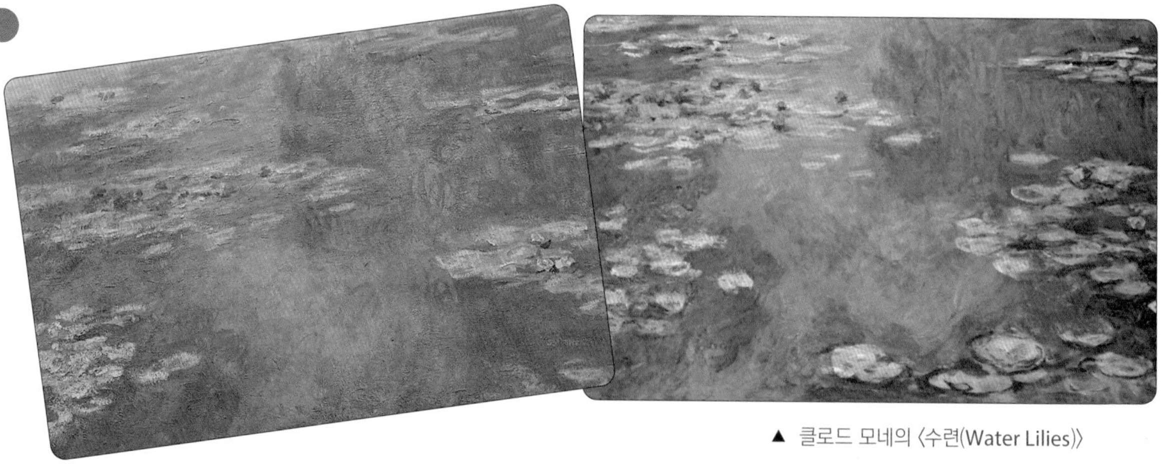

▲ 클로드 모네의 〈수련(Water Lilies)〉

Knowledge Bank 클로드 모네(Claude Monet, 1840–1926)

프랑스의 대표적인 인상파 화가 중 한 명으로, '빛의 화가'라고도 불린다. 이전의 화가들이 사물을 정확하게 묘사하는 데 중점을 둔 데 비해, 모네는 고정된 형태나 색감을 탈피하여 시시각각 변하는 빛에 따라 자신의 눈에 보이는 직관적인 이미지를 중시했다. '인상주의(Impressionism)'라는 말도 그의 작품 〈인상: 해돋이(Impression: Sunrise)〉에서 비롯되었다.

1 글의 제목으로 가장 알맞은 것은?

① A Judge Who Loved Monet's Paintings
② Monet: A Painter Who Loved Water Lilies
③ Monet and the Development of French Art
④ An Experience That Changed Monet's Painting Style
⑤ A Humorous Situation Caused by Monet's Painting Style

고난도

2 글의 빈칸에 들어갈 말로 가장 알맞은 것은?

① rich people
② the same place
③ different scenes
④ various objects
⑤ different flowers

3 글에 따르면, 모네가 약 250점의 수련 그림을 그린 이유는?

① 여러 사람들에게 선물하기 위해
② 그림 그리는 것을 연습하기 위해
③ 빛의 변화를 그림으로 담아내기 위해
④ 가장 좋아하는 꽃이 수련이었기 때문에
⑤ 다양한 장소에 핀 수련을 묘사하기 위해

4 글의 내용과 일치하면 T, 그렇지 않으면 F를 쓰시오.

(1) 판사는 사람들이 가져온 그림들이 모두 가짜라는 것을 밝혀냈다. ______
(2) 모네는 일정한 시간에 각기 다른 장소의 수련을 그렸다. ______

Words French 형 프랑스의, 프랑스인의 several 형 몇몇의, 여럿의 court 명 법정 scene 명 장면; *풍경 judge 명 판사 decide 동 결심하다; *결정하다 capture 동 포착하다, 담아내다 work 명 일; *작품 [문제] development 명 발달 humorous 형 재미있는 situation 명 상황 object 명 물건, 물체

Section 10

3

Think!
하프 소리를 들어 본 적이 있나요?

122 words

Do you know what the longest stringed instrument in the world is? It is the Earth Harp. Musician William Close invented it in 1999. He turns buildings and natural spaces into enormous harps. (①) The Earth Harp is still listed in the Guinness World Records as the longest stringed instrument. (②)

The harp has a large wooden base. (③) This is usually set on a stage. (④) They are attached to the tops of theaters, buildings, and even valleys. (⑤)

The musician stands on the stage near the base of the instrument. He wears cotton gloves coated with sticky *resin. He runs his hands along the strings and causes them to vibrate. This makes a beautiful sound that is much deeper than that of a normal harp.

*resin 송진(나무에서 나오는 끈끈한 물질로, 주로 현악기의 활에 바름)

1 글의 제목으로 가장 알맞은 것은?

① The Music That Earth Makes
② How to Choose a Good Harp
③ How to Be a Famous Musician
④ How Harps Are Made and Played
⑤ Turning Buildings and Nature into Harps

2 다음 문장이 들어갈 위치로 가장 알맞은 곳은?

Strings stretch from the base for hundreds of meters.

① ② ③ ④ ⑤

3 Earth Harp에 관한 글의 내용과 일치하는 것은?

① 길이가 길어서 기네스 세계 기록에 등재되었다.
② 악기의 하부가 금속으로 만들어져 있다.
③ 악기의 현들은 건축물에만 부착될 수 있다.
④ 연주할 때 악기의 하부와 떨어져 서야 한다.
⑤ 일반 하프보다는 가볍고 높은 소리를 낸다.

서술형

4 다음 빈칸에 알맞은 단어를 글에서 찾아 쓰시오.

The Earth Harp is a(n) ________ built by attaching long ________ to buildings, theaters, or natural spaces.

Words invent ⓢ 발명하다 natural ⓗ 자연의 (nature ⓜ 자연) enormous ⓗ 거대한 list ⓢ (명부·목록 등에) 기입[기재]하다 wooden ⓗ 나무로 된, 목재의 base ⓜ 맨 아랫부분, 하부 set ⓢ (특정한 장소·위치에) 놓다 (set-set-set) attach ⓢ 부착하다, 붙이다 valley ⓜ 계곡 instrument ⓜ 기구; *악기 cotton ⓜ 면직물 coat ⓢ 칠하다, 입히다 sticky ⓗ 끈적끈적한 run ⓢ (어떤 방향으로) 움직이다 along ⓟ ~을 따라 string ⓜ 끈, 줄; 악기의 현[줄] vibrate ⓢ 진동하다 [문제] stretch ⓢ 뻗어 있다

Section 10

4

Think!
Look at the painting on the right. What would you call it?

147 words

In a painting, a group of armed people gather together at night. It is *Night Watch*, one of Rembrandt's most famous works. ___(A)___, *Night Watch* is not its official name. Its real name is very long. So people started using the name *Night Watch* because it seemed to describe the painting well. However, it turns out that the nickname is wrong! ___(B)___, it is not a night scene at all!

After Rembrandt's death, layers of *varnish were added to the painting to protect it from dirt. This made the painting look dark. Naturally, people thought the painting showed a nighttime event. In the 1940s, however, the layers of varnish were removed and the colors were restored to their original condition. Soon, there were efforts to change its nickname to "Day Watch." But its original nickname was already famous, so the painting is still called *Night Watch* to this day!

*varnish 니스, 유약

1 Which is the best choice for the blanks (A) and (B)?

	(A)		(B)
①	Thus	……	Surprisingly
②	Thus	……	Actually
③	However	……	Similarly
④	However	……	Actually
⑤	As a result	……	Similarly

고난도 서술형

2 What does the underlined This refer to in the passage? Write it in Korean.

____

3 Write T if the statement is true or F if it is false.

(1) People failed to restore the original colors of the painting. ________

(2) Some people tried to change the nickname to "Day Watch." ________

서술형

4 Fill in the blanks with the words from the box.

remove	nickname	night	restore

Night Watch is the ________ of a painting by Rembrandt. People thought the painting showed a ________ scene. Actually, however, it became dark because of layers of varnish. The varnish was ________, but it is still called *Night Watch.*

Words armed (형) 무장한, 무기를 든 gather (동) 모이다 watch (명) 감시, 망 보기 official (형) 공식적인 describe (동) 묘사하다, 설명하다 turn out ~인 것으로 드러나다[밝혀지다] nickname (명) 별명 death (명) 죽음 layer (명) 층, 겹 protect (동) 보호하다 dirt (명) 먼지 naturally (부) 당연히, 자연스럽게 nighttime (명) 야간, 밤 remove (동) 제거하다 restore (동) 복원[복구]하다 original (형) 원래의 condition (명) 상태 effort (명) 노력

Review Test

1 단어의 뜻이 바르게 연결되지 않은 것을 고르시오.

① condition: 상태　② official: 공식적인　③ turn out: 돌다
④ vibrate: 진동하다　⑤ enormous: 거대한

2 다음 영영풀이에 해당하는 단어를 보기에서 골라 쓰시오.

보기	restore	protect	instrument	pitch

1) an object used for making music ____________
2) to bring something back to its normal condition ____________

3-4 다음 글을 읽고, 물음에 답하시오.

The violin and the viola are both orchestral *stringed instruments. However, 그들 사이에는 몇 가지 차이점이 있다. Most violins are around 35 centimeters long. On the other hand, the viola can be 45 centimeters long. The sounds of the two instruments are also different. The violin has a very high pitch. The viola produces a deeper sound than the violin, but not as deep as the cello. That places the viola in the middle of the stringed instrument family. The instruments' bows are also different. Violin bows are lighter than bows for violas. Furthermore, the part of the bow that is held in the hand, known as the "frog," is also different. On a violin bow, the frog is pointy. However, on a viola bow, it has a round shape.

*stringed instruments 현악기

수능유형 **3** 글의 내용과 일치하는 것을 고르시오.

① 바이올린은 비올라보다 보통 20cm 더 짧다.
② 비올라는 첼로보다 더 깊은 소리를 낸다.
③ 비올라는 소리로 현악기군에서 중간에 위치한다.
④ 바이올린의 활은 비올라의 활보다 무겁다.
⑤ 비올라의 활에서 프로그는 뾰족한 모양을 가지고 있다.

서술형 **4** 밑줄 친 우리말과 같은 뜻이 되도록 상자 안의 말을 바르게 배열하시오. (전치사구는 문장 뒤에 쓸 것)

them, are, differences, there, a few, between

____

5-6 다음 글을 읽고, 물음에 답하시오.

One day, several people brought paintings to court. Each of them said their painting had been painted by Monet. All of the paintings showed the same scene, but each one was a little different. (A) After he looked at the paintings, he said, "They all were!" (B) The judge knew a lot about art. (C) They wanted the judge to decide which one was really painted by Monet. Monet painted the same place at different times of the day to capture the change of light. For example, his most famous works of art show *water lilies in his garden at different times of the day.

*water lily (식물) 수련

5 문장 (A)~(C)를 글의 흐름에 알맞게 배열한 것을 고르시오.

① (A) – (B) – (C)　② (A) – (C) – (B)　③ (B) – (A) – (C)
④ (C) – (A) – (B)　⑤ (C) – (B) – (A)

6 다음 영영풀이가 나타내는 단어를 글에서 찾아 쓰시오.

a building or room where crimes are judged

____

7-8 다음 글을 읽고, 물음에 답하시오.

The Earth Harp is listed in the Guinness World Records as the longest stringed instrument. The harp has a large wooden base. This is usually set on a stage. Strings stretch from the base for hundreds of meters. They are attached __________ the tops of theaters, buildings, and even valleys. The musician stands on the stage near the base of the instrument. He wears cotton gloves coated with sticky *resin. He runs his hands along the strings and causes them to vibrate. This makes a beautiful sound that is much deeper than <u>that</u> of a normal harp.

*resin 송진(나무에서 나오는 끈끈한 물질로, 주로 현악기)

7 빈칸에 들어갈 말로 가장 알맞은 것을 고르시오.

① from　② into　③ of　④ on　⑤ to

서술형 **8** 밑줄 친 <u>that</u>이 가리키는 것을 우리말로 쓰시오.

____

세계 이색 악기들

허공에서 연주하는 악기
테레민(Theremin)

어떠한 물리적 접촉 없이 연주할 수 있는 악기가 있다는 것을 알고 있나요? 바로 '테레민'이라고 하는 악기입니다. 소련의 물리학자 '레옹 테레민'이 제작한 최초의 전자 악기예요. 이 악기의 본체에는 각각 두 개의 안테나와 발진기가 있어요. 그 발진기에서 나오는 전기장을 손으로 간섭해 소리를 만들어내요. 막대 모양 안테나에 손을 가까이하면 높은음을 내면서, 음정을 조절할 수 있어요. 고리 모양 안테나에 손을 가까이하면 세기가 작은 소리를 낼 수 있어서 이를 이용해 음량을 조절해요. 테레민은 으스스하면서도 웅장한 소리를 내서 공포영화의 배경음악에 자주 쓰여요. 테레민의 또 다른 매력 포인트는 이 음산한 소리와 반대되는, 아름다운 손짓으로 연주하는 연주자의 모습이에요!

천사의 악기와 저주 받은 악기
글라스 하프(Glass Harp)
글라스 하모니카 (Glass Harmonica)

여기 물로 연주를 하는 악기가 있습니다. 아주 청아하고 맑은 소리를 내서 천사의 악기라고도 불립니다. 이 악기의 이름은 글라스 하프예요. 글라스 하프는 물을 담은 유리잔에 젖은 손가락을 대고 문질러 소리를 내는 원리로 연주합니다. 유리잔에 물을 많이 넣으면 높은음의 소리가 나고, 적게 넣으면 낮은 소리가 나요. 연주자는 계속 손에 물을 묻혀 공연을 이어가야 해요.

이후, 글라스 하프가 발전하여 글라스 하모니카도 만들어졌어요. 그런데 이 악기는 글라스 하프와는 반대로 저주받은 악기라는 별명을 가졌답니다! 글라스 하모니카를 즐겨 연주하던 베토벤이 정상인의 100배에 달하는 납에 중독되어 있었고 그 납이 글라스 하모니카에서 나온 것이라고 여겼기 때문이에요. 유명한 음악가도 빠져버린 이 악기들의 소리가 정말 궁금하지 않나요?

Reading TUTOR 리딩 튜터

Junior 2

직독직해 Worksheet

1 왜 잠그지 않는 거야!

① You can often find something in common / among people / wearing suit jackets: / their bottom button is left open. / ② But why? /

③ One simple theory / behind this / is that it is practical. / ④ Jackets are made / to fit the body tightly. / ⑤ With the bottom button open, / the person can move more easily. / ⑥ This is especially true / for sitting down. /

⑦ There is another interesting theory. / ⑧ King Edward VII of England ruled / from 1901 to 1910. / ⑨ When he was the Prince of Wales, / elegant suits were popular / in court. / ⑩ However, / Edward VII loved eating so much / that he was overweight. / ⑪ He couldn't close / the bottom button of his jacket! / ⑫ To show respect to him, / people stopped / buttoning their bottom button / as well. / ⑬ Over time, / this has become today's practice / for jacket buttons. /

2 작은 삼각형의 비밀

① Most people own / at least / one comfortable sweatshirt. / ② However, / few people notice / the triangle shape / just below the collar. / ③ This shape was / on the very first sweatshirts. / ④ In the fashion industry, / it is sometimes called / the "V-stitch." / ⑤ It is made / from stretchable material, / like the waistband / on a pair of shorts. / ⑥ At first, / this extra piece of cloth / had a practical purpose. / ⑦ Sweatshirts were exercise clothing. / ⑧ People sweat a lot / when they exercise, / and / the sweat makes / clothing / wet and uncomfortable. / ⑨ The V-stitch had extra material / that soaked up sweat / and / reduced discomfort. / ⑩ In addition, / it allowed / people to put their head / through the collar / more easily. / Due to improvements / in the quality of sportswear, / the V-stitch is no longer necessary. / ⑪ But / many companies / still include the triangle / as a classic design feature. /

3 이 단추의 용도가 뭐야?

① Have you ever wondered / why there are buttons on jacket sleeves? / ② The origin is unclear, / but there may be a painful story / behind it. /

③ The idea may have come / from Napoleon. / ④ His soldiers often wiped their noses / on the sleeves of their jackets. / ⑤ Napoleon didn't like this dirty habit. / ⑥ He wanted a way / to stop it. / ⑦ So / he came up with / a clever but rather cruel solution. / ⑧ He had metal buttons sewn / onto the sleeves. /

⑨ Whenever the soldiers tried to wipe their noses / with their sleeves, / the rough metal scratched their faces. / ⑩ It was very painful. / ⑪ So / they started / to use handkerchiefs / instead of their sleeves. / (⑫ In the past, / soldiers had to carry lots of heavy equipment. /) ⑬ However, / jacket sleeves with buttons / later became fashionable / even among non-military people. /

4 수염을 기르려면 세금을~

① Many men around the world / have beards. / ② Interestingly, / Russian men / had to pay money / to have beards / under the rule / of Peter the Great, / a powerful Russian czar. /

③ Peter the Great / wanted to make / the country / more like Western Europe. / ⑤ He introduced many things / from Western Europe, / such as laws, a military system, and even fashion. / ⑥ At that time, / many Western European men shaved, / but / Russian men grew long beards. / ④ So / Peter the Great tried to / make all Russian men shave. / ⑦ If a man wanted to grow a beard, / he had to pay a tax. / ⑧ And / he had to carry a token / which showed / that he had already paid the tax. / ⑨ Peter the Great / even hired beard police / to collect the beard tax. / ⑩ If a man refused to pay, / the police shaved his beard off! /

1 파인애플은 맛있기만 한 게 아니야

① In some cultures, / the pineapple is considered a symbol / of welcoming others. /

② But / how did this idea get started? /

③ Europeans first learned about pineapples / in 1493. / ④ Christopher Columbus was taking his second trip / to the Caribbean. / ⑤ His crew found an unusual fruit. /

⑥ The outside was rough / like a pinecone. / ⑦ However, / the inside was like an apple. /

⑧ They brought the unique fruit back / to Europe. /

⑨ Later, European farmers tried / to grow pineapples. / ⑩ However, / the environment was not good / for growing them. / ⑪ It took almost two hundred years / to successfully cultivate pineapples. / ⑫ For this reason, / pineapples were very rare, / and they became the perfect gift / for guests. / ⑬ Hosts used pineapples / as decorations or in dishes / when guests visited them. / ⑭ This showed / how much the hosts valued their guests. /

2 무시무시한 음력 7월!

① Some Chinese people / are superstitious / about the seventh month / of the lunar calendar. / ② They believe / the gate / to the world of the dead / opens / at that time. / ③ That means / the spirits of the dead / can return / to earth. / ④ So / they call / the seventh month / the "ghost month." /

⑤ During this time, / Chinese people worry / that bad things will happen. / ⑥ So / they do not move / into a new house / or / get married. / Instead, / they try to make / the ghosts / happy. / ⑦ Some people make / lots of food / for the ghosts. / ⑧ Others burn / paper money / to give the ghosts comfort. / ⑨ They even have / a special "ghost festival" / on the fifteenth day / of the month. / ⑩ On that day, / people put paper lights / on rivers / to help / the ghosts / find their way / back home. /

3 빗자루를 왜 뛰어넘지?

① My friends / John and Olivia / had a beautiful wedding. / ② They gave rings / to each other. / ③ That is a typical custom. / ④ But / something surprising happened / at the party. /

⑤ "Let's jump the broom!" / the MC said. / ⑥ I had to ask / a woman next to me / what this meant. / ⑦ "They are going to jump / over a broom," / she said. / ⑧ "It shows / that they are husband and wife now!" / ⑨ She said / that jumping the broom / came from an African American tradition. / ⑩ During the 1800s, / marriage was banned / among African American slaves. / ⑪ To secretly show their love, / slaves jumped over a broom. / ⑫ This symbolized / sweeping the past away / and / linking families. /

⑬ Times have changed, / but / John and Olivia / wanted to keep this tradition / in their wedding. / ⑭ They even let guests try it! / ⑮ I thought / that was the best part / of their wedding. /

4 태국 원숭이는 복도 많네!

① On the last Sunday / of November, / there is a big party / in Lopburi, / Thailand. /

② Chefs prepare / fresh fruit, vegetables, and ice cream / in front of a temple. /

③ The food is served / for free. / (④ It is difficult / to keep food fresh / in hot weather. /)

⑤ Would you like to join / this party? / ⑥ Unfortunately, / it is only for / the more than

4,000 long-tailed monkeys / living in Lopburi! /

⑦ The people of Lopburi / hold the festival / to thank the monkeys. / ⑧ The

monkeys made / Lopburi / a famous tourist spot. / ⑨ Thousands of people / visit the

city / each year / to see the monkeys. / ⑩ The local people / also believe / that giving

food to the monkeys / can bring good luck / to the town. / ⑪ For these reasons, /

people set up the buffet / for the monkeys. /

1 바나나보다 중요해질지도 몰라!

① The food crisis around the world / is getting worse / due to the climate change. / ② Up to 783 million people regularly go hungry. / ③ The good news is / that there could be a solution. / ④ It is a plant / called enset. /

⑤ Enset is a staple food / in Ethiopia. / ⑥ It looks like a banana tree / and can grow / to a height of about 4 to 13 meters. / ⑦ Unlike the fruits of other plants, / the fruit of the enset cannot be eaten, / but / its roots and stems can. / ⑧ They are used / to make porridge and bread. /

⑨ There are several benefits / of enset / as the food of the future. / ⑩ It grows quickly / and can be harvested / in any season. / ⑪ The plant does not catch diseases / easily. / ⑫ It can also live / up to seven years / without water! / ⑬ It is possible / that enset will feed many people / despite worsening climate change. /

2 버터가 다 떨어졌다고요? 걱정 마세요!

① Here is / how you can easily make your own butter. / ② First, / fill half a jar / with heavy cream / and shake it / for a long time. / ③ The cream will start to thicken. / ④ Why does this happen? / ⑤ It's because / cream is a mixture of milk fat and water. / ⑥ When you shake it, / the fat molecules stick together. / ⑦ Eventually, / they will form yellow lumps. / ⑧ These lumps are butter. / ⑨ Now / place the lumps of butter / in a bowl of cold water. / ⑩ Rinse the butter / at least two times / in this way. / ⑪ Finally, / take out the butter / and squeeze it / until there is no more water. / ⑫ If you don't get all the water out, / your butter will quickly go bad. / ⑬ Once you finish squeezing, / your homemade butter will be ready!

3 실수가 나쁜 것만은 아니야~

① Some popular foods / may have been invented / by accident. / ② According to one story, / brownies were invented accidentally / by a woman / in the United States. / ③ She was trying to bake / a chocolate cake, / but she forgot to add / baking powder. / ④ Baking powder is the ingredient / that makes cakes rise. / ⑤ So her cake was flat. / ⑥ She served it / to her guests / anyway, / and they loved it! /

⑦ Some people say / tofu was also invented / by mistake. / ⑧ A Chinese man was cooking / for his elderly parents. / ⑨ They had trouble chewing their food / and could only eat soft food. / ⑩ He made soybean soup, / but they complained / it was tasteless. / ⑪ So he added salt / and cooked the soup / for a few more minutes. / ⑫ When it cooled down, / it turned into / a delicious soybean jelly. / ⑬ His parents loved it, / and now tofu is enjoyed / around the world. /

4 식당 인테리어에 이런 비밀이!

① Did you know / that there are secrets / behind the colors / used in restaurants?

② **Red and yellow** /

③ Think about the colors / inside fast-food restaurants. / ④ There are two common colors. / ⑤ Almost all fast-food restaurants / use red and yellow. / ⑥ Both are warm colors. / ⑦ Studies show / that warm colors / make people excited / and / cause them to eat more! / (⑧ Eating too much fast food / can be bad for your health.)

⑨ So / fast-food restaurants / use these colors / to make people eat a lot. /

⑩ **Green**

⑪ People think / that cool colors, / such as blue and green, / reduce their appetite / by making them calm. / ⑫ However, / green is actually linked / to food. / ⑬ People think of green / as the color / of nature and freshness. / ⑭ This makes it the color / of healthy, clean food. / ⑮ So / green is used / in restaurants / that sell fresh, healthy food. /

1 4초면 충분해요

① Chinstrap penguins live / in Antarctica. / ② Their name comes from the thin black line / that runs under their chin. / ③ These animals survive / in Antarctica's difficult conditions / with an unusual sleep pattern. / ④ They sleep / for very short periods, / about four seconds. / ⑤ This is called microsleep. / ⑥ Chinstraps have more than 10,000 microsleeps / each day. / ⑦ These add up to around 11 hours of sleep. / ⑧ The penguins do this / because a long, deep sleep could be dangerous. /

⑨ After the chinstrap penguins lay their eggs, / one parent goes hunting / for food. / ⑩ The other parent must protect the eggs or babies / at all times. / ⑪ This is because / birds / called brown skuas / want to eat them. / ⑫ However, / it is not easy / to be awake / for 24 hours a day. / ⑬ So, / chinstrap penguins need microsleep. / ⑭ They use it / to keep their eggs and babies safe. /

2 어질어질 꽃 냄새

① Most people think / that flowers are small and pretty, / have bright colors, / and smell nice. / ② But / the titan arum is different! / ③ We can find the titan arum / in Indonesia. / ④ It is one of the tallest flowers / in the world. / ⑤ It can grow / up to 10 centimeters / in one day! / ⑥ When the titan arum / finishes growing, / it is usually / around 3 meters tall. / ⑦ It does not bloom / as often as other flowers. / ⑧ And / when it does, / it does not have / a sweet smell. / (⑨ Some perfumes use / sweet flower scents. /) ⑩ Actually, / it smells terrible! / ⑪ People say / that it smells / like rotting meat. / ⑫ This is why / it is sometimes called / the "corpse flower." / ⑬ To make matters worse, / its bad smell can draw some insects / like beetles and flies. / ⑭ The insects even lay their eggs / in the flower. /

3 무지개색으로 빛나는 해변

① Once / there was a beach / in California / that was full of trash. / ② People threw garbage, / including cans, plastic, and a lot of glass, / onto it. /

⑧ In 1967, / the government stopped / people / from throwing their trash there. / ⑨ Projects were started / to clean up the area. / ⑩ Most of the trash / was removed. / ⑪ However, / one big problem remained: / how to get rid of / the small pieces of glass / covering the beach. /

⑤ Surprisingly, / Mother Nature / took care of the problem / by herself. / ⑥ Over the years, / the ocean's waves / broke down the glass / and / made it into tiny smooth pieces / that look like jewelry. / ⑦ They made the beach sparkle / with all the colors / of the rainbow! /

③ Today, / this place is known / as Glass Beach. / ④ Unlike in the past, / it is now a beautiful place / that many people want to visit!/

4 친환경 도시, 쿠리치바

① Curitiba, Brazil, / was once a city / that was full of / poor people and pollution. /

② In 1970, / however, / everything changed. / ③ A team of city workers / came together / to make Curitiba / one of the greenest cities / in the world. / ④ They thought of an idea / that could help / both poor families and the environment. / The idea was / to exchange trash for food. / ⑤ So, / they called / this / the Green Exchange Program. / ⑥ Poor people gave their trash / to the local centers / and / got food or bus tickets. / ⑦ Children could bring in / cans and bottles / and / receive school supplies / in return. / ⑧ Through this program, / people could get / what they needed / and / clean up the city / at the same time. / ⑨ The people also worked together / to plant flowers, trees, and grass. /

⑩ Now / Curitiba is cleaner and safer, / with 16 parks, 14 forests, and over 1,000 public green spaces / for people / to enjoy! /

1 왜 자꾸 늦을까?

① According to Hofstadter's law, / a project always takes a longer time / than planned. / ② Maybe / you have experience / with this. / ③ For example, / you have homework / that you think / will be easy. / ④ You leave a short amount of time / to complete it. / ⑤ In the end, / you almost miss the deadline. / ⑥ Things like this happen / because we believe too strongly / in our abilities. / ⑦ We usually think / we can work faster / than we really can. / ⑧ Also, / unexpected events often cause delays. /

⑨ Of course, / this is a problem. / ⑩ However, / there are some tips / that help you avoid Hofstadter's law. / ⑪ Compare your current plan with past ones / to make sure / that it is realistic. / ⑫ Also, / consider giving yourself extra time / to finish your project. / ⑬ This will help you / meet your deadline / despite any unexpected delays. /

2 다 바꾸고 싶어!

① Getting something new / can sometimes have an unexpected effect. /

② Suddenly / you feel unhappy with your old stuff / and want to buy more new things. /

③ This is called the Diderot effect. / ④ It was named after a French philosopher /

who was poor for most of his life. / ⑥ One day / he was given a beautiful red robe. /

⑤ When he brought it home, / it made his other things look ugly / in comparison. /

⑦ So / he started / replacing all his furniture and clothes with new items. / ⑧ This is /

how the Diderot effect leads you to a series of unplanned purchases. / ⑨ One new

thing causes / you to buy / more new things. / ⑩ As a result, / you end up with items /

you don't need. / ⑪ To prevent the Diderot effect, / try to purchase things / that fit

your current style / and match what you already have. /

3 분명히 집중했는데?

① Say / the colors of the words / in the box / below / as fast as you can! /

② Wasn't it easy? / ③ Now try this. / ④ Again, / say the color / that each word is written in. /

⑤ Did you find / that / more difficult? / ⑥ Did it take longer? / ⑦ Did you say the word / instead of the color? / ⑧ If so, / you experienced the Stroop Effect. / ⑨ It happens / because the brain needs / extra time / to work / when it handles / conflicting information. / ⑩ In this experiment, / the word *red* is written / in yellow. / ⑪ The word's meaning and its color / are conflicting. / ⑫ When there is conflicting information, / the brain generally does / the more familiar job / first. / ⑬ The brain is more familiar / with reading words / than with naming colors. / ⑭ So / words are recognized / more quickly / than colors. / ⑮ However, / the experiment asks / you / to say the color, / not the word. / ⑯ So / your brain / has to hold on to / the wrong answer / until the right answer comes. / ⑰ This slows down / your brain! /

4 조금만 더 도와줘~

① Your friend asks you to walk / to the playground / with her. / ② You say / you're busy, / so she asks you to walk / to the corner / instead. / ③ It's not far, / so you agree. / ④ When you get there, / she asks you to go / a little farther. / ⑤ The pattern repeats / until you arrive / at the playground. /

⑥ This is the "foot-in-the-door" technique. / ⑦ It is a classic strategy / in sales. / ⑧ A long time ago, / salespeople went / from house to house. / The people in the homes / could simply close the door / if they didn't want to buy anything. / ⑨ To prevent this, / salespeople would sometimes put their foot / in the way of the door / so it couldn't be closed. /

⑩ The foot-in-the-door technique / uses small requests. / ⑪ Each new request / is not that big. / ⑫ By focusing on getting / one small yes / after another, / this technique / often leads to a big yes. /

1 얕보면 안 되는 이것

① Have you ever cut your finger / on paper? / ② Paper cuts are usually small. / ③ However, / the pain they cause / is intense. / ④ Why do these minor injuries hurt / so much? /

⑤ One reason is / that our fingers are very sensitive. / ⑥ There are more pain receptors / in your fingers / than in most other parts of your body. / ⑦ So, / when you get a paper cut, / a lot of pain signals are sent / to the brain. / (⑧ The brain is the organ / that uses the most energy. /) ⑨ As a result, / we feel a strong pain. / ⑩ Also, / the edge of a piece of paper / is uneven. / ⑪ It's hard / to see this without a microscope. / ⑫ However, / the rough edge will damage your finger more / than a sharp knife would. /

⑬ No matter how small a paper cut is, / it will make you say, "Ouch!" /

2 이게 정말 내 목소리라니!

① Do you remember / the first time you heard / a recording / of your own voice? /

② You were probably surprised / by how it sounded. / But / that's how your voice sounds / to other people. / ③ The reason is / that sound travels / in waves. /

④ When another person speaks, / the sound waves travel / through the air. / ⑤ When they reach your ears, / you hear them. / ⑥ But / when you speak, / the sound waves also move / through the bones / of your head. / ⑦ So / they reach your ears / in two different ways, / which makes / your voice / sound lower and stronger. /

⑧ On the other hand, / when you hear a recording / of your voice, / the sound waves are traveling / only through the air. / ⑨ So / your voice sounds / higher and weaker. / ⑩ For this reason, / many people don't like / to hear recordings / of their own voice. /

3 키가 줄어들고 있다고?

① How tall are you? / ④ Surprisingly, / your answer depends on / what time of day / you measure yourself. / ③ It may sound strange, / but you're actually taller / in the morning / than you are / in the evening. / ② This is because / your spine contains / 33 small bones / that are connected / by discs. / ⑤ These discs are soft / and contain liquid. / ⑥ They allow / your spine to easily move / in many directions. /

⑦ During the day, / gravity pulls / the bones of your spine / downward. / ⑧ They squeeze the discs / and make them flatter. / ⑨ As a result, / you become / up to one centimeter / shorter. / ⑩ When you lie down / to sleep, / however, / gravity no longer causes / the bones to squeeze the discs. / ⑪ The discs get thicker, / and you gain back / your lost height. /

4 맛을 느끼려면 협력이 필요해

① When you have / a stuffed nose, / you cannot taste well. / ② Why is this? / ③ It is because / your nose helps you taste. / ④ The taste buds / on your tongue / only recognize basic tastes, / such as sweet, sour, bitter, and salty. / The rest of the taste / comes from smelling. / ⑤ When you eat something, / the scent of the food / goes into your nose / and / stimulates the nerve cells / in it. / ⑥ Then / these send information / about the taste / to the brain. / ⑦ However, / when your nose is stuffed, / the scent cannot reach / the nerve cells / because of the mucus. / ⑧ So / you cannot taste the food / well. /

⑨ Then, / does holding your nose work / when you want to avoid / tasting bitter medicine? / ⑩ It does not / because we don't use / our sense of smell / when tasting bitter flavors! /

1 덫이 걸렸다!

① Imagine / seeing an expensive item / in a store. / ② Then / you see an item / that is similar but cheaper. / ③ The cheaper item is still over your budget. / ④ But / it seems like a good deal. / ⑤ This is called / the anchoring effect. /

⑥ The anchoring effect happens / because of the way people process information. / ⑦ They usually rely the most / on the information / that they find first / —the "anchor." / ⑧ Once they have an anchor, / they compare other things to it. /

⑨ The anchoring effect can be a powerful tool / for selling products. / ⑩ That is because / it can change / the way customers think. / ⑪ For example, / many restaurants place a few expensive dishes / at the top of their menu. / ⑫ Customers see these items / first. / ⑬ So, / the other dishes seem cheap / even if they really aren't. /

2 친구 따라 물건을 산다고?

① When a product becomes popular, / do you buy it / even if you do not need it? /

② If so, / you are experiencing / the "bandwagon effect." /

③ The term comes from / American parades. / ④ In the past, / bandwagons would carry a band. / ⑤ When people heard the music, / they followed the bandwagon. / Soon, / more and more people gathered, / and / they formed a big crowd. / ⑥ But / most of them did not know / why they had joined the crowd. /

⑦ These days, / the term "bandwagon effect" is used / to describe the act / of people / doing something / just because others are doing it. / ⑧ We can see this / in our daily lives. / ⑨ Advertisements / that say things like / "Ten bottles are sold / every second" / also use this effect. / ⑩ But / you should not buy things / just because others do. / ⑪ Make sure / you buy items / only when you need them! /

3 나도 모르게 따라 하게 돼!

① Have you ever seen a TV advertisement / that really grabbed your attention? / ② Did it make you feel / like the person in it? / ③ If so, / you might have been influenced / by mirror neurons / in the brain. / ④ When you see someone doing something, / your brain's mirror neurons react / as if you were actually doing it / yourself. / ⑤ This can even cause you to copy / what you have seen. / ⑥ Marketing experts try / to use this effect. /

⑦ For example, / imagine there is a TV advertisement / for a hamburger. / ⑧ The advertisement may show the model / taking a bite of the hamburger. / ⑨ Due to mirror neurons, / people who watch the advertisement may start / to copy the model. / ⑩ Without even noticing it, / they might imitate / the model's emotions and facial expressions. / (⑪ People put lots of different things / on hamburgers. /) ⑫ Viewers may feel / like they have bitten the hamburger. / ⑬ As a result, / the advertisement makes them want the real thing! /

4 지글거리는 스테이크

① It is Friday night. / ② You enter / your favorite steak restaurant. / ③ You can smell / the delicious food. / ④ There is an open kitchen, / so / you can see the chef cooking. / ⑤ He puts a piece of meat / on the hot grill. / ⑥ It makes a sizzling sound / and / turns brown. / ⑦ All of these things / make your mouth water. /

⑧ Many restaurants know / that tasty food is not enough / to attract customers. / ⑨ The sights, smells, and sounds / of the food / all / affect a customer's experience. / ⑩ So / restaurants use these / to get more customers. / ⑪ If the entire experience is good, / customers enjoy the food / even more! /

⑫ So / when you visit / your favorite restaurant, / do not just taste the food. / ⑬ Pay attention to / how the restaurant satisfies / your other senses. / ⑭ Keep / your eyes, ears, and nose open / for a sizzling experience! /

1 스카치테이프가 자동차와 관계가 있다고?

① In the 1920s, / cars / with two different colors of paint / were popular. /

② Unfortunately, / this made life difficult / for car painters. /

③ First, / they painted the car / one color. / ④ Next, / they glued paper / over the parts / of the car / that had to stay / the original color. / ⑤ Finally, / they painted the car / a second color. / ⑥ When the paper was removed, / the car was two colors. / However, / it was nearly impossible / to completely remove the glue / from the cars. / ⑦ So / a man / named Richard Gurley Drew / decided / to find a solution. / ⑧ Two years later, / he invented paper tape / that could be removed / cleanly and easily. /

⑨ It was a great success, / but Drew wasn't satisfied. / ⑩ He began experimenting / with cellophane, / a new thin, clear plastic material / used for packaging. / ⑪ In 1930, / he invented the first clear tape. / ⑫ Today / we know his invention / as "Scotch tape." /

2 날씨 아래에 있다는 것은?

① If you are feeling a bit unwell, / you may say / that you're "under the weather." /

② What does our health have to do with the weather? / ③ There are several common theories / about the origin of this idiom. /

④ One popular theory suggests / that it came from the language of sailors. / ⑤ When the weather was bad, / the sea would be rough. / ⑥ This made the boat move / a lot, / which often made sailors ill. / ⑦ They had to go / below deck / to rest and get better. / ⑧ That meant / they were literally under the bad weather / taking place above deck. /

⑨ At first, / the idiom was only used / to talk about seasickness. / ⑩ As time went on, / it took on a wider meaning. / ⑪ Today, / "under the weather" can be used / for any type of illness. /

3 달을 닮은 빵

① Many people assume / that the croissant comes from France. / ② However, / it is actually based on / a type of Austrian bread, / the kipfel. / ③ Both the croissant and the kipfel / are shaped / like a crescent moon. / (④ When it is viewed / from Earth, / the moon changes shape / night after night. /)

⑤ According to legend, / the kipfel was created / in 1683 / after Austria defeated / the Ottoman Empire / in a battle. / ⑥ The Ottomans had surrounded / the city of Vienna. / ⑦ Luckily, / the city was protected / by tall walls. / ⑧ One night, / an Austrian baker / heard strange sounds / beneath his bakery. / ⑨ He realized / the Ottomans were digging a tunnel / under the city walls! / ⑩ He quickly alerted / the Austrian soldiers. / ⑪ The tunnel was destroyed, / and the city was saved! /

⑫ To celebrate, / he made some special bread. / ⑬ It was shaped / like the moon / on the Ottoman Empire's flag. / ⑭ Nearly 100 years later, / the kipfel was brought / to France, / where it became the croissant. /

4 오른손 좀 확인해 보겠습니다~

① When two people meet, / they often shake hands. / ② Today / this seems perfectly normal. / ③ But / why did people start / grabbing each other's hands / and shaking them / in the first place? /

④ It is believed that / it started / in ancient times. / ⑥ Paintings / from as early as the fifth century BC / show people / shaking hands. / ⑤ Many of these paintings / show soldiers. / ⑦ So / some experts think / shaking hands was a way / of checking for weapons. / ⑧ A person with a weapon / in his or her hand / couldn't grab / another person's hand. /

⑨ Also, / people sometimes hid weapons / in their sleeves. / ⑩ If someone did this, / moving the person's hand / up and down / would reveal the weapon. / ⑪ Since people usually carried weapons / in their right hands, / it was common / to always use the right hand / in a handshake. / ⑫ Eventually, / this became / a gesture of peace / between two people / who were meeting. /

1 세상에 이런 규칙이!

① The game of baseball is played / by two teams of nine players. / ② A player from one team throws a small ball. / ③ Then / a player from the other team tries to hit it / with a bat. / ④ Baseball has been popular / for more than 150 years. / ⑤ However, / some of the rules / in the 19th century / were very different / from the rules of today. /

⑥ For example, / batters could request the kind of pitch / they wanted. / ⑦ They would ask the pitchers / to throw the ball / either high or low. / ⑨ Another difference was the role of the umpires. / ⑩ Today, / they play a neutral role / by enforcing the rules. / ⑧ But / in the past / they would sometimes ask spectators / for help / in making decisions. / ⑪ That doesn't sound very fair, / does it? / ⑫ Fortunately, / these rules were later changed. /

2 환상의 쇼에 당신을 초대합니다

① Did you know / that there is a theater / in Las Vegas / that has a giant pool? /

② This is / where the show *O* is performed. / ③ It was created / by a Canadian circus. /

④ *O* sounds like *eau*, / the French word / for water. / ⑤ This name is fitting / because

the show takes place / in and around water. /

⑥ Eighty-five world-class acrobats, swimmers, and divers / use the giant pool /

in their performances. / ⑦ Gymnasts leap / through the air / on floating stages. /

⑧ Divers jump / into the pool / from breathtaking heights. / ⑨ Teams of swimmers /

move gracefully together / underwater. / ⑩ They dance / to the music / that plays /

through underwater speakers. / ⑪ There are also many scuba divers / in the water /

at all times. / ⑫ They help / the performers use air hoses / to breathe / beneath the

surface / of the pool. /

⑬ If you visit Las Vegas / someday, / how about seeing / this amazing show? /

3 럭비 선수들의 댄스 타임~

① The All Blacks are / New Zealand's national rugby team. / ② Before every international match, / they perform / a famous war dance. / ③ It is known as the *haka*. / ④ The *haka* is a tradition / of the Maori. / ⑤ The Maori lived in New Zealand / before the Europeans arrived. / ⑥ *Haka* dancers chant / and slap their bodies / while opening their eyes wide / and sticking out their tongues. /

⑦ In the past, / the dance was performed / to scare the enemy / before a battle. / ⑧ It was also used / to ask the war god for help. / ⑨ Over time, / however, / it became / more of a social event. / ⑩ Performing the *haka* / brought people together. / ⑪ It showed / their spirit and strength. / ⑫ Today you can see the *haka* / at many events, / including weddings and funerals. / ⑬ But the best place / to see the *haka* / is at an All Blacks rugby match! /

4 아무나 가질 수 없어요

① The most famous sports trophy / in the world / is given / to the winner / of the World Cup soccer tournament / every four years. / However, / there are two different World Cup trophies. /

② The first is the Jules Rimet Trophy. / ③ It was awarded / to the World Cup winner / from 1930 to 1970. / ④ Each winning team / kept the trophy / for four years / before giving it / to the next winner. / ⑤ However, / there was a special rule /—if a team won the World Cup / three times, / they could keep the trophy / forever. / ⑥ In 1970, / Brazil won the World Cup / for the third time / and / was given / the Jules Rimet Trophy. /

⑦ After this, / a new trophy / —the FIFA World Cup Trophy— / was designed, / and / the special rule was changed. / ⑧ Now, / no team can keep / the FIFA World Cup Trophy. / ⑨ Instead, / they get / a copy of the trophy. /

1 비슷하지만 다른 둘

① The violin and the viola are both orchestral stringed instruments. / ② However, / there are a few differences / between them. / ③ Most violins are around 35 centimeters long. / ④ On the other hand, / the viola can be 45 centimeters long. /

⑤ The sounds of the two instruments are also different. / ⑥ The violin has a very high pitch. / ⑦ The viola produces a deeper sound / than the violin, / but not as deep as the cello. ⑧ That places the viola / in the middle of the stringed instrument family. /

⑨ The instruments' bows are also different. / ⑩ Violin bows are lighter than bows for violas. / ⑪ Furthermore, / the part of the bow / that is held in the hand, / known as the "frog," / is also different. / ⑫ On a violin bow, / the frog is pointy. / (⑬ Basically, / a violin is made of wood. /) ⑭ However, / on a viola bow, / it has a round shape. /

2 모두 진품이 맞아요

① Claude Monet was / a famous French painter. / ② Here is an interesting story / about his paintings. / ③ One day, / several people brought paintings / to court. / ④ Each of them said / their painting had been painted / by Monet. / ⑤ All of the paintings / showed / the same scene, / but / each one was a little different. / ⑥ They wanted / the judge to decide / which one was really painted / by Monet. / ⑦ The judge knew a lot / about art. / ⑧ After he looked at the paintings, / he said, / "They all were!" /

⑨ Monet painted the same place / at different times / of the day / to capture / the change of light. / ⑩ For example, / his most famous works of art / show water lilies / in his garden / at different times / of the day. / ⑪ He made / about 250 / of these water lily paintings! /

3 제가 아는 그 악기가 맞나요?!

① Do you know / what the longest stringed instrument in the world is? / ② It is the Earth Harp. / ③ Musician William Close / invented it / in 1999. / ④ He turns / buildings and natural spaces / into enormous harps. / ⑤ The Earth Harp is still listed / in the Guinness World Records / as the longest stringed instrument. /

⑥ The harp has / a large wooden base. / ⑦ This is usually set / on a stage. / Strings stretch / from the base / for hundreds of meters. / ⑧ They are attached / to the tops / of theaters, buildings, and even valleys. /

⑨ The musician stands / on the stage / near the base of the instrument. / ⑩ He wears cotton gloves / coated with sticky resin. / ⑪ He runs his hands / along the strings / and causes / them to vibrate. / ⑫ This makes a beautiful sound / that is much deeper / than that of a normal harp. /

4 왜 이런 별명이?

① In a painting, / a group of armed people / gather together / at night. / ② It is *Night Watch*, / one of Rembrandt's most famous works. / ③ However, / *Night Watch* / is not its official name. / ④ Its real name / is very long. / ⑤ So / people started / using the name / *Night Watch* / because it seemed to describe / the painting / well. / ⑥ However, / it turns out / that the nickname is wrong! / ⑦ Actually, / it is not a night scene / at all! /

⑧ After Rembrandt's death, / layers of varnish / were added / to the painting / to protect it / from dirt. / ⑨ This made / the painting / look dark. / ⑩ Naturally, / people thought / the painting showed / a nighttime event. / ⑪ In the 1940s, / however, / the layers of varnish / were removed / and / the colors were restored / to their original condition. / ⑫ Soon, / there were efforts / to change its nickname / to "Day Watch." / ⑬ But / its original nickname / was already famous, / so / the painting is still called / *Night Watch* / to this day! /

Photo Credits

p. 18 Wachiwit / Shutterstock.com

p. 90 Hamara / Shutterstock.com

p. 108 Victor Velter / Shutterstock.com

p. 110 A.RICARDO / Shutterstock.com

p. 114 Ben Gingell / Shutterstock.com

Sampajano_Anizza / Shutterstock.com

others

www.shutterstock.com/

www.istockphoto.com/

commons.wikimedia.org/wiki/

BOOK
LIST

도/서/목/록

중등

문법

GRAMMAR Inside

많은 양의 문제로 체계적으로
학습하는 중학 영문법

Starter | Level 1 | Level 2 | Level 3

Reading Inside

문제로 마스터하는 중학영문법

많은 문제로 확실히 끝내는 중학 영문법

Level 1 | Level 2 | Level 3

문제로 마스터하는 고등 영문법

1316 GRAMMAR

기초부터 내신까지 중학 영문법 완성

Level 1 | Level 2 | Level 3

1316 Reading | 1316 Listening

GRAMMAR ZONE

대한민국 영문법 교재의 표준

입문 | 기초 | 기본 1 | 기본 2 | 종합
(각 Workbook 별매)

·중학영문법·
총정리 모의고사

내신 상위권을 위한 학교 문법 통합형 모의고사

Level 1 | Level 2 | Level 3

구문 · 서술형

중학 천문장

구문이 독해로 연결되는 해석 공식

Level 1 | Level 2 | Level 3

천문장

정말 기특한 구문독해

독해가 쉬워지는 중등 구문 독해서

입문 | 기본 | 완성

쓰기로 마스터하는 중학서술형

최신 중간·기말고사 빈출 서술형 마스터

1학년 | 2학년 | 3학년

어휘

주니어 능률 VOCA

대한민국 중등 어휘 교재의 표준

Starter 1 | Starter 2 | 입문 |
기본 | 실력 | 숙어

능률VOCA

대한민국 어휘서의 표준

어원편 Lite | 어원편 | 고교기본 |
고교필수 2000 | 수능완성 2200 | 숙어 | 고난도

해당 교재와 연계되는 시리즈

Reading TUTOR 리딩 튜터

Junior 2

정답 및 해설

NE 능률

Reading TUTOR 리딩 튜터

Junior 2

정답 및 해설

Section 01 Fashion

본책 • pp. 8-9

1

정답 1 ③ 2 ⑤ 3 그가 먹는 것을 좋아해서 과체중이었기 때문에 4 practice, open

문제 해설

1 정장 재킷의 맨 아래 단추를 잠그지 않는 두 가지 설에 관한 글이므로, 주제로는 ③ '재킷의 아래 단추가 열려 있는 이유'가 가장 알맞다.
① 정장 재킷의 인기 상승
② 에드워드 7세 왕이 패션 유행을 창조한 방법
④ 재킷의 단추 수 뒤에 숨겨진 비밀
⑤ 사람들이 일상생활에서 정장을 입기 시작한 시기

2 ⑤: 에드워드 7세가 정장 재킷 맨 아래 단추와 관련한 법을 제정했다는 내용은 글에 언급되지 않았다.
①은 문장 ①에, ②는 문장 ⑤에, ③은 문장 ⑨에, ④는 문장 ⑫에 언급되어 있다.

3 문장 ⑩에 언급되어 있다.

4 보기 | 존경 닫힌 관행 열려 있는

정장 재킷의 맨 아래 단추를 열어 두는 관행은 에드워드 7세 왕에 의해 시작되었을 수도 있다.

본문 직독 직해

① You can often find something in common / among people / wearing suit jackets: / their bottom button is left open. / ② But why? /
당신은 흔히 공통점을 발견할 수 있다 / 사람들 사이에서 / 정장 재킷을 입은 / 맨 아래 단추가 열려 있다 / 하지만 왜일까

③ One simple theory / behind this / is that it is practical. / ④ Jackets are made / to fit the body tightly. / ⑤ With the bottom button open, / the person can move more easily. / ⑥ This is especially true / for sitting down. /
한 가지 간단한 이론은 / 이것 뒤에 숨겨진 / 그것이 실용적이라는 것이다 / 재킷은 만들어진다 / 몸에 꼭 맞게 / 맨 아래 단추가 열려 있어서 / 사람은 더 쉽게 움직일 수 있다 / 이것은 / 특히 해당된다 / 앉을 때에

⑦ There is another interesting theory. / ⑧ King Edward VII of England ruled / from 1901 to 1910. / ⑨ When he was the Prince of Wales, / elegant suits were popular / in court. /
또 다른 흥미로운 이론이 있다 / 영국의 왕 에드워드 7세는 통치했다 / 1901년부터 1910년까지 / 그가 웨일스의 왕자였을 때 / 우아한 정장은 인기가 있었다 / 궁정에서

⑩ However, / Edward VII loved eating so much / that he was overweight. / ⑪ He couldn't close / the bottom button of his jacket! / ⑫ To show respect to him, / people stopped / buttoning their bottom button / as well. / ⑬ Over time, / this has become today's practice / for jacket buttons. /
하지만 / 에드워드 7세는 먹는 것을 너무 좋아해서 / 과체중이었다 / 그는 잠글 수가 없었다 / 재킷의 맨 아래 단추를 / 그에 대한 존경을 표하기 위해 / 사람들도 멈췄다 / 맨 아래 단추를 잠그는 것을 / 역시 / 시간이 지나면서 / 이것은 오늘날의 관행이 되었다 / 재킷 단추에 대한

본문 해석

당신은 정장 재킷을 입은 사람들 사이에서 흔히 공통점을 발견할 수 있다. 맨 아래 단추가 열려 있다. 하지만 왜일까?

이것 뒤에 숨겨진 한 가지 간단한 이론은 그것이 실용적이라는 것이다. 재킷은 몸에 꼭 맞게 만들어진다. 맨 아래 단추가 열려 있어서, 사람은 더 쉽게 움직일 수 있다. 이것은 특히 앉을 때에 해당된다.

또 다른 흥미로운 이론이 있다. 영국의 왕 에드워드 7세는 1901년부터 1910년까지 통치했다. 그가 웨일스의 왕자였을 때, 우아한 정장은 궁정에서 인기가 있었다. 하지만, 에드워드 7세는 먹는 것을 너무 좋아해서 과체중이었다. 그는 재킷의 맨 아래 단추를 잠글 수가 없었다! 그에 대한 존경을 표하기 위해, 사람들도 역시 맨 아래 단추를 잠그는 것을 멈췄다. 시간이 지나면서, 이것은 재킷 단추에 대한 오늘날의 관행이 되었다.

구문 해설

① You can often find something in common among people [**wearing** suit jackets]: … .
→ [ ]는 people을 수식하는 현재분사구이다.

③ One simple theory [behind this] is [**that** it is practical].
→ 첫 번째 [ ]는 One simple theory를 수식하는 전치사구이다.
→ that은 명사절을 이끄는 접속사로, 두 번째 [ ]는 문장의 보어로 쓰였다.

⑤ **With the bottom button open**, the person can move more easily.
→ 「with+목적어+형용사」는 '~가 …한 채로'의 의미이다.

⑩ However, Edward VII loved eating **so much that he was** overweight.
→ 「so+부사+that+주어+동사」는 '너무 ~해서 …하다'의 의미이다.

⑫ **To show** respect to him, people *stopped buttoning* their bottom button as well.
→ To show는 '보여주기 위해'의 의미로, 〈목적〉을 나타내는 부사적 용법의 to부정사이다.
→ 「stop+v-ing」는 '~하는 것을 멈추다'의 의미이다.

⑬ Over time, this **has become** today's practice for jacket buttons.
→ has become은 '되었다'의 의미로 〈결과〉를 나타내는 현재완료(have[has]+p.p.)이다.

2

본책 • pp. 10-11

정답 1 ② 2 ⑤ 3 (1) F (2) T 4 (1) 땀을 흡수하여 불쾌함을 줄여 준다. (2) 사람들이 머리를 칼라 안으로 더 쉽게 집어넣게 해 준다.

문제 해설

1 운동복 상의[맨투맨 티]에 있는 삼각형 모양의 V 스티치의 용도에 관한 글이므로, 제목으로는 ② '맨투맨 티에 삼각형이 있는 이유'가 가장 알맞다.
① 땀을 조절하는 직물들 ③ 맨투맨 티는 어떻게 발명되었는가
④ 땀의 해결책: 새로운 맨투맨 티 ⑤ 가장 유행하는 운동복

2 '운동복의 품질 향상으로, V 스티치가 더는 필요 없게 되었다'는 내용의 주어진 문장은 V 스티치의 초기 용도를 추가로 설명한 문장 ⑩과 많은 회사들이 여전히 이 삼각형을 포함시킨다는 내용의 문장 ⑪ 사이인 ⑤의 위치가 가장 알맞다.

3 (1) 문장 ⑤에서 신축성 있는 소재로 만들어진다고 했다.
(2) 문장 ⑥에 언급되어 있다.

4 문장 ⑨-⑩에 언급되어 있다.

본문 직독 직해

① Most people own / at least / one comfortable sweatshirt. / ② However, / few people
대부분의 사람들은 가지고 있다 적어도 하나의 편안한 맨투맨 티를 그러나 의식하는 사람들은

notice / the triangle shape / just below the collar. / ③ This shape was / on the very first
거의 없다 삼각형 모양을 칼라 바로 아래의 이 모양은 있었다 최초의

sweatshirts. / ④ In the fashion industry, / it is sometimes called / the "V-stitch." / ⑤ It is
맨투맨 티 위에 패션업계에서 그것은 때때로 불린다 'V 스티치'라고 그것은

made / from stretchable material, / like the waistband / on a pair of shorts. / ⑥ At first, /
만들어진다 신축성 있는 소재로 허리 밴드처럼 한 벌의 반바지의 처음에

this extra piece of cloth / had a practical purpose. / ⑦ Sweatshirts were exercise clothing. /
이 여분의 천 조각은 실용적인 목적이 있었다 맨투맨 티는 운동복이었다

⑧ People sweat a lot / when they exercise, / and / the sweat makes / clothing / wet and
사람들은 땀을 많이 흘린다 그들이 운동할 때 그리고 그 땀은 만든다 옷을 축축하고

uncomfortable. / ⑨ The V-stitch had extra material / that soaked up sweat / and / reduced
불편하게 V 스티치에는 여분의 직물이 있었다 땀을 흡수하는 그리고

discomfort. / ⑩ In addition, / it allowed / people to put their head / through the collar /
불쾌함을 줄여 주는 게다가 그것은 ~하게 해 주었다 사람들이 그들의 머리를 집어넣도록 칼라를 통과해

more easily. / Due to improvements / in the quality of sportswear, / the V-stitch is no
더 쉽게 향상 덕분에 운동복의 품질에 있어서 V 스티치는 더는

longer necessary. / ⑪ But / many companies / still include the triangle / as a classic design
필요하지 않다 그러나 많은 회사들이 여전히 그 삼각형을 포함시킨다 고전적인 디자인

feature. /
특징으로

본문 해석

대부분의 사람들은 편안한 맨투맨 티를 적어도 하나는 가지고 있다. 그러나 칼라 바로 아래에 있는 삼각형 모양을 의식하는 사람들은 거의 없다. 이 모양은 최초의 맨투맨 티에 있었다. 패션 업계에서 그것은 때때로 'V 스티치'라고 불린다. 그것은 한 벌의 반바지에 있는 허리 밴드처럼 신축성 있는 소재로 만들어진다. 처음에 이 여분의 천 조각은 실용적인 목적이 있었다. 맨투맨 티는 운동복이었다. 사람들은 운동할 때 땀을 많이 흘리고, 그 땀은 옷을 축축하고 불편하게 만든다. V 스티치에는 땀을 흡수하여 불쾌함을 줄여 주는 여분의 직물이 있었다. 게다가, 그것은 사람들이 머리를 칼라를 통과해 더 쉽게 집어넣게 해 주었다. 운동복의 품질 향상으로, V 스티치가 더는 필요하지 않다. 그러나 많은 회사들이 여전히 이 삼각형을 고전적인 디자인 특징으로 포함시킨다.

구문 해설

⑧ People sweat a lot when they exercise, and the sweat **makes clothing *wet*** and ***uncomfortable***.
→ 「make+목적어+형용사」는 '~을 …하게 만들다'의 의미이다.
→ make의 목적격 보어로 쓰인 형용사 wet과 uncomfortable이 접속사 and로 병렬 연결되어 있다.

⑨ The V-stitch had **extra material** [**that** *soaked up* sweat and *reduced* discomfort].
→ [ ]는 선행사 extra material을 수식하는 주격 관계대명사절이다.
→ 관계대명사절의 동사 soaked up과 reduced가 접속사 and로 병렬 연결되어 있다.

⑩ In addition, it **allowed people to put** their head through the collar more easily.
→ 「allow+목적어+to-v」는 '~가 …하게 하다'의 의미이다.

⑪ But many companies still include the triangle **as** a classic design feature.
→ as는 '~로(서)'라는 의미의 전치사이다.

3

정답 1 ③ 2 ④ 3 군인들이 재킷의 소매에 콧물을 닦는 것 4 metal buttons

문제 해설

1 재킷의 소매에 단추를 달게 된 이유에 관한 글이므로, 제목으로는 ③ '의외의 장소에서 온 패션'이 가장 알맞다.
① 단추에 가장 적합한 소재
② 나폴레옹의 단추와의 전쟁
④ 군인들의 장비 문제
⑤ 사람들이 나폴레옹처럼 옷을 입는 것을 좋아했던 이유

2 나폴레옹이 소매에 금속 단추를 달게 해서 군인들이 콧물을 닦을 때 소매 대신 손수건으로 닦기 시작했다는 내용 중에 과거에 군인들은 많은 무거운 장비를 가지고 다녀야 했다는 내용의 (d)는 글의 흐름과 무관하다.

3 문장 ④에 언급되어 있다.

4 나폴레옹은 군인들의 나쁜 습관을 고치길 원해서 그는 군인들을 긁게 될 금속 단추를 그들의 재킷 소매에 추가했다.

본문 직독 직해

① Have you ever wondered / why there are buttons on jacket sleeves? / ② The origin is unclear, / but there may be a painful story / behind it. /
여러분은 궁금해한 적이 있는가 / 왜 재킷의 소매에 단추가 있는지 / 기원은 불분명하다 / 하지만 고통스러운 이야기가 있을 수 있다 / 그 뒤에는

③ The idea may have come / from Napoleon. / ④ His soldiers often wiped their noses / on the sleeves of their jackets. / ⑤ Napoleon didn't like this dirty habit. / ⑥ He wanted a way / to stop it. / ⑦ So / he came up with / a clever but rather cruel solution. / ⑧ He had metal buttons sewn / onto the sleeves. /
그 아이디어는 비롯된 것일 수도 있다 / 나폴레옹에게서 / 그의 군인들은 종종 콧물을 닦았다 / 재킷 소매에 / 나폴레옹은 이 더러운 습관을 좋아하지 않았다 / 그는 방법을 원했다 / 그것을 멈출 / 그래서 / 그는 생각해 냈다 / 영리하지만 다소 잔인한 해결책을 / 그는 금속 단추를 꿰매게 했다 / 소매에

⑨ Whenever the soldiers tried to wipe their noses / with their sleeves, / the rough metal scratched their faces. / ⑩ It was very painful. / ⑪ So / they started / to use handkerchiefs / instead of their sleeves. / (⑫ In the past, / soldiers had to carry lots of heavy equipment. /) ⑬ However, / jacket sleeves with buttons / later became fashionable / even among non-military people. /
군인들이 그들의 코를 닦으려고 할 때마다 / 소매로 / 거친 금속이 그들의 얼굴을 긁었다 / 그것은 매우 고통스러웠다 / 그래서 / 그들은 시작했다 / 손수건을 사용하는 것을 / 그들의 소매 대신에 / 과거에 / 군인들은 많은 무거운 장비를 가지고 다녀야 했다 / 그러나 / 단추가 달린 재킷 소매는 / 나중에 유행하게 되었다 / 심지어 군인이 아닌 사람들 사이에서도

본문 해석

여러분은 왜 재킷의 소매에 단추가 있는지 궁금해한 적이 있는가? 기원은 불분명하지만, 그 뒤에는 고통스러운 이야기가 있을 수 있다.

그 아이디어는 나폴레옹에게서 비롯된 것일 수도 있다. 그의 군인들은 종종 재킷 소매에 콧물을 닦았다. 나폴레옹은 이 더러운 습관을 좋아하지 않았다. 그는 그것을 멈출 방법을 원했다. 그래서 그는 영리하지만 다소 잔인한 해결책을 생각해 냈다. 그는 소매에 금속 단추를 꿰매게 했다.

군인들이 소매로 그들의 코를 닦으려 할 때마다, 거친 금속이 그들의 얼굴을 긁었다. 그것은 매우 고통스러웠다. 그래서 그들은 소매 대신에 손수건을 사용하기 시작했다. (과거에 군인들은 많은 무거운 장비를 가지고 다녀야 했다.) 그러나 단추가 달린 재킷 소매는 나중에 군인이 아닌 사람들 사이에서도 유행하게 되었다.

구문 해설

① **Have** you ever **wondered** [why there are buttons on jacket sleeves]?

→ have wondered는 '궁금해한 적이 있다'의 의미로, 〈경험〉을 나타내는 현재완료(have[has]+p.p.)이다.

→ [ ]는 동사 have wondered의 목적어 역할을 하는 간접의문문이다.

③ The idea **may have come** from Napoleon.

→ 「may have p.p.」는 '~했을지도 모른다'의 의미이다.

⑥ He wanted a way **to stop** it.

→ to stop은 a way를 수식하는 형용사적 용법의 to부정사이다.

⑦ So he came up with a **clever** but **rather cruel** solution.

→ 명사 solution을 수식하는 형용사 clever와 cruel이 접속사 but으로 병렬 연결되어 있다. 부사 rather는 형용사 cruel을 수식한다.

⑧ He **had metal buttons sewn** onto the sleeves.

→ 「have+목적어+p.p.」는 '~가 …되도록 하다'의 의미로, 목적어와 목적격 보어가 수동의 관계이므로 목적격 보어로 과거분사가 왔다.

⑪ So they **started to use** handkerchiefs instead of their sleeves.

→ 「start+to-v[v-ing]」는 '~하기 시작하다'의 의미이다.

⑫ In the past, soldiers **had to carry** lots of heavy equipment.

→ 「had to+동사원형」은 '~해야 했다'의 의미이다.

4

본책 • pp. 14-15

정답 1 ① 2 ③ 3 ④ 4 (1) T (2) T

문제 해설

1 과거 러시아의 표트르 대제가 남성들이 수염을 기르지 못하도록 세금을 부과한 것에 관한 글로, 주제로는 ① '러시아의 특이한 세금'이 가장 알맞다.

[문제] 글의 주제로 가장 알맞은 것은?

② 현대 남성들의 수염 스타일 ③ 역사상 가장 강력한 군주
④ 전 세계의 흥미로운 직업들 ⑤ 서유럽이 세계에 미친 영향

2 빈칸 뒤에 표트르 대제가 서유럽으로부터 법률, 군사 제도, 패션 등을 들여왔다는 내용이 이어지므로, 그가 러시아를 서유럽처럼 만들고 싶어 했음을 알 수 있다. 따라서, 빈칸에는 ③ '서유럽과 더 비슷한'이 가장 알맞다.

[문제] 글의 빈칸에 들어갈 말로 가장 알맞은 것은?

① 남성들에게 더 좋은 ② 이전보다 더 큰
④ 더 아름답고 유명한 ⑤ 다른 나라들보다 더 부유한

3 러시아의 표트르 대제가 서유럽으로부터 많은 것을 도입했다는 내용의 (B), 그 당시에 많은 서유럽 남성들이 면도를 했지만, 러시아 남성들은 긴 수염을 길렀다는 내용의 (C), 그래서 표트르 대제는 러시아 남성들도 면도를 하게 하려고 했다는 내용의 (A)의 흐름으로 이어지는 것이 가장 자연스럽다.

[문제] 문장 (A)~(C)의 순서로 가장 알맞은 것은?

4 (1) 문장 ⑦-⑧에 언급되어 있다.
(2) 문장 ⑨-⑩에 언급되어 있다.
[문제] 글의 내용과 일치하면 T, 그렇지 않으면 F를 쓰시오.
(1) 한 남성이 수염 세금을 내면, 그는 징표를 받았다.
(2) 경찰은 세금을 징수했고, 지불하지 않은 사람의 수염을 깎았다.

본문 직독 직해

① Many men around the world / have beards. / ② Interestingly, / Russian men /
전 세계의 많은 남성들은 / 수염이 있다 / 흥미롭게도 / 러시아 남성들은

had to pay money / to have beards / under the rule / of Peter the Great, / a powerful
돈을 내야 했다 / 수염을 갖기 위해 / 통치하에서 / 표트르 대제의 / 강력한

Russian czar. /
러시아 군주인

③ Peter the Great / wanted to make / the country / more like Western Europe. /
표트르 대제는 / 만들기를 원했다 / 국가를 / 서유럽과 더 비슷하게

⑤ He introduced many things / from Western Europe, / such as laws, a military system,
그는 많은 것들을 도입했다 / 서유럽으로부터 / 법률, 군사 제도,

and even fashion. / ⑥ At that time, / many Western European men shaved, / but / Russian
그리고 심지어 패션과 같은 / 그 당시에 / 많은 서유럽 남성들은 면도를 했다 / 하지만 / 러시아

men grew long beards. / ④ So / Peter the Great tried to / make all Russian men shave. /
남성들은 긴 수염을 길렀다 / 그래서 / 표트르 대제는 ~하려고 노력했다 / 모든 러시아 남성들이 면도하게 만들려고

⑦ If a man wanted to grow a beard, / he had to pay a tax. / ⑧ And / he had to carry a token /
만약 어떤 남성이 수염을 기르기를 원했다면 / 그는 세금을 지불해야 했다 / 그리고 / 그는 징표를 가지고 다녀야 했다

which showed / that he had already paid the tax. / ⑨ Peter the Great / even hired beard police /
보여주는 / 그가 이미 세금을 지불했었다는 것을 / 표트르 대제는 / 심지어 수염 경찰을 고용했다

to collect the beard tax. / ⑩ If a man refused to pay, / the police shaved his beard off! /
수염 세금을 징수하기 위해 / 만약 어떤 남성이 (세금을) 지불하기를 거부했다면 / 경찰은 그의 수염을 깎아 버렸다

본문 해석

전 세계의 많은 남성들은 수염이 있다. 흥미롭게도, 러시아 남성들은 강력한 러시아 군주인 표트르 대제의 통치하에서 수염을 갖기 위해 돈을 내야 했다.

표트르 대제는 국가를 서유럽과 더 비슷하게 만들기를 원했다. (B) 그는 서유럽으로부터 법률, 군사 제도, 그리고 심지어 패션과 같은 많은 것들을 도입했다. (C) 그 당시에, 많은 서유럽 남성들은 면도를 했지만, 러시아 남성들은 긴 수염을 길렀다. (A) 그래서 표트르 대제는 모든 러시아 남성들이 면도하게 하려고 노력했다. 만약 어떤 남성이 수염을 기르기를 원했다면, 그는 세금을 지불해야 했다. 그리고 그는 이미 세금을 지불했었다는 것을 보여주는 징표를 가지고 다녀야 했다. 표트르 대제는 심지어 수염 세금을 징수하기 위해 수염 경찰을 고용했다. 만약 어떤 남성이 (세금을) 지불하기를 거부했다면, 경찰은 그의 수염을 깎아 버렸다!

구문 해설

② Interestingly, Russian men had to pay money **to have** beards under the rule of *Peter the Great, a powerful Russian czar*.
→ to have는 '갖기 위해'의 의미로, 〈목적〉을 나타내는 부사적 용법의 to부정사이다.
→ Peter the Great와 a powerful Russian czar는 동격 관계이다.

④ So Peter the Great tried to **make all Russian men shave**.

→ 「make+목적어+동사원형」은 '~가 …하게 하다'의 의미이다.

⑧ And he had to carry **a token** [**which** showed that he *had* already *paid* the tax].

→ [ ]는 선행사 a token을 수식하는 주격 관계대명사절이다.

→ had paid는 과거완료(had+p.p.)로, 기준이 되는 과거 시점(showed)보다 먼저 일어난 일을 나타낸다.

⑨ Peter the Great even hired beard police **to collect** the beard tax.

→ to collect는 '징수하기 위해'라는 의미로, 〈목적〉을 나타내는 부사적 용법의 to부정사이다.

Review Test

본책 • pp. 16-17

정답 1 ⑤ 2 1) ⓑ 2) ⓐ 3) ⓒ 3 ④ 4 loved eating so much that he was overweight 5 ⑤
6 운동복의 품질 향상 때문에 7 ④ 8 habit

문제 해설

1 ⑤ sew: 바느질하다

2 1) beard((턱)수염): ⓑ 남성의 얼굴에서 자라는 털
2) comfortable(편안한): ⓐ 입기에 쾌적한
3) clever(영리한): ⓒ 똑똑하고 빨리 배우는

3 ④는 현재진행형의 현재분사로 쓰이고, 밑줄 친 buttoning과 나머지는 동명사로 쓰였다.
① 농구하는 것은 즐겁다.
② 제인은 소설 읽기를 좋아한다.
③ 춤추는 것은 그녀가 살아있다고 느끼게 해준다.
④ 앤디는 부엌에서 요리하고 있다.
⑤ 나의 직업은 영어를 가르치는 것이다.

4 '너무 ~해서 …하다'의 의미인 「so+형용사/부사+that+주어+동사」를 이용한다.

5 ⑤ 마지막 문장에서 많은 회사들이 V 스티치를 디자인 특징으로 포함시킨다고 했다.

6 V 스티치는 운동복의 품질 향상 때문에 더 이상 필요하지 않다고 했다.

Q. 왜 V 스티치는 더 이상 필요 없는가?

7 나폴레옹이 이 더러운 습관을 좋아하지 않았다는 내용 다음에, this dirty habit을 it으로 받아 그 더러운 습관을 나폴레옹이 고치고 싶어 했다는 (C)가 이어지고, 그래서 영리하지만 다소 잔인한 해결책을 내놓았다는 (A)가 나온 후, 그 해결책이 바로 소매에 금속 단추를 다는 것이었다고 설명하는 (B)로 이어지는 것이 자연스럽다.

8 어떤 사람이 규칙적이고 반복적으로 하는 것

Section 02 Culture

1

본책 • pp. 20-21

정답 1 ⑤ 2 ② 3 (유럽의) 환경이 파인애플을 재배하기에 좋지 않았기 때문에 4 welcoming, rare

문제 해설

1 파인애플이 환대의 의미를 가지게 된 이유에 관한 글이므로, 제목으로는 ⑤ '파인애플로 당신의 손님을 맞이해라'가 가장 알맞다.

① 손님을 접대하는 가장 중요한 규칙 ② 파인애플의 비극적인 역사

③ 유럽 최초의 파인애플 재배 ④ 유럽인들이 파인애플 먹는 것을 좋아하는 이유

2 ②: 문장 ④-⑤에서 카리브해로의 두 번째 여행에서 파인애플을 발견했다고 언급되어 있다.
①은 문장 ③에, ③은 문장 ⑧에, ④는 문장 ⑫에, ⑤는 문장 ⑬에 언급되어 있다.

3 문장 ⑩을 통해 알 수 있다.

Q: 왜 파인애플을 성공적으로 재배하는 데 200년이 걸렸는가?

4

파인애플은 오랫동안 유럽에서 희귀했기 때문에 다른 사람들을 환영하는 상징이 되었다.

본문 직독 직해

① In some cultures, / the pineapple is considered a symbol / of welcoming others. / ② But / how did this idea get started? /
일부 문화권에서 / 파인애플은 상징으로 여겨진다 / 다른 사람들을 환영하는 / 하지만 / 이 생각은 어떻게 시작되었을까?

③ Europeans first learned about pineapples / in 1493. / ④ Christopher Columbus was taking his second trip / to the Caribbean. / ⑤ His crew found an unusual fruit. / ⑥ The outside was rough / like a pinecone. / ⑦ However, / the inside was like an apple. / ⑧ They brought the unique fruit back / to Europe. /
유럽인들은 파인애플에 대해 처음 알게 되었다 / 1493년에 / 크리스토퍼 콜럼버스는 두 번째 여행을 가고 있었다 / 카리브해로 / 그의 선원들은 특이한 과일을 발견했다 / 겉은 거칠었다 / 솔방울처럼 / 하지만 / 속은 사과 같았다 / 그들은 그 독특한 과일을 가져왔다 / 유럽으로

⑨ Later, European farmers tried / to grow pineapples. / ⑩ However, / the environment was not good / for growing them. / ⑪ It took almost two hundred years / to successfully cultivate pineapples. / ⑫ For this reason, / pineapples were very rare, / and they became the perfect gift / for guests. / ⑬ Hosts used pineapples / as decorations or in dishes / when guests visited them. / ⑭ This showed / how much the hosts valued their guests. /
후에, 유럽의 농부들은 노력했다 / 파인애플을 재배하려고 / 그러나 / 환경이 좋지 않았다 / 그것들을 재배하기에 / 거의 200년이 걸렸다 / 성공적으로 파인애플을 재배하는 데 / 이러한 이유로 / 파인애플은 매우 희귀했다 / 그리고 그것은 완벽한 선물이 되었다 / 손님을 위한 / 주인은 파인애플을 사용했다 / 장식으로 또는 요리에 / 손님들이 그들을 방문하면 / 이것은 보여 주었다 / 그 주인이 얼마나 손님을 소중하게 생각하는지

본문 해석

일부 문화권에서, 파인애플은 다른 사람들을 환영하는 상징으로 여겨진다. 하지만 이 생각은 어떻게 시작되었을까?

유럽인들은 1493년에 파인애플에 대해 처음 알게 되었다. 크리스토퍼 콜럼버스는 카리브해로 두 번째 여행을

가고 있었다. 그의 선원들은 특이한 과일을 발견했다. 겉은 솔방울처럼 거칠었다. 하지만 속은 사과 같았다. 그들은 그 독특한 과일을 유럽으로 가져왔다.

후에, 유럽의 농부들은 파인애플을 재배하려고 노력했다. 그러나 환경이 파인애플을 재배하기에 좋지 않았다. 성공적으로 파인애플을 재배하는 데 거의 200년이 걸렸다. 이러한 이유로, 파인애플은 매우 희귀했고, 그것은 손님을 위한 완벽한 선물이 되었다. 손님들이 방문하면 주인은 장식으로 또는 요리에 파인애플을 사용했다. 이것은 그 주인이 얼마나 손님을 소중하게 생각하는지 보여 주었다.

구문 해설

① In some cultures, the pineapple **is considered** a symbol [of {*welcoming* others}].
→ is considered는 '여겨진다'의 의미로, 「be+p.p.」의 수동태이다.
→ [ ]는 a symbol을 수식하는 전치사구이다.
→ { }는 전치사 of의 목적어 역할을 하는 동명사구이다.

⑨ Later, European farmers **tried to grow** pineapples.
→ 「try+to-v」는 '~하려고 노력하다'의 의미이다.

⑪ **It took** almost **two hundred years to** successfully **cultivate** pineapples.
→ 「it takes+시간/노력/돈 + to-v」는 '~하는 데 …가 들다'의 의미이다.

⑭ This showed [how much the hosts valued their guests].
→ [ ]는 「의문사+주어+동사」의 간접의문문으로, 동사 show의 목적어 역할을 한다.

본책 • pp. 22-23

2

정답 1 ④ 2 ② 3 ④ 4 귀신들이 그들의 집으로 돌아가는 길을 찾는 것을 돕기 위해

문제 해설

1 귀신의 달이라고 불리는 음력 7월에 나쁜 일들이 생기지 않도록 조심하는 중국인들의 여러 행동을 설명하고 있으므로, 제목으로는 ④ '귀신의 달에는 조심하세요'가 가장 알맞다.
① 새로운 세계로 가는 문 ② 왜 사람들이 귀신을 믿는가
③ 중국의 월별 전통 ⑤ 중국의 미신이 주는 교훈

2 '대신에, 그들은 귀신들을 기쁘게 만들려고 노력한다'는 주어진 문장은, 귀신들을 위해 많은 음식을 만들고 귀신들에게 위안을 주기 위해 지폐를 태운다는 구체적인 노력의 예시 앞인 ②의 위치가 알맞다.

3 문장 ②-③에 언급되어 있다.

4 문장 ⑩에 언급되어 있다.

본문 직독 직해

① Some Chinese people (어떤 중국인들은) / are superstitious (미신을 믿는다) / about the seventh month (7월에 대한) / of the lunar calendar (음력의). / ② They believe (그들은 믿는다) / the gate (문이) / to the world of the dead (죽은 사람들의 세계로 가는) / opens (열린다) / at that time (그때에). / ③ That (그것은) means (의미한다) / the spirits of the dead (죽은 사람들의 영혼이) / can return (돌아올 수 있다는 것을) / to earth (이승으로). / ④ So (그래서) / they call (그들은 부른다) / the seventh month (7월을) / the "ghost month." ('귀신의 달'이라고) /

⑤ During this time, / Chinese people worry / that bad things will happen. / ⑥ So / they do
이 기간 동안에 / 중국인들은 걱정한다 / 나쁜 일들이 일어날 것을 / 그래서 그들은

not move / into a new house / or / get married. / Instead, / they try to make / the ghosts /
이사하지 않는다 새집으로 / 또는 결혼을 하지 않는다 대신에 / 그들은 만들려고 노력한다 귀신들을

happy. / ⑦ Some people make / lots of food / for the ghosts. / ⑧ Others burn / paper money /
기쁘게 / 어떤 사람들은 만든다 / 많은 음식을 / 귀신들을 위해 / 다른 사람들은 태운다 지폐를

to give the ghosts comfort. / ⑨ They even have / a special "ghost festival" / on the fifteenth
귀신들에게 위안을 주기 위해 / 그들은 심지어 연다 / 특별한 '귀신제'를 / 15일에

day / of the month. / ⑩ On that day, / people put paper lights / on rivers / to help / the ghosts /
그달의 / 그날 / 사람들은 종이등을 놓는다 / 강에 / 돕기 위해 귀신들이

find their way / back home. /
그들의 길을 찾는 것을 / 집으로 돌아가는

본문 해석

어떤 중국인들은 음력 7월에 대한 미신을 믿는다. 그들은 그때에 죽은 사람들의 세계로 가는 문이 열린다고 믿는다. 그것은 죽은 사람들의 영혼이 이승으로 돌아올 수 있다는 것을 의미한다. 그래서 그들은 7월을 '귀신의 달'이라고 부른다.

이 기간 동안에, 중국인들은 나쁜 일들이 일어날 것을 걱정한다. 그래서 그들은 새집으로 이사를 하거나 결혼을 하지 않는다. 대신에, 그들은 귀신들을 기쁘게 만들려고 노력한다. 어떤 사람들은 귀신들을 위해 많은 음식을 만든다. 다른 사람들은 귀신들에게 위안을 주기 위해 지폐를 태운다. 그들은 심지어 그달의 15일에는 특별한 '귀신제'를 열기도 한다. 그날, 사람들은 귀신들이 그들의 집으로 돌아가는 길을 찾는 것을 돕기 위해 강에 종이등을 띄운다.

구문 해설

② They believe [(**that**) the gate {to the world of *the dead*} opens at that time].
→ [ ]는 동사 believe의 목적어 역할을 하는 명사절로, 접속사 that이 생략되었다.
→ { }는 앞의 명사 the gate를 수식하는 전치사구이다.
→ 「the+형용사」는 '~한 사람들'의 의미이다.

⑧ Others burn paper money **to *give*** *the ghosts comfort*.
→ to give는 '주기 위해'의 의미로, 〈목적〉을 나타내는 부사적 용법의 to부정사이다.
→ 「give A B」는 'A에게 B를 주다'의 의미이다.

⑩ On that day, people put paper lights on rivers to **help the ghosts find** their way back home.
→ 「help+목적어+동사원형[to-v]」은 '~가 …하는 것을 돕다'의 의미이다.

본책 • pp. 24-25

3

정답 1 ③ 2 ① 3 ② 4 (1) T (2) F

문제 해설

1 아프리카계 미국인들의 결혼식 전통인 빗자루 넘기의 유래와 의미에 관한 글로, 주제로는 ③ '독특한 결혼 전통'이 가장 알맞다.
① 현대의 결혼 풍습 ② 결혼반지의 기원
④ 결혼의 문제점 ⑤ 전통을 지키는 것의 중요성

2 ⓐ는 반지를 주는 전형적인 결혼식 풍습을 가리키고, 나머지는 모두 빗자루를 넘는 것을 가리킨다.

3 문장 ⑮를 통해 알 수 있다.

4 (1) 문장 ⑩에 언급되어 있다.
(2) 문장 ⑫에서 빗자루를 넘는 것은 과거를 털어 버리고 가족을 잇는다는 의미라고 했다. 새집과 관련된 내용은 언급되지 않았다.

본문 직독 직해

① My friends / John and Olivia / had a beautiful wedding. / ② They gave rings / to each other. / ③ That is a typical custom. / ④ But / something surprising happened / at the party. /
내 친구들인 / John과 Olivia는 / 아름다운 결혼식을 했다 / 그들은 반지를 주었다 / 서로에게 / 그것은 전형적인 풍습이다 / 그런데 / 놀라운 무언가가 일어났다 / 그 파티에서

⑤ "Let's jump the broom!" / the MC said. / ⑥ I had to ask / a woman next to me / what this meant. / ⑦ "They are going to jump / over a broom," / she said. / ⑧ "It shows / that they are husband and wife now!" / ⑨ She said / that jumping the broom / came from an African American tradition. / ⑩ During the 1800s, / marriage was banned / among African American slaves. / ⑪ To secretly show their love, / slaves jumped over a broom. / ⑫ This symbolized / sweeping the past away / and / linking families. /
빗자루를 넘자고요 / 사회자가 말했다 / 나는 물어야 했다 / 내 옆에 있는 여성에게 / 이것이 무엇을 의미하는지 / 그들이 뛰어넘을 거예요 / 빗자루 위로 / 그녀가 말했다 / 그것은 보여주지요 / 그들이 이제 남편과 아내라는 것을 / 그녀는 말했다 / 빗자루를 넘는 것이 / 아프리카계 미국인들의 전통에서 왔다고 / 1800년대 동안에 / 결혼은 금지되었다 / 아프리카계 미국인 노예들 사이에서 / 그들의 사랑을 비밀스럽게 보여주기 위해 / 노예들은 빗자루를 뛰어넘었다 / 이것은 상징했다 / 과거를 털어 버리는 것을 / 그리고 / 가족을 잇는 것을

⑬ Times have changed, / but / John and Olivia / wanted to keep this tradition / in their wedding. / ⑭ They even let guests try it! / ⑮ I thought / that was the best part / of their wedding. /
시대가 바뀌었다 / 하지만 / John과 Olivia는 / 이 전통을 지키기를 원했다 / 그들의 결혼식에서 / 그들은 심지어 하객들이 그것을 시도해 보게 했다 / 나는 생각했다 / 그것이 가장 멋진 부분이라고 / 그들의 결혼식에서

본문 해석

내 친구들인 John과 Olivia가 아름다운 결혼식을 했다. 그들은 서로에게 반지를 주었다. 그것은 전형적인 풍습이다. 그런데 그 파티에서 놀라운 무언가가 일어났다.

"빗자루를 넘자고요!"라고 사회자가 말했다. 나는 이것이 무엇을 의미하는지 내 옆에 있는 여성에게 물어야 했다. "그들이 빗자루 위로 뛰어넘을 거예요."라고 그녀가 말했다. "그것은 이제 그들이 남편과 아내라는 것을 보여주지요!" 그녀는 빗자루를 넘는 것이 아프리카계 미국인들의 전통에서 왔다고 말했다. 1800년대 동안에, 아프리카계 미국인 노예들 사이에서 결혼은 금지되었다. 그들의 사랑을 비밀스럽게 보여주기 위해, 노예들은 빗자루를 뛰어넘었다. 이것은 과거를 털어 버리고 가족을 잇는 것을 상징했다.

시대가 바뀌었지만, John과 Olivia는 그들의 결혼식에서 이 전통을 지키기를 원했다. 그들은 심지어 하객들이 그것(빗자루 넘기)을 시도해 보게 했다! 나는 그것이 그들의 결혼식에서 가장 멋진 부분이라고 생각했다.

구문 해설

④ But **something surprising** happened at the party.

→ -thing으로 끝나는 대명사는 형용사가 뒤에서 수식한다.

⑥ I **had to** ***ask*** *a woman next to me* *what this meant*.

→ 「had to + 동사원형」은 '~해야 했다'의 의미이다.

→ 「ask A B」는 'A에게 B를 묻다'의 의미이다. a woman next to me가 A, what this meant가 B에 해당한다.

→ what this meant는 「의문사 + 주어 + 동사」의 간접의문문이다.

⑨ She said [**that** *jumping the broom* came from an African American tradition].

→ that은 명사절을 이끄는 접속사로, [ ]는 동사 said의 목적어 역할을 한다.

→ jumping the broom은 that절의 주어 역할을 하는 동명사구이다.

⑫ This symbolized **sweeping** the past away and **linking** families.

→ 동사 symbolized의 목적어 역할을 하는 동명사 sweeping과 linking이 접속사 and로 병렬 연결되어 있다.

⑭ They even **let guests try** it!

→ 「let + 목적어 + 동사원형」은 '~가 …하게 하다'의 의미이다.

본책 • pp. 26-27

4

정답 1 ③ 2 ① 3 ④ 4 good luck

문제 해설

1 원숭이 축제에 요리사들이 원숭이들을 위한 음식을 준비한다는 내용 중에, 무더운 날씨에 음식을 신선하게 보관하는 것은 어렵다는 내용의 (c)는 글의 흐름과 무관하다.

[문제] 글의 (a)~(e) 중, 전체 흐름과 관계없는 문장은?

2 빈칸 뒤에서 매년 수천 명의 사람들이 그 원숭이들을 보러 도시를 찾는다고 했으므로, 빈칸에는 ① '유명한 관광지'가 가장 알맞다.

[문제] 글의 빈칸에 들어갈 말로 가장 알맞은 것은?

② 원숭이들에게 안전한 지역 ③ 많은 축제가 있는 도시

④ 소원을 빌기에 좋은 장소 ⑤ 세계에서 가장 깨끗한 도시

3 ④: 문장 ⑥에서 축제는 Lopburi에 사는 4천 마리가 넘는 원숭이들을 위한 것이라고 했다.

①, ②는 문장 ①에, ③은 문장 ②-③에, ⑤는 문장 ⑪에 언급되어 있다.

[문제] 원숭이 축제에 관한 글의 내용과 일치하지 않는 것은?

4 문장 ⑦, ⑩에 언급되어 있다.

[문제] 다음 빈칸에 알맞은 단어를 글에서 찾아 쓰시오.

> Lopburi의 사람들은 원숭이들에게 감사를 표하기 위해 그리고 마을에 행운을 가져오기 위해 그들에게 음식을 준다.

본문 직독 직해

① On the last Sunday / of November, / there is a big party / in Lopburi, / Thailand. /
마지막 일요일에 11월의 성대한 파티가 있다 Lopburi에서 태국의

② Chefs prepare / fresh fruit, vegetables, and ice cream / in front of a temple. / ③ The food is
요리사들은 준비한다 신선한 과일, 채소, 그리고 아이스크림을 사찰 앞에 그 음식은

served / for free. / (④ It is difficult / to keep food fresh / in hot weather. /) ⑤ Would you like to
제공된다 무료로 어렵다 음식을 신선하게 보관하는 것은 무더운 날씨에 당신은 참여하고 싶은가

join / this party? / ⑥ Unfortunately, / it is only for / the more than 4,000 long-tailed monkeys /
이 파티에 유감스럽게도 그것은 오직 ~을 위한 것이다 4천 마리가 넘는 긴 꼬리원숭이들을

living in Lopburi! /
Lopburi에 사는

⑦ The people of Lopburi / hold the festival / to thank the monkeys. / ⑧ The monkeys
Lopburi의 사람들은 그 축제를 개최한다 원숭이들에게 감사를 표하기 위해 그 원숭이들은

made / Lopburi / a famous tourist spot. / ⑨ Thousands of people / visit the city / each year /
만들었다 Lopburi를 유명한 관광지로 수천 명의 사람들이 그 도시를 방문한다 매년

to see the monkeys. / ⑩ The local people / also believe / that giving food to the monkeys /
그 원숭이들을 보기 위해 지역 사람들은 또한 믿는다 원숭이들에게 음식을 주는 것이

can bring good luck / to the town. / ⑪ For these reasons, / people set up the buffet / for the
행운을 가져올 수 있다고 마을에 이런 이유들로 사람들은 뷔페를 마련한다

monkeys. /
원숭이들을 위해

본문 해석

11월의 마지막 일요일에, 태국의 Lopburi에서는 성대한 파티가 있다. 요리사들은 신선한 과일, 채소, 그리고 아이스크림을 사찰 앞에 준비한다. 그 음식은 무료로 제공된다. (무더운 날씨에 음식을 신선하게 보관하는 것은 어렵다.) 당신은 이 파티에 참여하고 싶은가? 유감스럽게도, 그것은 오직 Lopburi에 사는 4천 마리가 넘는 긴 꼬리 원숭이들을 위한 것이다!

Lopburi의 사람들은 그 원숭이들에게 감사를 표하기 위해 그 축제를 개최한다. 그 원숭이들은 Lopburi를 유명한 관광지로 만들었다. 수천 명의 사람들이 매년 그 원숭이들을 보기 위해 그 도시를 방문한다. 지역 사람들은 또한 원숭이들에게 음식을 주는 것이 마을에 행운을 가져올 수 있다고 믿는다. 이런 이유들로, 사람들은 원숭이들을 위해 뷔페를 마련한다.

구문 해설

④ It is difficult **to** ***keep food fresh*** in hot weather.
→ It은 가주어, to keep food fresh는 진주어이다.
→ 「keep+목적어+형용사」는 '~을 …하게 유지하다'의 의미이다.

⑥ Unfortunately, it is only for the **more than** 4,000 long-tailed monkeys [*living* in Lopburi]!
→ more than은 '~ 이상, ~보다 더 많은'의 의미이다.
→ [ ]는 the more … monkeys를 수식하는 현재분사구이다.

⑧ The monkeys **made Lopburi a famous tourist spot.**
→ 「make A B」는 'A를 B로 만들다'의 의미이다.

⑩ The local people also believe [**that** *giving food to the monkeys* can bring good luck…].
→ that은 명사절을 이끄는 접속사로, [ ]는 동사 believe의 목적어 역할을 한다.
→ giving food to the monkeys는 that절의 주어 역할을 하는 동명사구이다.

Review Test

본책 • pp. 28-29

정답 1 ② 2 ② 3 ③ 4 how much the hosts valued their guests 5 ⑤ 6 귀신들에게 위안을 주기 위해 7 ③ 8 broom, families

문제 해설

1 ② local: 지역의

2 banned(금지된다)와 반대 의미의 단어는 ② 'allowed(허용된다)'이다.

> 껌을 씹는 것은 싱가포르에서 금지된다.

① 의미했다 ③ 준비했다 ④ 소중하게 생각했다 ⑤ 참여했다

3 빈칸 앞에서 파인애플이 재배하기 어려워 그것을 성공적으로 재배하기까지 200년이나 걸렸다고 했으므로, 빈칸에는 ③ '희귀한'이 가장 알맞다.

① 큰 ② 흔한 ④ 신 ⑤ 다채로운

4 동사 show의 목적어로 「how much+주어+동사」 어순의 간접의문문을 쓴다.

5 ⓔ는 '귀신들'을 가리키고, 나머지는 모두 '중국인들'을 가리킨다.

6 귀신들에게 위안을 주기 위해서 지폐를 태운다고 했다.

> Q. 왜 중국인들이 지폐를 태우는가?

7 결혼식에서 빗자루를 뛰어넘는 아프리카계 미국인들의 전통 역사를 설명하는 내용 중에, 결혼 케이크에 관해 설명하는 (c)는 글의 전체 흐름과 무관하다.

8
> John과 Olivia의 결혼식에서 그들은 빗자루를 뛰어넘었다. 이 전통은 과거를 털어 버리고 가족을 이어주는 것을 상징한다.

Section 03 Food

본책 • pp. 32-33

1

정답 1 ⑤ 2 ③ 3 뿌리와 줄기 4 hungry, diseases, water

문제 해설

1 세계의 식량 부족 문제의 해결책이 될 수 있는 에티오피아의 주식인 엔셋이라는 식물에 관한 글이므로, 제목으로는 ⑤ '이 에티오피아 식물이 세계 기아를 해결할 수 있을까?'가 가장 알맞다.

① 너무 많은 엔셋을 먹는 것의 위험성 ② 왜 일부 식물들은 쉽게 병에 걸릴까?

③ 바나나와 비슷한 모양과 맛의 과일 ④ 전 세계 기아의 주요 원인

2 글의 첫 문단에 기후 변화로 인한 세계 기아의 문제점을 언급했고, 빈칸 뒤쪽에는 엔셋이 여러 환경 속에서 잘 자라나기 때문에 악화되는 기후 변화에도 사람들을 먹여 살릴 것이라고 했다. 그러므로 빈칸에는 ③ '미래의 식량'이 가장 알맞다.

① 현지에서 기른 작물 ② 멸종되고 있는 식물

④ 에티오피아의 국민 요리 ⑤ 전 세계적으로 판매되는 상품

3 문장 ⑦을 통해 알 수 있다.

Q: 엔셋의 어느 부분을 먹을 수 있는가?

4 엔셋은 빠르게 자라고, 쉽게 병에 걸리지 않으며, 물 없이도 오래 살 수 있기 때문에 사람들이 굶주리는 것을 막을 수 있다.

본문 직독 직해

① The food crisis around the world / is getting worse / due to the climate change. / ② Up to 783 million people regularly go hungry. / ③ The good news is / that there could be a solution. / ④ It is a plant / called enset. /

전 세계의 식량 위기가 / 더 악화되고 있다 / 기후 변화 때문에 / 7억 8천 3백만 명에 이르는 사람들이 정기적으로 굶주리고 있다 / 좋은 소식은 / 해결책이 있을 수 있다는 것이다 / 그것은 식물이다 / 엔셋이라고 불리는

⑤ Enset is a staple food / in Ethiopia. / ⑥ It looks like a banana tree / and can grow / to a height of about 4 to 13 meters. / ⑦ Unlike the fruits of other plants, / the fruit of the enset cannot be eaten, / but / its roots and stems can. / ⑧ They are used / to make porridge and bread. /

엔셋은 주식이다 / 에티오피아의 / 그것은 바나나 나무처럼 생겼다 / 그리고 자랄 수 있다 / 약 4미터에서 13미터 높이까지 / 다른 식물들의 열매들과 달리 / 엔셋의 열매는 먹을 수 없다 / 하지만 / 그것의 뿌리와 줄기는 먹을 수 있다 / 그것들은 사용된다 / 포리지와 빵을 만드는 데

⑨ There are several benefits / of enset / as the food of the future. / ⑩ It grows quickly / and can be harvested / in any season. / ⑪ The plant does not catch diseases / easily. / ⑫ It can also live / up to seven years / without water! / ⑬ It is possible / that enset will feed many people / despite worsening climate change. /

몇 가지 이점이 있다 / 엔셋의 / 미래의 식량으로서 / 그것은 빨리 자란다 / 그리고 수확할 수 있다 / 어떤 계절에도 / 이 식물은 병에 걸리지 않는다 / 쉽게 / 또한 살 수 있다 / 7년까지 / 물 없이도 / 가능성이 있다 / 엔셋은 많은 사람들을 먹여 살릴 것이라는 / 악화되고 있는 기후 변화에도 불구하고

본문 해석

기후 변화 때문에 전 세계의 식량 위기가 더 악화되고 있다. 7억 8천 3백만 명에 이르는 사람들이 정기적으로 굶주리고 있다. 좋은 소식은 해결책이 있을 수 있다는 것이다. 그것은 바로 엔셋이라고 불리는 식물이다.

엔셋은 에티오피아의 주식이다. 그것은 바나나 나무처럼 생겼고 약 4미터에서 13미터까지의 높이까지 자랄 수 있다. 다른 식물들의 열매들과 달리, 엔셋의 열매는 먹을 수 없지만, 그것의 뿌리와 줄기는 먹을 수 있다. 그것들은 포리지와 빵을 만드는 데 사용된다.

미래의 식량으로서 엔셋의 몇 가지 이점이 있다. 그것은 빨리 자라고 어떤 계절에도 수확할 수 있다. 이 식물은 쉽게 병에 걸리지 않는다. 또한 물 없이도 7년까지 살 수 있다! 악화되고 있는 기후 변화에도 불구하고 엔셋은 많은 사람들을 먹여 살릴 가능성이 있다.

구문 해설

① The food crisis [around the world] is **getting worse** *due to* the climate change.
- → [ ]는 The food crisis를 수식하는 전치사구이다.
- → 「get+비교급」은 '더 ~해지다'의 의미이다.
- → due to는 '~ 때문에'라는 의미의 전치사이므로 뒤에 명사(구)가 왔다.

③ The good news is [**that** there could be a solution].
- → that은 명사절을 이끄는 접속사로, [ ]는 문장의 보어 역할을 한다.

④ It is a plant [**called** enset].
- → [ ]는 a plant를 수식하는 과거분사이구다.

⑥ It ***looks* like** a banana tree and *can grow* to a height of about 4 to 13 meters.
- → look like는 '~처럼 보이다'의 의미이다.
- → 동사 looks와 can grow가 접속사 and로 병렬 연결되어 있다.

⑦ **Unlike** the fruits of other plants, the fruit of the enset cannot be eaten, but its roots and stems can (be eaten).
- → unlike는 '~와 달리'의 의미로, 전치사로 쓰였다.
- → can 뒤는 앞 절의 be eaten이 반복을 피하기 위해 생략되었다.

⑧ They **are used to make** porridge and bread.
- → 「be used+to-v」는 '~하는 데 사용되다'의 의미이다.

⑬ **It** is possible [**that** enset will feed many people *despite* worsening climate change]!
- → It은 가주어 [ ]가 진주어이다.
- → despite는 '~에도 불구하고'의 의미인 전치사이다.
- → worsening은 뒤의 명사 climate change를 수식하는 현재분사이다.

2

본책 • pp. 34-35

정답 1 ⑤ 2 크림이 걸쭉해지기 시작하는 것 3 (1) F (2) T 4 shake, butter

문제 해설

1 손수 버터를 만드는 방법에 관한 글이므로, 제목으로는 ⑤ '유지가 많은 크림으로 손수 만든 버터'가 가장 알맞다.
① 유지가 많은 크림의 기원
② 버터 제조의 새로운 추세
③ 크림을 만드는 것 뒤에 숨겨진 과학
④ 버터가 당신의 건강에 나쁜 이유

2 바로 앞 문장에 언급되어 있다.

3 (1) 문장 ⑨에서 버터를 차가운 물이 담긴 그릇에 넣으라고 했다.
(2) 문장 ⑫에 언급되어 있다.
(1) 버터를 만들려면 그 노란색 덩어리를 따뜻한 물에 넣어야 한다.
(2) 손수 만든 버터는 잘 짜내지 않으면 상할 것이다.

4 당신이 크림을 흔든 후에, 당신은 덩어리를 갖게 되는데, 이것이 버터이다.

본문 직독 직해

① Here is / how you can easily make your own butter. / ② First, / fill half a jar / with heavy
여기에 있다 당신이 쉽게 당신만의 버터를 만들 수 있는 방법이 먼저 병의 반을 채워라 유지가 많은
cream / and shake it / for a long time. / ③ The cream will start to thicken. / ④ Why does this
크림으로 그리고 그것을 흔들어라 오랫동안 크림이 걸쭉해지기 시작할 것이다 왜 이런 일이 일어날까
happen? / ⑤ It's because / cream is a mixture of milk fat and water. / ⑥ When you shake it, /
그것은 ~ 때문이다 크림은 유지방과 물의 혼합물이기 당신이 그것을 흔들면
the fat molecules stick together. / ⑦ Eventually, / they will form yellow lumps. / ⑧ These
지방 분자들은 서로 붙는다 결국 그것들은 노란 덩어리를 형성할 것이다 이
lumps are butter. / ⑨ Now / place the lumps of butter / in a bowl of cold water. / ⑩ Rinse the
덩어리가 버터이다 이제 버터 덩어리를 넣어라 차가운 물이 담긴 그릇에 버터를 헹궈라
butter / at least two times / in this way. / ⑪ Finally, / take out the butter / and squeeze it / until
최소 두 번 이런 방법으로 마지막으로 버터를 꺼내라 그리고 그것을 짜라
there is no more water. / ⑫ If you don't get all the water out, / your butter will quickly go bad. /
물이 더 이상 없을 때까지 만약 당신이 물을 모두 나오게 하지 못하면 당신의 버터는 빠르게 상할 것이다
⑬ Once you finish squeezing, / your homemade butter will be ready!
일단 짜는 것이 끝나면 손수 만든 버터가 준비될 것이다

본문 해석

여기에 당신이 쉽게 당신만의 버터를 만들 수 있는 방법이 있다. 먼저, 유지가 많은 크림으로 병의 반을 채우고 그것을 오랫동안 흔들어라. 크림이 걸쭉해지기 시작할 것이다. 왜 이런 일이 일어날까? 크림은 유지방과 물의 혼합물이기 때문이다. 당신이 그것을 흔들면, 지방 분자들은 서로 붙는다. 결국, 그것들은 노란 덩어리를 형성할 것이다. 이 덩어리가 버터이다. 이제 차가운 물이 담긴 그릇에 버터 덩어리를 넣어라. 이런 방법으로 버터를 최소 두 번 헹궈라. 마지막으로 버터를 꺼내 더 이상 물이 없을 때까지 그것을 짜라. 만약 당신이 물을 모두 나오게 하지 못하면, 당신의 버터는 빠르게 상할 것이다. 일단 짜는 것이 끝나면, 손수 만든 버터가 준비될 것이다!

구문 해설

① Here is [**how** you can easily make your own butter].
→ [ ]는 관계부사절로, how는 '~하는 방법[방식]'의 의미이다. 방법을 나타내는 선행사 the way와 관계부사 how는 같이 쓸 수 없으므로 둘 중 하나는 반드시 생략한다.

② First, **fill** half a jar with heavy cream and **shake** it for a long time.
→ 명령문의 동사원형 fill과 shake가 접속사 and로 병렬 연결되어 있다.

⑤ **It's because** cream is a mixture [of milk fat and water].
→ it's because ~는 '그것은 ~ 때문이다'의 의미로, 뒤에 이유에 해당하는 내용이 온다.
→ [ ]는 a mixture를 수식하는 전치사구이다.

⑨ Now **place the lumps of butter in a bowl of cold water.**

→ 「place A in B」는 'A를 B에 두다'의 의미로, the lumps of butter가 A, a bowl of cold water가 B에 해당한다.

⑪ Finally, **take out** the butter and **squeeze** it *until* there is no more water.

→ 명령문의 동사원형 take out과 squeeze가 접속사 and로 병렬 연결되어 있다.

→ until은 '~할 때까지'의 의미인 접속사이다.

⑫ **If** you don't get all the water out, your butter will quickly go bad.

→ if는 '만약 ~한다면'의 의미로, 〈조건〉을 나타내는 접속사이다.

⑬ **Once** you *finish squeezing*, your homemade butter will be ready!

→ once 는 '일단 ~하면'의 의미로, 〈조건〉을 나타내는 접속사이다.

→ 「finish+v-ing」는 '~하는 것을 마치다'의 의미로, finish는 동명사(squeezing)를 목적어로 취한다.

본책 • pp. 36-37

3

정답 1 ⑤ 2 ② 3 (1) F (2) T 4 forgot, soft

문제 해설

1 우연히 발명된 두 가지 음식에 관한 글이므로, 제목으로는 ⑤ '한 쌍의[두 가지] 맛있는 실수'가 가장 알맞다.
① 두 개의 문화, 하나의 요리법 ② 두부로 만든 브라우니
③ 사고로 다친 요리사들 ④ 노인들을 위한 최고의 음식들

2 빈칸 앞에서 케이크를 부풀어 오르게 만드는 재료인 베이킹파우더를 넣지 않았다고 했으므로, 빈칸에는 ② '납작한'이 가장 알맞다.
① 건조한 ③ 부드러운 ④ 쫄깃쫄깃한 ⑤ 달콤한

3 (1) 문장 ⑥에서 손님들이 여자가 만든 초콜릿 케이크를 아주 좋아했다고 했다.
(2) 문장 ⑫에 언급되어 있다.

4

보기	노력했다	잊었다	부드러운	딱딱한

브라우니는 한 미국인 여성이 케이크에 베이킹파우더를 넣는 것을 잊었을 때 발명되었다. 두부는 자신의 연로한 부모님을 위해 부드러운 음식을 만들려고 했던 한 중국인 남성에 의해 발명되었다.

본문 직독 직해

① Some popular foods / may have been invented / by accident. / ② According to one story, / brownies were invented accidentally / by a woman / in the United States. / ③ She was trying to bake / a chocolate cake, / but she forgot to add / baking powder. / ④ Baking powder is the ingredient / that makes cakes rise. / ⑤ So her cake was flat. / ⑥ She served it / to her guests / anyway, / and they loved it! /

어떤 인기 있는 음식들은 / 발명되었을 수도 있다 / 우연히 / 한 이야기에 따르면 / 브라우니는 우연히 발명되었다 / 한 여성에 의해 / 미국의 / 그녀는 구우려고 노력 중이었다 / 초콜릿 케이크를 / 그러나 그녀는 넣는 것을 잊었다 / 베이킹파우더를 / 베이킹파우더는 재료이다 / 케이크를 부풀어 오르게 만드는 / 그래서 그녀의 케이크는 납작했다 / 그녀는 그것을 대접했다 / 그녀의 손님들에게 / 어쨌든 / 그리고 그들은 그것을 아주 좋아했다

⑦ Some people say / tofu was also invented / by mistake. / ⑧ A Chinese man was cooking /
어떤 사람들은 말한다 두부 역시 발명되었다고 실수로 한 중국인 남성이 요리를 하고 있었다

for his elderly parents. / ⑨ They had trouble chewing their food / and could only eat soft food. /
그의 연로한 부모님을 위해 그들은 음식을 씹는 데 어려움이 있었다 그리고 부드러운 음식만을 먹을 수 있었다

⑩ He made soybean soup, / but they complained / it was tasteless. / ⑪ So he added salt /
그는 콩 수프를 만들었다 그러나 그들은 불평했다 그것이 맛없다고 그래서 그는 소금을 넣었다

and cooked the soup / for a few more minutes. / ⑫ When it cooled down, / it turned into / a
그리고 그 수프를 조리했다 몇 분 더 그것이 식었을 때 그것은 ~로 변했다

delicious soybean jelly. / ⑬ His parents loved it, / and now tofu is enjoyed / around the world. /
맛있는 콩 젤리 그의 부모님은 그것을 아주 좋아했다 그리고 이제 두부는 즐겨진다 전 세계에서

본문 해석

어떤 인기 있는 음식들은 우연히 발명되었을 수도 있다. 한 이야기에 따르면, 브라우니는 미국의 한 여성에 의해 우연히 발명되었다. 그녀는 초콜릿 케이크를 구우려고 하고 있었는데, 그녀는 베이킹파우더를 넣는 것을 잊어버렸다. 베이킹파우더는 케이크를 부풀어 오르게 만드는 재료이다. 그래서 그녀의 케이크는 납작했다. 그녀는 어쨌든 그것을 자신의 손님들에게 대접했고, 그들은 그것을 아주 좋아했다!

어떤 사람들은 두부 역시 실수로 발명되었다고 말한다. 한 중국인 남성이 자신의 연로한 부모님을 위해 요리를 하고 있었다. 그들은 음식을 씹는 데 어려움이 있었고 부드러운 음식만 먹을 수 있었다. 그는 콩 수프를 만들었지만, 그들은 그것이 맛이 없다고 불평했다. 그래서 그는 소금을 넣고 수프를 몇 분 더 조리했다. 그것이 식자, 그것은 맛있는 콩 젤리로 변했다. 그의 부모님은 그것을 아주 좋아했고, 두부는 이제 전 세계에서 즐겨진다.

구문 해설

① Some popular foods **may have** *been invented* by accident.
→ 「may have + p.p.」는 '~했을지도 모른다'의 의미로 과거의 일에 대한 추측을 나타낸다.
→ 음식은 '발명되는' 것이므로 수동태(been invented)가 쓰였다.

③ She was **trying to bake** a chocolate cake, but she *forgot to add* baking powder.
→ 「try + to-v」는 '~하려고 노력하다'의 의미이다.
→ 「forget + to-v」는 '~할 것을 잊다'의 의미이다.

④ Baking powder is **the ingredient** [**that** *makes cakes rise*].
→ [ ]는 선행사 the ingredient를 수식하는 주격 관계대명사절이다.
→ 「make + 목적어 + 동사원형」은 '~가 …하게 하다'의 의미이다.

⑨ They **had trouble chewing** their food and could only eat soft food.
→ 「have trouble + v-ing」는 '~하는 데 어려움을 겪다'의 의미이다.

⑩ He made soybean soup, but they complained [(**that**) it was tasteless].
→ [ ]는 동사 complained의 목적어 역할을 하는 명사절로, 접속사 that이 생략되었다.

본책 • pp. 38-39

4

정답 1 ④ 2 ③ 3 ③ 4 warm colors, more

문제 해설

1 난색을 사용하는 패스트푸드 식당들에 대한 내용 중에, 패스트푸드를 너무 많이 먹는 것은 건강에 좋지 않을 수 있다는 내용의 (d)는 글의 흐름과 무관하다.

[문제] 글의 (a)~(e) 중, 전체 흐름과 관계없는 것은?

2 ③: 문장 ⑪에서 한색은 사람들을 차분하게 만들어서 식욕을 줄인다고 했다.
①은 문장 ⑤에, ②는 문장 ⑦에, ④는 문장 ⑬에, ⑤는 문장 ⑮에 언급되어 있다.
[문제] 글의 내용과 일치하지 않는 것은?
① 패스트푸드 식당들은 빨간색과 노란색을 많이 사용한다.
② 난색은 사람을 들뜨게 만들 수 있다.
③ 한색은 사람들을 더 먹게 만들 수 있다.
④ 녹색은 자연의 색이라고 여겨진다.
⑤ 건강에 좋은 음식을 파는 식당들은 녹색을 많이 사용한다.

3 빈칸 앞에서는 사람들이 파란색이나 녹색 같은 한색들은 식욕을 줄인다고 생각한다고 했고, 빈칸 뒤에서는 녹색은 사실 음식과 연결되고, 건강하고 깨끗한 음식의 색으로 여겨진다고 했으므로, 빈칸에는 역접의 의미를 나타내는 ③ '하지만'이 가장 알맞다.
[문제] 글의 빈칸에 들어갈 말로 가장 알맞은 것은?
① 요약하면 ② 비슷하게 ④ 게다가 ⑤ 예를 들어

4 문장 ⑤-⑦에 언급되어 있다.
[문제] 다음 빈칸에 알맞은 단어나 표현을 글에서 찾아 쓰시오.

많은 패스트푸드 식당들이 난색을 사용하는데, 이것들은 사람들이 더 많이 먹게 하기 때문이다.

본문 직독 직해

① Did you know / that there are secrets / behind the colors / used in restaurants?
알고 있었나 / 비밀이 있다는 것을 / 색에 / 레스토랑에서 사용되는

② **Red and yellow** /
빨간색과 노란색

③ Think about the colors / inside fast-food restaurants. / ④ There are two common colors. /
색들에 대해 생각해 봐라 / 패스트푸드 식당들 안의 / 두 가지 공통된 색들이 있다

⑤ Almost all fast-food restaurants / use red and yellow. / ⑥ Both are warm colors. / ⑦ Studies show / that warm colors / make people excited / and / cause them to eat more! / (⑧ Eating too much fast food / can be bad for your health.) ⑨ So / fast-food restaurants / use these colors / to make people eat a lot. /
거의 모든 패스트푸드 식당들은 / 빨간색과 노란색을 사용한다 / 둘 다 난색이다 / 연구들은 보여준다 / 난색들이 / 사람들을 들뜨게 만든다는 것을 / 그리고 / 그들이 더 많이 먹게 야기한다는 것을 / 패스트푸드를 너무 많이 먹는 것은 / 건강에 좋지 않을 수 있다 / 그래서 / 패스트푸드 식당들은 / 이러한 색들을 사용한다 / 사람들을 많이 먹게 만들기 위해

⑩ **Green**
녹색

⑪ People think / that cool colors, / such as blue and green, / reduce their appetite / by making them calm. / ⑫ However, / green is actually linked / to food. / ⑬ People think of green / as the color / of nature and freshness. / ⑭ This makes it the color / of healthy, clean food. /
사람들은 생각한다 / 한색들이 / 파란색이나 녹색 같은 / 그들의 식욕을 줄인다고 / 그들을 차분하게 만들어서 / 하지만 / 녹색은 사실 연결된다 / 음식과 / 사람들은 녹색을 생각한다 / 색으로 / 자연과 신선함의 / 이것은 그것을 색으로 만든다 / 건강에 좋고 깨끗한 음식의

⑮ So / green is used / in restaurants / that sell fresh, healthy food. /
그래서 / 녹색은 사용된다 / 식당들에서 / 신선하고 건강에 좋은 음식을 파는

본문 해석

레스토랑에서 사용되는 색에 비밀이 있다는 것을 알고 있었나?

빨간색과 노란색

패스트푸드 식당들 안의 색들에 대해 생각해 봐라. 두 가지 공통된 색들이 있다. 거의 모든 패스트푸드 식당들은 빨간색과 노란색을 사용한다. 둘 다 난색이다. 연구들은 난색들이 사람들을 들뜨게 만들고 그들이 더 많이 먹게 한다는 것을 보여준다! (패스트푸드를 너무 많이 먹는 것은 건강에 좋지 않을 수 있다.) 그래서 패스트푸드 식당들은 사람들이 많이 먹게 만들기 위해 이러한 색들을 사용한다.

녹색

사람들은 파란색이나 녹색 같은 한색들이 그들을 차분하게 만들어서 그들의 식욕을 줄인다고 생각한다. 하지만, 녹색은 사실 음식과 연결된다. 사람들은 녹색을 자연과 신선함의 색이라고 생각한다. 이것은 그것(녹색)을 건강에 좋고 깨끗한 음식의 색으로 만든다. 그래서 녹색은 신선하고 건강에 좋은 음식을 파는 식당들에서 사용된다.

구문 해설

① Did you know [**that** there are secrets behind the colors {**used** in restaurants}]?
- → that은 명사절을 이끄는 접속사로, [ ]는 동사 know의 목적어 역할을 한다.
- → { }는 colors를 수식하는 과거분사구이다.

⑦ Studies show [**that** warm colors *make people excited* and cause them to eat more]!
- → that은 명사절을 이끄는 접속사로, [ ]는 동사 show의 목적어 역할을 하는 명사절이다.
- → 「make+목적어+형용사」는 '~을 …하게 만들다'의 의미이다.
- → 「cause+목적어+to-v」는 '~가 …하게 야기하다'의 의미이다.

⑨ So fast-food restaurants use these colors to **make people eat** a lot.
- → 「make+목적어+동사원형」은 '~가 …하게 하다'의 의미이다.

⑫ However, green is actually **linked to** food.
- → 「A be linked to B」는 「link A to B(A를 B에 연결하다)」의 수동태 표현으로, 'A는 B에 연결되다'라는 의미이다.

⑬ People **think of green as the color of nature and freshness.**
- → 「think of A as B」는 'A를 B로 생각하다[여기다]'의 의미이다.

⑭ This **makes it the color of healthy, clean food.**
- → 「make A B」는 'A를 B로 만들다'의 의미로, 여기서는 it이 A, the color of healthy, clean food가 B에 해당한다.

Review Test

본책 • pp. 40-41

정답 1 ① 2 1) serve 2) calm 3 ③ 4 It is possible that enset will feed many people
5 ⑤ 6 ingredient 7 사람들이 많이 먹게 만드는 색이라서 8 ④

문제 해설

1 ① fill: 채우다

2 1) '누군가에게 음식이나 음료를 주다'라는 의미의 단어는 'serve(제공하다, 대접하다)'이다.
2) '속상하거나 불안하거나 흥분하지 않은'이라는 의미의 단어는 'calm(차분한)'이다.

3 엔셋을 어느 지역에서나 쉽게 재배할 수 있다고는 언급하지 않았다.

4 가주어 it, 진주어 that절을 이용하여 배열한다.

5 ⓔ는 콩 젤리, 즉 지금의 두부를 가리키고, 나머지는 콩 수프를 가리킨다.

6 | 음식, 제품 등을 만드는 데 사용되는 품목 중 하나 |

7 난색이 사람들이 많이 먹게 만들기 때문에 사용한다고 했다.
| Q. 왜 패스트푸드 식당이 난색을 사용하는가? |

8 주어진 문장의 This는 사람들이 녹색을 자연과 신선함의 색으로 생각하는 것을 가리키며, it은 녹색을 가리키므로, '이것은 그것(녹색)을 건강에 좋고 깨끗한 음식의 색으로 만든다.'라는 내용의 주어진 문장은 ④의 위치에 들어가는 것이 가장 알맞다.

Section 04 Nature & Environment

본책 • pp. 44-45

1

정답 1 ⑤ 2 ④ 3 ④ 4 short, protect

문제 해설

1 턱끈펭귄이 마이크로 수면을 하는 이유에 관한 글이므로, 제목으로는 ⑤ '종 생존을 위한 특이한 수면 패턴'이 가장 알맞다.

① 동물들이 그들의 이름을 얻는 방법 ② 펭귄은 낮에 잠을 잘까?
③ 남극에 사는 것의 위험성 ④ 동물들이 겨울에 더 오래 자는 이유

2 빈칸 앞에서 턱끈펭귄이 짧은 마이크로 수면을 한다는 설명이 나오고, 빈칸 뒤의 단락에서 갈색 도둑갈매기로부터 새끼를 보호하기 위해 마이크로 수면이 필요하다고 했으므로, 빈칸에는 ④ '위험한'이 가장 알맞다.

① 안전한 ② 건강한 ③ 중요한 ⑤ 불편한

3 ④: 문장 ⑨에서 턱끈펭귄의 한 부모가 먹이를 사냥하러 간다고 했다.
①은 문장 ②에, ②는 문장 ④에, ③은 문장 ⑦에, ⑤는 문장 ⑪에 언급되어 있다.

4 턱끈펭귄은 다른 새들로부터 자신의 알을 보호하기 위해 매우 짧은 시간 동안 잠을 잔다.

본문 직독 직해

① Chinstrap penguins live / in Antarctica. / ② Their name comes from the thin black line / that runs under their chin. / ③ These animals survive / in Antarctica's difficult conditions / with an unusual sleep pattern. / ④ They sleep / for very short periods, / about four seconds. / ⑤ This is called microsleep. / ⑥ Chinstraps have more than 10,000 microsleeps / each day. / ⑦ These add up to around 11 hours of sleep. / ⑧ The penguins do this / because a long, deep sleep could be dangerous. /

턱끈펭귄은 산다 / 남극에 / 그들의 이름은 가는 검은 선에서 유래한다 / 턱 밑으로 이어지는 / 이 동물들은 생존한다 / 남극의 어려운 환경에서 / 특이한 수면 패턴으로 / 그들은 잠을 잔다 / 매우 짧은 시간 동안 / 약 4초 정도의 / 이것은 마이크로 수면이라고 불린다 / 턱끈펭귄은 10,000번 넘게 마이크로 수면을 한다 / 매일 / 이것들은 결국 약 11시간의 수면 시간이 된다 / 펭귄들은 이렇게 한다 / 길고 깊은 수면은 위험할 수 있기 때문에

⑨ After the chinstrap penguins lay their eggs, / one parent goes hunting / for food. / ⑩ The other parent must protect the eggs or babies / at all times. / ⑪ This is because / birds / called brown skuas / want to eat them. / ⑫ However, / it is not easy / to be awake / for 24 hours a day. / ⑬ So, / chinstrap penguins need microsleep. / ⑭ They use it / to keep their eggs and babies safe. /

턱끈펭귄이 알을 낳은 후 / 한 부모는 사냥하러 간다 / 먹이를 / 다른 부모는 알이나 새끼를 보호해야 한다 / 항상 / 이것은 때문이다 / 새들이 / 갈색 도둑갈매기라고 불리는 / 그것들을 먹고 싶어 하기 / 하지만 / 쉽지 않다 / 깨어 있는 것은 / 하루에 24시간 동안 / 그래서 / 턱끈펭귄은 마이크로 수면이 필요하다 / 그들은 그것을 이용한다 / 알과 새끼를 안전하게 지키기 위해

본문 해석

턱끈펭귄은 남극에 산다. 그들의 이름은 턱 밑으로 이어지는 가는 검은 선에서 유래한다. 이 동물들은 남극의 어려운 환경에서 특이한 수면 패턴으로 생존한다. 그들은 약 4초 정도의 매우 짧은 시간 동안 잠을 잔다. 이것은

마이크로 수면이라고 불린다. 턱끈펭귄은 매일 10,000번 넘게 마이크로 수면을 한다. 이것들은 결국 약 11시간의 수면 시간이 된다. 펭귄들은 길고 깊은 수면은 위험할 수 있기 때문에 이렇게 한다.

턱끈펭귄이 알을 낳은 후, 한 부모는 먹이를 사냥하러 간다. 다른 부모는 항상 알이나 새끼를 보호해야 한다. 이것은 갈색 도둑갈매기라고 불리는 새들이 그것들을 먹고 싶어 하기 때문이다. 하지만, 하루에 24시간 동안 깨어 있는 것은 쉽지 않다. 그래서 턱끈펭귄은 마이크로 수면이 필요하다. 그들은 알과 새끼를 안전하게 지키기 위해 그것을 이용한다.

구문 해설

② Their name comes from **the thin black line** [**that** runs under their chin].
→ that은 the thin black line을 선행사로 하는 주격 관계대명사이다.

⑤ This **is called** microsleep.
→ is called는 '~라고 불린다'의 의미로, 「be+p.p.」의 수동태이다.

⑧ The penguins **do this** because a long, deep sleep could be dangerous.
→ do this는 have more than 10,000 microsleeps each day를 가리킨다.

⑩ The other parent **must protect** the eggs or babies at all times.
→ '~해야 한다'의 의미인 〈의무〉를 나타내는 조동사 must 뒤에 동사원형 protect가 왔다.

⑪ **This is because** birds [*called* brown skuas] want to eat them.
→ this is because ~는 '이것은 ~ 때문이다'의 의미로, 뒤에 이유에 해당하는 내용이 온다.
→ [ ]는 birds를 수식하는 과거분사구이다.

⑫ However, **it** is not easy **to be awake for 24 hours a day.**
→ it은 가주어이고, to be awake for 24 hours a day가 진주어이다.

⑭ They use it **to *keep*** *their eggs and babies safe.*
→ to keep은 '유지하기 위해'의 의미로, 〈목적〉을 나타내는 부사적 용법의 to부정사이다.
→ 「keep+목적어+형용사」는 '~을 …하게 유지하다'의 의미이다.

2

본책 • pp. 46-47

정답 1 ⑤ 2 ①, ③ 3 ③ 4 썩어가는 고기 같은 냄새가 나서

문제 해설

1 빈칸 앞에서 사람들이 일반적으로 꽃에 대해 가지고 있는 생각을 설명하고, 빈칸 뒤에서 보통의 꽃과 다른 특징을 지닌 titan arum에 관해 설명하고 있으므로, 빈칸에는 ⑤ '다른'이 가장 알맞다.
① 강한 ② 알록달록한 ③ 아름다운 ④ 흔한

2 문장 ③을 통해 서식지를, ⑥을 통해 크기를 알 수 있다.

3 titan arum은 냄새가 좋지 않다고 설명하는 내용 중에, 일부 향수들은 달콤한 꽃 향기를 사용한다는 내용의 (c)는 글의 흐름과 무관하다.

4 문장 ⑪-⑫에 언급되어 있다.

본문 직독 직해

① Most people think / that flowers are small and pretty, / have bright colors, / and
대부분의 사람들은 생각한다 꽃들이 작고 예쁘고 밝은색을 가지고 있고

smell nice. / ② But / the titan arum is different! / ③ We can find the titan arum / in
그리고 좋은 냄새가 난다고 하지만 titan arum은 다르다 우리는 titan arum을 발견할 수 있다

Indonesia. / ④ It is one of the tallest flowers / in the world. / ⑤ It can grow / up to 10
인도네시아에서 그것은 가장 키가 큰 꽃들 중 하나이다 세계에서 그것은 자랄 수 있다

centimeters / in one day! / ⑥ When the titan arum / finishes growing, / it is usually /
10센티미터까지 하루 사이에 titan arum이 성장하는 것을 끝낼 때 그것은 보통 ~이다

around 3 meters tall. / ⑦ It does not bloom / as often as other flowers. / ⑧ And / when it
키가 약 3미터 그것은 꽃을 피우지 않는다 다른 꽃들만큼 자주 그리고 그것이

does, / it does not have / a sweet smell. / (⑨ Some perfumes use / sweet flower scents. /)
할[필] 때 그것은 가지고 있지 않다 달콤한 냄새를 일부 향수들은 사용한다 달콤한 꽃 향기를

⑩ Actually, / it smells terrible! / ⑪ People say / that it smells / like rotting meat. / ⑫ This
사실 그것은 끔찍한 냄새가 난다 사람들은 말한다 그것은 냄새가 난다고 썩어가는 고기 같은 이것이

is why / it is sometimes called / the "corpse flower." / ⑬ To make matters worse, / its bad smell
~한 이유이다 그것이 때때로 불리는 '시체꽃'이라고 설상가상으로 그것의 나쁜 냄새는

can draw some insects / like beetles and flies. / ⑭ The insects even lay their eggs / in the flower. /
몇몇 곤충들을 끌 수 있다 딱정벌레나 파리 같은 그 곤충들은 심지어 알도 낳는다 그 꽃 안에

본문 해석

대부분의 사람들은 꽃들이 작고 예쁘며, 밝은색을 가지고 있고, 좋은 향기가 난다고 생각한다. 하지만 titan arum은 다르다! 우리는 titan arum을 인도네시아에서 발견할 수 있다. 그것은 세계에서 가장 키가 큰 꽃들 중 하나이다. 그것은 하루 사이에 10센티미터까지 자랄 수 있다! titan arum이 성장하는 것을 끝낼 때, 그것은 보통 키가 약 3미터이다. 그것은 다른 꽃들만큼 자주 꽃을 피우지 않는다. 그리고 그것이 필 때, 그것은 달콤한 향기를 가지고 있지 않다. (일부 향수들은 달콤한 꽃 향기를 사용한다.) 사실, 그것은 끔찍한 냄새가 난다! 사람들은 그것이 썩어가는 고기 같은 냄새가 난다고 말한다. 이것이 그것(titan arum)이 때때로 '시체꽃'이라고 불리는 이유이다. 설상가상으로, 그것의 나쁜 냄새는 딱정벌레나 파리 같은 곤충들을 끌 수 있다. 그 곤충들은 심지어 그 꽃 안에 알도 낳는다.

구문 해설

① Most people think [**that** flowers *are* small and pretty, *have* bright colors, and *smell* nice].
- that은 명사절을 이끄는 접속사로, [ ]는 동사 think의 목적어 역할을 한다.
- are, have, smell은 명사절의 동사로 「A, B, and C」의 구조로 병렬 연결되어 있다.
- 「smell + 형용사」는 '~한 냄새가 나다'의 의미이다.

④ It is **one of the tallest flowers** in the world.
- 「one of the + 최상급 + 복수 명사」는 '가장 ~한 …들 중 하나'의 의미이다.

⑥ When the titan arum **finishes growing**, it is usually around 3 meters tall.
- 「finish + v-ing」는 '~하는 것을 끝내다'의 의미로, finish는 동명사(growing)를 목적어로 취한다.

⑫ **This is why** it is sometimes called the "corpse flower."
- this is why ~는 '이것이 ~한 이유이다'의 의미로, 뒤에 결과에 해당하는 내용이 온다.

3

정답 1 ② 2 ⑤ 3 ③ 4 (1) T (2) F

문제 해설

1 한때 쓰레기로 가득 차 있던 해변이 정부의 노력과 대자연의 정화를 통해 아름다운 해변으로 거듭났다는 내용의 글로, 주제로는 ② 'Glass Beach가 어떻게 만들어졌는가'가 가장 알맞다.

① 곤경에 빠진 해변 ③ 세계의 유명한 해변들
④ 해변을 깨끗하게 하려는 정부의 노력들 ⑤ 해변에서 쓰레기를 치우는 과정

2 정부가 Glass Beach를 치우기 위한 프로젝트를 시작했지만 작은 유리 조각들을 제거하는 문제가 남아 있었다는 내용의 (C), 놀랍게도 대자연이 혼자 그 문제를 처리했고 유리 조각들을 보석같이 만들었다는 내용의 (B), 덕분에 오늘날 Glass Beach가 많은 사람들이 방문하고 싶어 하는 아름다운 장소가 되었다는 내용의 (A)의 흐름으로 이어지는 것이 가장 자연스럽다.

3 ⓒ는 the glass(유리)를 가리키고, 나머지는 모두 Glass Beach를 가리킨다.

4 (1) 문장 ①에 언급되어 있다.
(2) 문장 ⑧-⑪에서 정부가 Glass Beach의 쓰레기 대부분을 치웠지만 작은 유리 조각들을 제거하는 문제가 남아 있었다고 했고, 문장 ⑤에서 대자연이 혼자 그 문제를 처리했다고 했다.

본문 직독 직해

① Once / there was a beach / in California / that was full of trash. / ② People threw garbage, / including cans, plastic, and a lot of glass, / onto it. /
예전에 / 해변이 있었다 / 캘리포니아에 / 쓰레기로 가득 차 있던 / 사람들은 쓰레기를 버렸다 / 캔, 플라스틱, 그리고 많은 유리를 포함하여 / 그곳에

⑧ In 1967, / the government stopped / people / from throwing their trash there. /
1967년에 / 정부는 막았다 / 사람들이 / 그들의 쓰레기를 그곳에 버리는 것을

⑨ Projects were started / to clean up the area. / ⑩ Most of the trash / was removed. /
프로젝트들이 시작되었다 / 그 지역을 치우기 위해 / 대부분의 쓰레기는 / 치워졌다

⑪ However, / one big problem remained: / how to get rid of / the small pieces of glass / covering the beach. /
하지만 / 한 가지 큰 문제가 남아 있었다 / 어떻게 ~을 제거할 것인가 / 작은 유리 조각들 / 해변을 덮고 있는

⑤ Surprisingly, / Mother Nature / took care of the problem / by herself. / ⑥ Over the years, / the ocean's waves / broke down the glass / and / made it into tiny smooth pieces / that look like jewelry. / ⑦ They made the beach sparkle / with all the colors / of the rainbow! /
놀랍게도 / 대자연은 / 그 문제를 처리했다 / 혼자 / 수년간 / 바다의 파도가 / 유리를 부수었다 / 그리고 / 그것을 아주 작은 매끄러운 조각들로 만들었다 / 보석처럼 보이는 / 그것들은 해변이 반짝이게 만들었다 / 모든 색으로 / 무지개의

③ Today, / this place is known / as Glass Beach. / ④ Unlike in the past, / it is now a beautiful place / that many people want to visit! /
오늘날 / 이 장소는 알려져 있다 / Glass Beach로 / 과거와는 달리 / 그곳은 이제 아름다운 장소이다 / 많은 사람들이 방문하고 싶어 하는

본문 해석

예전에 캘리포니아에는 쓰레기로 가득 찬 해변이 있었다. 사람들이 캔, 플라스틱, 그리고 많은 유리를 포함하여 쓰레기를 그곳에 버렸다.

(C) 1967년에, 정부는 사람들이 그곳에 쓰레기를 버리는 것을 막았다. 그 지역을 치우기 위해 프로젝트들이

시작되었다. 대부분의 쓰레기는 치워졌다. 하지만, 한 가지 큰 문제가 남아 있었는데, 해변을 덮고 있는 작은 유리 조각들을 어떻게 제거할 것인가 하는 것이었다.

(B) 놀랍게도, 대자연은 그 문제를 혼자 처리했다. 수년간, 바다의 파도가 유리를 부수고 그것을 보석처럼 보이는 아주 작고 매끄러운 조각들로 만들었다. 그것들은 해변이 무지개의 모든 색으로 반짝이게 했다!

(A) 오늘날, 이 장소는 Glass Beach로 알려져 있다. 과거와는 달리, 그곳은 이제 많은 사람들이 방문하고 싶어 하는 아름다운 장소이다!

구문 해설

① Once there was **a beach** in California [**that** was full of trash].
→ [ ]는 선행사 a beach를 수식하는 주격 관계대명사절이다.

④ **Unlike** in the past, it is now *a beautiful place* [*that* many people want to visit]!
→ unlike는 '~와는 달리'의 의미인 전치사이다.
→ [ ]는 선행사 a beautiful place를 수식하는 목적격 관계대명사절이다.

⑦ They **made the beach sparkle** with all the colors of the rainbow!
→ 「make+목적어+동사원형」은 '~가 …하게 하다'의 의미이다.

⑧ In 1967, the government **stopped people from throwing** their trash there.
→ 「stop+목적어+from+v-ing」는 '~가 …하는 것을 막다'의 의미이다.

⑪ However, **one big problem** remained: [*how to get rid of* the small pieces of glass {covering the beach}].
→ 콜론(:)은 앞의 내용을 보충하거나 부연 설명할 때 사용되며, one big problem과 [ ]는 동격 관계이다.
→ 「how+to-v」는 '어떻게 ~할지'의 의미이다.
→ { }는 the small pieces of glass를 수식하는 현재분사구이다.

본책 • pp. 50-51

4

정답 1 ⑤ 2 ④ 3 ② 4 (1) pollution (2) environment (3) trash

문제 해설

1 브라질의 도시 Curitiba가 빈곤과 환경 오염 문제를 극복하기 위해 한 노력들과 그 성과를 설명하는 글로, 제목으로는 ⑤ '어떻게 쿠리치바의 사람들이 도시의 문제들을 극복했는가'가 가장 알맞다.
[문제] 글의 제목으로 가장 알맞은 것은?
① 브라질 쿠리치바의 특징들 ② 쿠리치바에서 방문해 볼 만한 많은 관광 명소들
③ 왜 쿠리치바의 사람들이 빈곤으로 고통받는가 ④ 재활용: 환경을 보호하기 위한 최고의 방법

2 빈칸 다음에 쓰레기를 음식이나 필요한 물품으로 교환해 줘서 가난한 사람을 돕는 동시에 도시를 깨끗이 했으며, 사람들이 함께 꽃과 나무와 풀을 심었다는 내용이 나오므로, 빈칸에는 ④ '가장 친환경적인 도시들 중 하나'가 가장 알맞다.
[문제] 글의 빈칸에 들어갈 말로 가장 알맞은 것은?
① 가장 안전한 도시 ② 가장 흥미로운 도시
③ 가장 부유한 도시들 중 하나 ⑤ 가장 인기 있는 관광지

3 '그 아이디어는 쓰레기를 음식으로 교환하는 것이었다'는 내용의 주어진 문장은 쿠리치바의 빈곤 가정과 환경 둘 다 도울 수 있는 아이디어를 생각해냈다는 문장 ④뒤, 그래서 그것을 Green Exchange 프로그램이라고 부르기 시작했다는 문장 ⑤ 앞인 ②의 위치에 오는 것이 가장 알맞다.

[문제] 다음 문장이 들어갈 위치로 가장 알맞은 것은?

4 [문제] 다음 빈칸에 알맞은 단어를 상자에서 골라 쓰시오.

쓰레기	오염	공간	환경

쿠리치바
가난한 사람들과 (1) 오염으로 가득 차 있던 도시였다

⬇

친환경적으로 되기 위한 노력
- Green Exchange 프로그램을 시작했다
- 가난한 사람들과 (2) 환경 둘 다 도왔다
- (3) 쓰레기를 받는 대신에 사람들에게 음식을 주었다
- 꽃과 나무와 풀을 심었다

⬇

더 깨끗하고 더 안전한 도시가 되었다

본문 직독 직해

① Curitiba, Brazil, / was once a city / that was full of / poor people and pollution. /
브라질의 Curitiba는 한때 도시였다 ~로 가득 차 있던 가난한 사람들과 오염

② In 1970, / however, / everything changed. / ③ A team of city workers / came together /
1970년에 그러나 모든 것이 달라졌다 시 근로자들 팀이 모였다

to make Curitiba / one of the greenest cities / in the world. / ④ They thought of an idea / that
Curitiba를 만들기 위해 가장 친환경적인 도시들 중 하나로 세계에서 그들은 아이디어를 생각해 냈다

could help / both poor families and the environment. / The idea was / to exchange trash for
도울 수 있는 빈곤 가정과 환경 둘 다 그 아이디어는 ~였다 쓰레기를 음식으로

food. / ⑤ So, / they called / this / the Green Exchange Program. / ⑥ Poor people gave their
교환하는 것 그래서 그들은 불렀다 이것을 Green Exchange 프로그램이라고 가난한 사람들은 그들의 쓰레기를 주었다

trash / to the local centers / and / got food or bus tickets. / ⑦ Children could bring in / cans
지역 센터들에 그리고 음식이나 버스표를 얻었다 아이들은 가져올 수 있었다 캔과

and bottles / and / receive school supplies / in return. / ⑧ Through this program, / people
병을 그리고 학용품을 받을 수 있었다 보상으로 이 프로그램을 통해 사람들은

could get / what they needed / and / clean up the city / at the same time. / ⑨ The people also
얻을 수 있었다 그들이 필요로 하는 것을 그리고 도시를 깨끗이 치울 수 있었다 동시에 사람들은 또한

worked together / to plant flowers, trees, and grass. /
함께 일했다 꽃과 나무와 풀을 심기 위해

⑩ Now / Curitiba is cleaner and safer, / with 16 parks, 14 forests, and over 1,000 public
이제 Curitiba는 더 깨끗하고 더 안전하다 16개의 공원, 14개의 숲, 그리고 1,000개 이상의 공공

green spaces / for people / to enjoy! /
녹지들과 더불어 사람들이 즐길 수 있는

본문 해석

브라질의 Curitiba(쿠리치바)는 한때 가난한 사람들과 오염으로 가득 차 있던 도시였다. 그러나, 1970년에 모든 것이 달라졌다. 시 근로자들 팀이 Curitiba를 세계에서 가장 친환경적인 도시들 중 하나로 만들기 위해 모였다. 그들은 빈곤 가정과 환경 둘 다 도울 수 있는 아이디어를 생각해 냈다. 그 아이디어는 쓰레기를 음식으로 교환하는 것이었다. 그래서 그들은 이것을 Green Exchange 프로그램이라고 불렀다. 가난한 사람들은 그들의 쓰레기를 지

역 센터들에 주고 음식이나 버스표를 얻었다. 아이들은 캔과 병을 가져와서 보상으로 학용품을 받을 수 있었다. 이 프로그램을 통해, 사람들은 그들이 필요로 하는 것을 얻고 동시에 도시를 깨끗이 치울 수 있었다. 사람들은 또한 꽃과 나무와 풀을 심기 위해 함께 일했다.

이제 Curitiba는 사람들이 즐길 수 있는 16개의 공원, 14개의 숲, 그리고 1,000개 이상의 공공녹지들과 더불어 더 깨끗하고 더 안전하다!

구문 해설

③ A team of city workers came together to **make Curitiba *one of the greenest cities* in the world.**

➔ 「make A B」는 'A를 B로 만들다'의 의미이다. Curitiba가 A, one of the greenest cities in the world가 B에 해당한다.

➔ 「one of the + 최상급 + 복수 명사」는 '가장 ~한 것들 중 하나'의 의미이다.

④ They thought of **an idea** [**that** could help *both* poor families *and* the environment].

➔ [ ]는 선행사 an idea를 수식하는 주격 관계대명사절이다.

➔ 「both A and B」는 'A와 B 둘 다'의 의미이다.

⑤ So, they **called this the Green Exchange Program.**

➔ 「call A B」는 'A를 B라고 부르다'의 의미이다. this가 A, the Green Exchange Program이 B에 해당한다.

⑧ **Through** this program, people could *get* [what they needed] and *clean up* the city at the same time.

➔ through는 '~을 통하여'라는 의미의 전치사이다.

➔ 동사원형 get과 clean up이 접속사 and로 병렬 연결되어 있다.

➔ what은 선행사를 포함하는 관계대명사로, '~하는 것'의 의미이며, [ ]는 동사 get의 목적어 역할을 한다.

⑩ Now Curitiba is cleaner and safer, with [16 parks, 14 forests, and over 1,000 public green spaces] **for people** *to enjoy*!

➔ for people은 to부정사(to enjoy)의 의미상의 주어이다.

➔ to enjoy는 [ ]를 수식하는 형용사적 용법의 to부정사이다.

Review Test

본책 • pp. 52-53

정답 1 ④ 2 ① 3 ③ 4 microsleep 5 one of the tallest flowers in the world 6 ⑤ 7 ② 8 school supplies

문제 해설

1 ④ common: 흔한

2 get rid of(~을 처리하다[없애다])와 비슷한 의미의 단어는 ① 'remove(제거하다, 치우다)'이다.

> 내 등에서 벌레를 없애 주세요.

② 던지다 ③ 가리다 ④ 받다 ⑤ 교환하다

3 '이것은 마이크로 수면이라고 불린다'는 주어진 문장은 마이크로 수면이 무엇인지 설명한 문장과 턱끈펭귄이 하루에 만 번 넘게 마이크로 수면을 한다는 문장 사이인 ③의 위치에 들어가는 것이 가장 알맞다.

4 it은 바로 앞 문장의 microsleep을 가리킨다.

5 '가장 ~한 것[사람]들 중 하나'라는 의미의 「one of the+최상급+복수 명사」를 이용한다.

6 빈칸 앞에 titan arum이 끔찍한 냄새가 나서 '시체꽃'으로 불린다는 내용이 언급되었고, 빈칸 뒤에는 그 냄새가 곤충들을 꽃으로 이끌어 그 꽃 안에 알을 낳기까지 한다는 또 다른 안 좋은 점이 언급되었으므로, 빈칸에는 ⑤ 'To make matters worse(설상가상으로)'가 알맞다.
① 요약해서 ② 그러므로 ③ 대신에 ④ 반면에

7 빈곤 가정과 환경 둘 다 도울 수 있다는 아이디어를 생각해 냈다는 (B) 뒤에, 그 아이디어가 쓰레기를 음식으로 교환하는 것이라고 설명하는 (A)가 오고, 그것을 Green Exchange 프로그램이라고 불렀다는 (C)의 흐름으로 이어지는 것이 가장 자연스럽다.

8

> Green Exchange 프로그램에서, 아이들은 캔과 병을 주고 학용품을 받았다.

Section 05 Psychology

본책 • pp. 56-57

1

정답 1 ② 2 프로젝트가 항상 계획된 것보다 더 오랜 시간이 걸리는 것 3 (1) F (2) F (3) T
4 more, project

문제 해설

1 프로젝트는 항상 계획한 것보다 더 오랜 시간이 걸린다는 호프스태터의 법칙에 관한 글이므로, 제목으로는 ② '호프스태터의 법칙: 왜 당신의 계획이 실패하는가'가 가장 알맞다.
① 늦더라도 하지 않는 것보다는 낫다
③ 호프스태터 법칙의 흥미로운 역사
④ 호프스태터의 법칙은 왜 유용하지 않을 수도 있는가
⑤ 자신을 다른 사람들과 비교하는 것의 이점

2 문장 ①에 언급되어 있다.

3 (1) 문장 ①에서 호프스태터의 법칙은 일을 끝마치는 데 계획보다 더 오랜 시간이 걸리는 것을 말한다고 했다.
(2) 문장 ⑥에서 사람들은 자신의 능력을 강하게 믿는 경향이 있다고 했다.
(3) 문장 ⑪에 언급되어 있다.

4

보기	프로젝트	더 적은	계획	더 많은

호프스태터의 법칙에 따르면 우리는 우리가 예상한 것보다 프로젝트를 마치는 데 항상 더 많은 시간이 필요하다.

본문 직독 직해

① According to Hofstadter's law, / a project always takes a longer time / than planned. /
호프스태터의 법칙에 따르면 프로젝트는 항상 더 오랜 시간이 걸린다 계획된 것보다

② Maybe / you have experience / with this. / ③ For example, / you have homework / that you think / will be easy. / ④ You leave a short amount of time / to complete it. / ⑤ In the end, / you almost miss the deadline. / ⑥ Things like this happen / because we believe too strongly / in our abilities. / ⑦ We usually think / we can work faster / than we really can. / ⑧ Also, / unexpected events often cause delays. /
아마도 당신은 경험이 있을 것이다 이것에 대한 예를 들어 당신은 숙제가 있다 당신이 생각하는 쉬울 것이라고 당신은 짧은 시간을 남겨 둔다 그것을 완료하는 데 결국 당신은 기한을 놓칠 뻔한다 이러한 일들은 발생한다 우리가 너무 강하게 믿기 때문에 우리의 능력을 우리는 보통 생각한다 우리가 더 빠르게 작업할 수 있다고 우리가 실제로 할 수 있는 것보다 또한 예상치 못한 일들이 자주 지연을 일으킨다

⑨ Of course, / this is a problem. / ⑩ However, / there are some tips / that help you avoid Hofstadter's law. / ⑪ Compare your current plan with past ones / to make sure / that it is realistic. / ⑫ Also, / consider giving yourself extra time / to finish your project. / ⑬ This will help you / meet your deadline / despite any unexpected delays. /
물론 이것은 문제이다 하지만 몇 가지 방법이 있다 당신이 호프스태터의 법칙을 피할 수 있도록 도와주는 당신의 현재 계획을 과거의 계획들과 비교해라 확인하기 위해 그것이 현실적인지 또한 스스로에게 여분의 시간을 주는 것을 고려해라 당신의 프로젝트를 마치기 위해 이것은 당신을 도와줄 것이다 마감일을 지키도록 어떤 예상치 못한 지연에도 불구하고

본문 해석

호프스태터의 법칙에 따르면, 프로젝트는 항상 계획된 것보다 더 오랜 시간이 걸린다. 아마도 당신은 이것에 대한 경험이 있을 것이다. 예를 들어, 당신은 쉬울 것이라고 생각하는 숙제가 있다. 당신은 그것을 완료하는 데 짧은 시간을 남겨 둔다. 결국, 당신은 기한을 놓칠 뻔한다. 이러한 일들은 우리가 우리의 능력을 너무 강하게 믿기 때문에 발생한다. 우리는 보통 자신이 실제로 할 수 있는 것보다 더 빠르게 작업할 수 있다고 생각한다. 또한, 예상치 못한 일들이 자주 지연을 일으킨다.

물론, 이것은 문제이다. 하지만, 당신이 호프스태터의 법칙을 피할 수 있도록 도와주는 몇 가지 방법이 있다. 계획이 현실적인지 확인하기 위해 당신의 현재 계획을 과거의 계획들과 비교해라. 또한, 당신의 프로젝트를 마치기 위해 스스로에게 여분의 시간을 주는 것을 고려해라. 이것은 당신이 어떤 예상치 못한 지연에도 불구하고 마감일을 지키도록 도와줄 것이다.

구문 해설

③ For example, you have **homework** [**that** {you think} will be easy].
→ [ ]는 선행사 homework를 수식하는 주격 관계대명사절이며, you think가 삽입되었다.

⑦ We usually think [(**that**) we can work faster than we really can].
→ [ ]는 동사 think의 목적어 역할을 하는 명사절로, 접속사 that이 생략되어 있다.

⑩ However, there are **some tips** [**that** *help you avoid* Hofstadter's law].
→ [ ]는 선행사 some tips를 수식하는 주격 관계대명사절이다.
→ 「help+목적어+동사원형[to-v]」은 '~가 …하는 것을 돕다'의 의미이다.

⑪ **Compare your current plan with past ones** *to make sure* [that it is realistic].
→ 「compare A with B」는 'A와 B를 비교하다'의 의미이다. A는 your current plan, B는 past ones에 해당한다. ones는 plans를 대신한다.
→ to make sure는 '확인하기 위해'의 의미로, 〈목적〉을 나타내는 부사적 용법의 to부정사이다.
→ that은 명사절을 이끄는 접속사로, [ ]는 make sure의 목적어 역할을 한다.

⑫ Also, **consider giving** yourself extra time *to finish* your project.
→ 「consider+v-ing」는 '~하는 것을 고려하다'의 의미이다.
→ to finish는 '마치기 위해'의 의미로, 〈목적〉을 나타내는 부사적 용법의 to부정사이다.

⑬ This will **help you meet** your deadline despite any unexpected delays.
→ 「help+목적어+동사원형[to-v]」은 '~가 …하는 것을 돕다'의 의미이다.

2

본책 • pp. 58-59

정답 1 ⑤ 2 ③ 3 ⑤ 4 replace, fit

문제 해설

1 어떤 새로운 물건으로 인해 그 물건과 어울리는 다른 새로운 제품을 계속 구매하고 싶어 하는 디드로 효과에 관한 글이므로, 주제로는 ⑤가 가장 알맞다.

2 디드로 효과는 한 프랑스 철학자의 이름을 따서 지어졌다는 내용 뒤에, 그가 빨간 가운을 받았다는 내용의 (B), 그가 그것을 집으로 가져온 후 다른 기존 물건들과 비교하게 되었다는 내용의 (A), 결국 새로운 가구와 옷으로 모두 교체했다는 내용의 (C)로 이어지는 흐름이 가장 알맞다.

3 빈칸 앞에서 프랑스 철학자가 아름다운 가운을 받고 난 뒤 그의 물건들을 새로운 것들로 교체하기 시작했다는 내용이 나오고, 빈칸 뒤에서는 한 가지 새로운 것이 더 많은 새로운 것들을 구매하게 만든다고 하였으므로 빈칸에는 ⑤ '당신을 계획하지 않은 일련의 구매로 이끈다'가 가장 알맞다.

① 선물을 주는 참된 이유를 밝힌다
② 당신이 당신의 모든 소유물을 정리할 수 있도록 도와준다
③ 당신이 돈을 낭비하는 것을 막는다
④ 당신의 현재 스타일을 훨씬 더 최신 유행으로 만든다

4 보기 | 보다 교체하다 사다 맞다

사람들은 새로운 것을 얻으면 때때로 그들의 오래된 물건을 교체하고 싶어 한다. 우리는 우리가 이미 가진 것과 맞는 물건들을 선택함으로써 이를 방지할 수 있다.

본문 직독 직해

① Getting something new / can sometimes have an unexpected effect. / ② Suddenly / you
새로운 것을 얻는 것은 때때로 예상치 못한 효과를 가질 수 있다 갑자기 당신은

feel unhappy with your old stuff / and want to buy more new things. / ③ This is called the
당신의 오래된 물건들에 만족하지 못하고 더 많은 새로운 것들을 사고 싶어 한다 이것은

Diderot effect. / ④ It was named after a French philosopher / who was poor for most of his
디드로 효과라고 불린다 그것은 프랑스 철학자의 이름을 따서 지어졌다 삶의 대부분을 가난하게 보냈던

life. / ⑥ One day / he was given a beautiful red robe. / ⑤ When he brought it home, / it made
어느 날 그는 아름다운 빨간 가운을 받았다 그가 그것을 집에 가지고 왔을 때 그것은

his other things look ugly / in comparison. / ⑦ So / he started / replacing all his furniture and
그의 다른 물건들을 보기 흉하게 만들었다 비교적 그래서 그는 시작했다 그의 모든 가구와

clothes with new items. / ⑧ This is / how the Diderot effect leads you to a series of unplanned
옷을 새로운 물품들로 교체하는 것을 이것이 ~이다 디드로 효과가 당신을 계획하지 않은 일련의 구매로 이끄는 방법

purchases. / ⑨ One new thing causes / you to buy / more new things. / ⑩ As a result, / you end
한 가지 새로운 것은 야기한다 당신이 사도록 더 많은 새로운 것들을 결과적으로 당신은

up with items / you don't need. / ⑪ To prevent the Diderot effect, / try to purchase things /
물건들을 갖게 된다 필요하지 않은 디드로 효과를 방지하기 위해 물건들을 구매하려고 노력해라

that fit your current style / and match what you already have. /
당신의 현재 스타일에 맞는 그리고 당신이 이미 가지고 있는 것과 어울리는

본문 해석

새로운 것을 얻는 것은 때때로 예상치 못한 효과를 가질 수 있다. 갑자기 당신은 당신의 오래된 물건들에 만족하지 못하고 더 많은 새로운 것들을 사고 싶어 한다. 이것은 디드로 효과라고 불린다. 그것은 삶의 대부분을 가난하게 보냈던 프랑스 철학자의 이름을 따서 지어졌다. (B) 어느 날 그는 아름다운 빨간 가운을 받았다. (A) 그가 그것을 집에 가지고 왔을 때, 그것은 그의 다른 물건들을 비교적 보기 흉하게 만들었다. (C) 그래서 그는 그의 모든 가구와 옷을 새로운 물품들로 교체하기 시작했다. 이것이 디드로 효과가 당신을 계획하지 않은 일련의 구매로 이끄는 방법이다. 한 가지 새로운 것은 당신이 더 많은 새로운 것들을 구매하게 만든다. 결과적으로, 당신은 필요하지 않은 물건들을 갖게 된다. 디드로 효과를 방지하기 위해, 당신의 현재 스타일에 맞으며 당신이 이미 가지고 있는 것과 어울리는 물건들을 구매하려고 노력해라.

구문 해설

① Getting **something new** can sometimes have an unexpected effect.
→ -thing으로 끝나는 대명사는 형용사가 뒤에서 수식하므로, 형용사 new가 something 뒤에 왔다.

② Suddenly you ***feel* unhappy** with your old stuff and *want* to buy more new things.
→ 「feel+형용사」는 '~하게 느끼다'의 의미이다.

→ 문장의 동사 feel과 want가 접속사 and로 병렬 연결되어 있다.

④ It **was named after** *a French philosopher* [*who* was poor for most of his life].

→ was named after는 '~의 이름을 따서 지어졌다'의 의미로, 「be+p.p.」의 수동태이다.

→ [ ]는 선행사 a French philosopher를 수식하는 주격 관계대명사절이다.

⑦ So he **started *replacing*** *all his furniture and clothes with new items.*

→ 「start+v-ing[to-v]」는 '~하기 시작하다'의 의미이다.

→ 「replace A with B」는 'A를 B로 바꾸다'의 의미이다. 여기에서 A는 all his furniture and clothes이고 B는 new items이다.

⑧ This is [**how** the Diderot effect leads you to a series of unplanned purchases].

→ [ ]는 관계부사절로, how는 '~하는 방법[방식]'의 의미이다. 방법을 나타내는 선행사 the way와 관계부사 how는 같이 쓸 수 없으므로, 둘 중 하나는 반드시 생략한다.

⑩ As a result, you end up with **items** [(**which**[**that**]) you don't need].

→ [ ]는 선행사 items를 수식하는 목적격 관계대명사절로, 앞에 관계대명사 which[that]가 생략되었다.

⑪ **To prevent** the Diderot effect, *try to purchase* things [that **fit** your current style and **match** *what* you already have].

→ To prevent는 '방지하기 위해'의 의미로, 〈목적〉을 나타내는 부사적 용법의 to부정사이다.

→ 「try+to-v」는 '~하려고 노력하다'의 의미이다.

→ [ ]는 선행사 things를 수식하는 주격 관계대명사절이다.

→ [ ]의 동사 fit과 match는 접속사 and로 병렬 연결되어 있다.

→ what은 선행사를 포함하는 관계대명사로, '~하는 것'의 의미이다.

3

본책 • pp. 60-61

정답 1 ⑤ 2 ⑤ 3 (1) F (2) T 4 ④

문제 해설

1 문장 ⑨를 통해 알 수 있다.

2 빈칸 앞에서 올바른 답이 떠오를 때까지 뇌는 잘못된 답을 계속 갖고 있어야 한다고 했으므로, 뇌의 속도가 느려진다는 것을 알 수 있다. 따라서, 빈칸에는 ⑤ '늦춘다'가 가장 알맞다.
① 진정시킨다 ② 깨운다 ③ 속도를 낸다 ④ 자극한다

3 (1) 문장 ⑫에서 뇌는 일반적으로 상충되는 정보 중 더 친숙한 일을 먼저 한다고 했다.
(2) 문장 ⑬에 언급되어 있다.

4 스트룹 효과는 상충되는 정보를 처리할 때 발생한다고 했으므로, 도형의 형태와 그 명칭이 일치하지 않는 ④가 가장 알맞다.

본문 직독 직해

① Say / the colors of the words / in the box / below / as fast as you can! /
말해 보라 / 단어들의 색들을 / 상자에 있는 / 아래의 / 가능한 한 빨리

② Wasn't it easy? / ③ Now try this. / ④ Again, / say the color / that each word is written in. /
그것은 쉽지 않았는가 / 이제 이것을 시도해 봐라 / 다시 / 색을 말해 보라 / 각 단어가 쓰여 있는

⑤ Did you find / that / more difficult? / ⑥ Did it take longer? / ⑦ Did you say the word /
당신은 생각했는가 그것이 더 어렵다고 시간이 더 오래 걸렸는가 당신은 단어를 말했는가

instead of the color? / ⑧ If so, / you experienced the Stroop Effect. / ⑨ It happens / because
색 대신에 만약 그렇다면 당신은 스트룹 효과를 경험했다 그것은 발생한다

the brain needs / extra time / to work / when it handles / conflicting information. /
뇌가 필요로 하기 때문에 추가의 시간을 일할 그것이 다룰 때 상충되는 정보를

⑩ In this experiment, / the word *red* is written / in yellow. / ⑪ The word's meaning and
이 실험에서 '빨강'이라는 단어는 쓰여 있다 노란색으로 단어의 의미와

its color / are conflicting. / ⑫ When there is conflicting information, / the brain generally
그것의 색이 상충된다 상충되는 정보가 있을 때 뇌는 일반적으로

does / the more familiar job / first. / ⑬ The brain is more familiar / with reading words /
한다 더 친숙한 일을 먼저 뇌는 더 친숙하다 단어를 읽는 것에

than with naming colors. / ⑭ So / words are recognized / more quickly / than colors. /
색의 이름을 말하는 것보다 그래서 단어들은 인식된다 더 빨리 색들보다

⑮ However, / the experiment asks / you / to say the color, / not the word. / ⑯ So / your brain /
하지만 그 실험은 요청한다 당신에게 색을 말하라고 단어가 아니라 그래서 당신의 뇌는

has to hold on to / the wrong answer / until the right answer comes. / ⑰ This slows down /
~을 계속 보유해야 한다 잘못된 답 올바른 답이 떠오를 때까지 이것은 늦춘다

your brain! /
당신의 뇌를

본문 해석

아래 상자에 있는 단어들의 색들을 가능한 한 빨리 말해 보라!

빨강초록파랑분홍노랑

그것은 쉽지 않았는가? 이제 이것을 시도해 봐라. 다시, 각 단어가 쓰여 있는 색을 말해 보라.

빨강초록파랑분홍노랑

당신은 그것이 더 어렵다고 생각했는가? 시간이 더 오래 걸렸는가? 색 대신에 단어를 말했는가? 만약 그렇다면, 당신은 스트룹 효과(Stroop Effect)를 경험했다. 그것은 뇌가 상충되는 정보를 다룰 때 일할 추가의 시간을 필요로 하기 때문에 발생한다. 이 실험에서, '빨강'이라는 단어는 노란색으로 쓰여 있다. 단어의 의미와 그것의 색이 상충된다. 상충되는 정보가 있을 때, 뇌는 일반적으로 더 친숙한 일을 먼저 한다. 뇌는 색의 이름을 말하는 것보다 단어를 읽는 것에 더 친숙하다. 그래서 단어들이 색들보다 더 빨리 인식된다. 하지만, 그 실험은 당신에게 단어가 아니라 색을 말하라고 요청한다. 그래서 당신의 뇌는 올바른 답이 떠오를 때까지 잘못된 답을 계속 보유해야 한다. 이것은 당신의 뇌를 늦춘다!

구문 해설

① Say the colors of the words in the box below **as fast as you can**!

→ 「as + 형용사[부사]의 원급 + as + 주어 + can」은 '가능한 한 ~한[하게]'의 의미이다.

④ Again, say **the color** [**that** each word is written in].

→ that은 the color를 선행사로 하는 목적격 관계대명사이다.

⑤ Did you **find that more difficult**?

→ 「find + 목적어 + 형용사」는 '~가 …하다고 생각하다'의 의미이다.

⑨ It happens because the brain needs extra time **to work** ... .

→ to work는 명사구 extra time을 수식하는 형용사적 용법의 to부정사이다.

⑬ The brain **is** more **familiar with** *reading words* than **with** *naming colors*.
→ be familiar with ~는 '~에 친숙[익숙]하다'의 의미이다.
→ reading words와 naming colors는 전치사 with의 목적어 역할을 하는 동명사구로, 접속사 than에 병렬 연결되어 있다.

본책 • pp. 62-63

4

정답 1 ② 2 ③ 3 ⑤ 4 small

문제 해설

1 작은 부탁에 대한 승낙을 연달아 얻어 결과적으로 큰 부탁에 대한 승낙을 이끌어 내는 기법에 관한 글이므로, 제목으로는 ② '큰 부탁을 하는 한 가지 방법'이 가장 알맞다.
[문제] 글의 제목으로 가장 알맞은 것은?
① 작은 행동들이 차이를 만든다 ③ 영업 기법은 정말 효과가 있을까?
④ 장사의 비결들: 무언가를 판매하는 방법 ⑤ 문간에 발 들여놓기 기법 피하기

2 '집에 있던 사람들이 아무것도 사고 싶지 않다면 그저 문을 닫으면 되었다'는 내용의 주어진 문장은 과거의 판매원들의 방문 판매에 대해 언급한 문장 ⑧ 뒤에 오는 것이 자연스럽다. 또한, 문장 ⑨의 this가 주어진 문장의 내용 전체를 가리키므로, ③의 위치가 가장 알맞다.
[문제] 다음 문장이 들어갈 위치로 가장 알맞은 곳은?

3 문간에 발 들여놓기 기법은 작은 부탁을 연달아 하는 것을 통해 결과적으로 큰 승낙을 얻어 내는 것이므로, 한 문제씩 연달아 도와 달라고 요청하는 ⑤가 가장 알맞다.
[문제] '문간에 발 들여놓기' 기법의 사례로 가장 알맞은 것은?
① "이것은 한정판입니다. 하나만 남았습니다."
② "이 케이크를 구매하시면 두 개의 쿠키를 공짜로 드립니다!"
③ "만약 100달러가 비싸다고 생각하신다면 이 제품을 90달러에 드리겠습니다."
④ "솔직하게 말씀드릴게요. 제가 지금 매우 바쁩니다. 그것을 대신 해 주세요."
⑤ "1번 문제풀이를 도와주셔서 감사해요. 그 다음 것도 해주시겠어요?"

4 문장 ⑩-⑫를 통해 알 수 있다.
[문제] 다음 빈칸에 알맞은 단어 하나를 글에서 찾아 쓰시오.

> '문간에 발 들여놓기' 기법은 요청하는 데 사용될 수 있다. 먼저 당신은 작은 부탁을 한다. 그런 다음 당신은 원하는 것을 얻어 낼 때까지 계속해서 작은 부탁들을 더 한다.

본문 직독 직해

① Your friend asks you to walk / to the playground / with her. / ② You say / you're busy, / so she asks you to walk / to the corner / instead. / ③ It's not far, / so you agree. / ④ When you get there, / she asks you to go / a little farther. / ⑤ The pattern repeats / until you arrive / at the playground. /

당신의 친구가 당신에게 걸어가 달라고 부탁한다 / 운동장까지 / 그녀와 함께 / 당신은 말한다 / 당신은 바쁘다고 / 그래서 그녀는 당신에게 걸어가 달라고 부탁한다 / (길)모퉁이까지 / 대신에 / 그곳은 멀지 않다 / 그래서 당신은 승낙한다 / 당신이 그곳에 도착하자 / 그녀는 당신에게 가자고 부탁한다 / 조금 더 멀리 / 그 패턴은 반복된다 / 당신이 도착할 때까지 / 운동장에

⑥ This is the "foot-in-the-door" technique. / ⑦ It is a classic strategy / in sales. /
이것은 '문간에 발 들여놓기' 기법이다 이것은 대표적인 전략이다 영업에서

⑧ A long time ago, / salespeople went / from house to house. / The people in the homes /
오래전에 판매원들은 다녔다 집집마다 집에 있던 사람들은

could simply close the door / if they didn't want to buy anything. / ⑨ To prevent this, /
그저 문을 닫으면 되었다 만약 그들이 무언가를 사는 것을 원하지 않으면 이것을 막기 위해

salespeople would sometimes put their foot / in the way of the door / so it couldn't be closed. /
판매원들은 때때로 그들의 발을 놓곤 했다 문간에 그것이 닫히지 않도록

⑩ The foot-in-the-door technique / uses small requests. / ⑪ Each new request / is not that
문간에 발 들여놓기 기법은 작은 요청들을 사용한다 각각의 새로운 요청은 그렇게 크지

big. / ⑫ By focusing on getting / one small yes / after another, / this technique / often leads to
않다 얻어 내는 것에 집중함으로써 하나의 작은 승낙을 연달아 이 기법은 흔히 큰 승낙으로

a big yes. /
이어진다

본문 해석

당신의 친구가 당신에게 그녀와 함께 운동장까지 걸어가자고 부탁한다. 당신이 바쁘다고 말해서, 그녀는 당신에게 대신 길모퉁이까지 걸어가자고 부탁한다. 그곳(길모퉁이)은 멀지 않아서, 당신은 승낙한다. 당신이 그곳에 도착하자, 그녀는 조금 더 멀리 가자고 부탁한다. 이 패턴은 당신이 운동장에 도착할 때까지 반복된다.

이것은 '문간에 발 들여놓기(foot-in-the-door)' 기법이다. 이것은 영업의 대표적인 전략이다. 오래전에 판매원들은 집집마다 다녔다. 집에 있던 사람들이 아무것도 사고 싶지 않다면 그저 문을 닫으면 되었다. 이것을 막기 위해, 판매원들은 문이 닫히지 않도록 때때로 문간에 발을 들여놓곤 했다.

문간에 발 들여놓기 기법은 작은 요청들을 사용한다. 각각의 새로운 요청은 그다지 크지 않다. 작은 승낙을 연달아 얻어 내는 것에 집중함으로써, 이 기법은 흔히 큰 승낙으로 이어진다.

구문 해설

① Your friend **asks you to walk** to the playground with her.

→ 「ask+목적어+to-v」는 '~에게 …해 달라고 부탁하다'의 의미이다.

⑤ The pattern repeats **until** you arrive at the playground.

→ until은 '~할 때까지'의 의미인 접속사이다.

⑨ **To prevent** this, salespeople *would* sometimes put their foot in the way of the door so it couldn't be closed.

→ To prevent는 '막기 위해'의 의미로, 〈목적〉을 나타내는 부사적 용법의 to부정사이다.

→ would는 '~하곤 했다'의 의미인 조동사로, 〈과거의 습관〉을 나타낸다.

→ so (that) ~는 '~하도록'의 의미로, 〈목적〉을 나타내는 접속사이다.

⑫ **By focusing** on *getting one small yes after another*, this technique often leads to a big yes.

→ 「by+v-ing」는 '~함으로써'의 의미이다.

→ getting one small yes after another는 동사구 focus on의 목적어 역할을 하는 동명사구이다.

Review Test

본책 • pp. 64-65

정답 1 ⑤ 2 ② 3 ⑤ 4 ⓐ: homework ⓑ: current plan 5 ③ 6 try to purchase things that fit your current style 7 ④ 8 repeat

문제 해설

1 ⑤ replace: 대신하다

2 arrives(도착한다)와 반대 의미의 단어는 ② 'leaves(떠난다)'이다.

그 기차는 10분 후에 <u>도착한다</u>.

① 놓치다 ③ 피하다 ④ 비교하다 ⑤ 맞다

3 호프스태터의 법칙을 설명하며 숙제를 예로 들어 설명하고 있으므로, 빈칸에는 'For example(예를 들어)'이 가장 알맞다.

4 ⓐ: 바로 앞 문장에 언급된 homework를 가리킨다.
ⓑ: 같은 문장의 current plan을 가리킨다.

5 주어진 문장은 '그것은 삶의 대부분을 가난하게 보냈던 프랑스 철학자의 이름을 따서 지어졌다'는 내용으로, 디드로 효과를 언급한 문장과 프랑스 철학자 이야기를 시작하며 그를 he로 쓴 문장 사이인 ③에 위치하는 것이 알맞다.

6 '~하려고 노력하다'라는 의미의 「try+to-v」를 쓰며, 주격 관계대명사인 that이 선행사 things를 수식하도록 쓴다.

7 빈칸 뒤에서 새로운 요구들은 그렇게 크지 않다고 했고, 작은 승낙을 연달아 얻어 내는 것이 큰 승낙으로 이어진다고 했으므로, 빈칸에는 ④ '작은 요청들'이 가장 알맞다.
① 직접적인 명령들 ② 복잡한 과업들 ③ 큰 요구들 ⑤ 즉각적인 행동들

8

되풀이해서 일어나다

Section 06 Body & Health

본책 • pp. 68-69

1

정답 1 ③ 2 ② 3 ④ 4 (1) hurt (2) sensitive (3) rough

문제 해설

1 종이에 베이는 것이 상처는 작지만 통증은 심한 이유를 설명하는 내용의 글이므로, 제목으로는 ③ '종이에 베인 상처: 보이는 것보다 더 아프다!'가 가장 알맞다.
① 종이에 베이는 것을 피하는 방법
② 종이에 베인 상처를 치료하는 가장 좋은 방법
④ 뇌가 고통을 감지하는 놀라운 방법
⑤ 아이들이 어른들보다 종이에 더 베이는 이유

2 앞 문장에서 종이에 베인 상처는 작다는 내용이 나오고, 빈칸이 있는 문장은 However(그러나)로 문장을 시작하고 있으므로, 빈칸에는 앞의 내용과 대조의 의미를 나타내는 ② '극심한'이 가장 알맞다.
① 가벼운 ③ 예상되는 ④ 위험한 ⑤ 예방할 수 있는

3 종이에 베이면 몹시 아픈 이유를 설명하는 내용 중에, 뇌는 가장 많은 에너지를 사용하는 기관이라는 내용의 (d)는 글의 흐름과 무관하다.

4

문제	종이에 베인 상처는 많이 (1) 아프다.
이유	•우리의 손가락은 많은 통증 수용기를 가지고 있기 때문에 매우 (2) 민감하다. •종이의 가장자리는 고르지 않고 (3) 거칠다.

본문 직독 직해

① Have you ever cut your finger / on paper? / ② Paper cuts are usually small. / ③ However, /
당신은 손가락을 베인 적이 있는가 종이에 종이에 베인 상처는 보통 작다 하지만
the pain they cause / is intense. / ④ Why do these minor injuries hurt / so much? /
그것이 유발하는 통증은 심하다 왜 이 작은 상처가 아픈 걸까 그렇게 많이
⑤ One reason is / that our fingers are very sensitive. / ⑥ There are more pain receptors / in
한 가지 이유는 ~이다 우리의 손가락은 매우 민감하다는 것 더 많은 통증 수용기가 있다
your fingers / than in most other parts of your body. / ⑦ So, / when you get a paper cut, / a lot
당신의 손가락에는 다른 대부분의 신체 부위보다 그래서 당신이 종이에 베이면 많은
of pain signals are sent / to the brain. / (⑧ The brain is the organ / that uses the most energy. /)
통증 신호가 전달된다 뇌로 뇌는 기관이다 가장 많은 에너지를 사용하는
⑨ As a result, / we feel a strong pain. / ⑩ Also, / the edge of a piece of paper / is uneven. /
결과적으로 우리는 강한 통증을 느낀다 또한 종이의 가장자리는 고르지 않다
⑪ It's hard / to see this without a microscope. / ⑫ However, / the rough edge will damage your
어렵다 이것을 현미경 없이 보기는 하지만 그 거친 가장자리는 당신의 손가락을
finger more / than a sharp knife would. /
더 손상시킬 것이다 날카로운 칼보다
⑬ No matter how small a paper cut is, / it will make you say, "Ouch!" /
종이에 베인 상처가 아무리 작더라도 그것은 당신이 "아야!"라고 말하게 할 것이다

본문 해석

당신은 종이에 손가락을 베인 적이 있는가? 종이에 베인 상처는 보통 작다. 하지만 그것이 유발하는 통증은 심하다. 왜 이 작은 상처가 그렇게 많이 아픈 걸까?

한 가지 이유는 우리의 손가락은 매우 민감하기 때문이다. 당신의 손가락에는 다른 대부분의 신체 부위보다 더 많은 통증 수용기가 있다. 그래서 당신이 종이에 베이면, 많은 통증 신호가 뇌로 전달된다. (뇌는 가장 많은 에너지를 사용하는 기관이다.) 결과적으로, 우리는 강한 통증을 느낀다. 또한, 종이의 가장자리는 고르지 않다. 현미경 없이 이것을 보기는 어렵다. 하지만 그 거친 가장자리는 날카로운 칼보다 당신의 손가락을 더 손상시킬 것이다.

종이에 베인 상처가 아무리 작더라도, 그것은 당신이 "아야!"라고 말하게 할 것이다.

구문 해설

① **Have** you ever **cut** your finger on paper?

→ have cut은 '베어본 적이 있다'의 의미로, 〈경험〉을 나타내는 현재완료(have[has]+p.p.)이다.

③ However, **the pain** [(**which[that]**) they cause] is intense.

→ [ ]는 선행사 the pain을 수식하는 목적격 관계대명사절로, 관계대명사 which[that]가 생략되었다.

⑤ One reason is [**that** our fingers are very sensitive].

→ that은 명사절을 이끄는 접속사로, [ ]는 동사 is의 보어 역할을 한다.

⑥ There are **more** pain receptors *in your fingers* **than** *in most other parts of your body*.

→ 「형용사의 비교급+than」은 '~보다 더 …한'의 의미이다

→ in your fingers와 in most other parts of your body는 부사구로, 접속사 than으로 병렬 연결되어 있다.

⑦ So, when you get a paper cut, a lot of pain signals **are sent** to the brain.

→ are sent는 '전달된다'의 의미로, 「be+p.p.」의 수동태이다.

⑧ The brain is **the organ** [**that** uses the most energy].

→ [ ]는 선행사 the organ을 수식하는 주격 관계대명사절이다.

⑩ Also, the edge of **a piece of** paper is uneven.

→ '종이'를 의미하는 paper는 셀 수 없는 명사이므로, a piece of를 이용하여 수를 나타내었다.

⑪ **It**'s hard [**to see** *this* without a microscope].

→ It은 가주어, [ ]는 진주어이다.

→ this는 앞 문장의 '종이의 가장자리가 고르지 않다는 것'을 가리킨다.

⑫ However, the rough edge will damage your finger more than a sharp knife would (damage your finger).

→ would 뒤에는 damage your finger가 생략되어 있다.

⑬ **No matter how** small a paper cut is, it will *make you say*, "Ouch!"

→ no matter how는 '아무리[어떤 방법으로] ~ 하더라도'의 의미이다.

→ 「make+목적어+동사원형」은 '~을 …하게 하다'의 의미이다.

본책 • pp. 70-71

2

정답 1 ① 2 ① 3 ⑤ 4 (1) bones (2) lower (3) higher

문제 해설

1 말할 때의 목소리와 녹음된 목소리가 다른 이유에 관해 설명하는 글이므로, 제목으로는 ① '당신의 목소리의 진짜 소리'가 가장 알맞다.

② 음파가 형성되는 방법 ③ 당신의 목소리를 개선하는 방법들

④ 소리를 녹음하는 것의 문제점 ⑤ 인간의 귀의 놀라운 구조

2 주어진 문장은 '그러나 그것이 당신의 목소리가 다른 사람들에게 들리는 방식이다'라는 내용으로, 녹음된 자신의 목소리를 듣고 놀란 경험에 대한 문장 뒤인 ①의 위치가 가장 알맞다.

3 빈칸 앞에서 말할 때 음파의 이동 방식을 설명하고 있고, 빈칸 뒤에서는 녹음된 목소리를 들을 때 음파의 이동 방식을 설명하고 있으므로, 빈칸에는 대조를 나타내는 ⑤ '반면에'가 가장 알맞다.
① 요약하면 ② 게다가 ③ 예를 들어 ④ 결과적으로

4 **당신의 목소리가 당신에게 들리는 방식**

당신이 다른 사람들에게 말할 때	당신이 자신의 목소리가 녹음된 것을 들을 때
음파가 공기와 당신의 (1) 뼈를 통해 이동한다.	음파가 공기 중으로만 이동한다.
그래서 당신의 목소리는 (2) 더 낮고 더 선명하게 들린다.	그래서 당신의 목소리는 (3) 더 높고 더 약하게 들린다.

본문 직독 직해

① Do you remember / the first time you heard / a recording / of your own voice? /
당신은 기억하는가 / 당신이 처음으로 들었을 때를 / 녹음된 것을 / 당신 자신의 목소리의

② You were probably surprised / by how it sounded. / But / that's how your voice sounds / to other people. / ③ The reason is / that sound travels / in waves. /
당신은 아마 놀랐을 것이다 / 그것이 들리는 방식에 / 그러나 / 그것이 당신의 목소리가 들리는 방식이다 / 다른 사람들에게 / 그 이유는 ~이다 / 소리는 이동한다 / 파동을 통해

④ When another person speaks, / the sound waves travel / through the air. / ⑤ When they reach your ears, / you hear them. / ⑥ But / when you speak, / the sound waves also move / through the bones / of your head. / ⑦ So / they reach your ears / in two different ways, / which makes / your voice / sound lower and stronger. /
다른 사람이 말할 때 / 그 음파는 이동한다 / 공기를 통해서 / 그것들이 당신의 귀에 도달할 때 / 당신은 그것들을 듣는다 / 그러나 / 당신이 말을 할 때 / 그 음파는 또한 이동한다 / 뼈들을 통과하여 / 당신의 머리의 / 그래서 / 그것들은 당신의 귀에 도달한다 / 두 가지 다른 경로로 / 그리고 그것은 만든다 / 당신의 목소리가 / 더 낮고 더 선명하게 들리게

⑧ On the other hand, / when you hear a recording / of your voice, / the sound waves / are traveling / only through the air. / ⑨ So / your voice sounds / higher and weaker. /
반면에 / 당신이 녹음된 것을 들을 때 / 당신의 목소리의 / 그 음파는 / 이동하고 있다 / 오직 공기를 통해서 / 그래서 / 당신의 목소리는 들린다 / 더 높고 더 약하게

⑩ For this reason, / many people don't like / to hear recordings / of their own voice. /
이러한 이유 때문에 / 많은 사람들은 좋아하지 않는다 / 녹음된 것을 듣는 것을 / 그들 자신의 목소리의

본문 해석

당신은 처음으로 자신의 목소리가 녹음된 것을 들었을 때를 기억하는가? 당신은 아마 그것이 들리는 방식에 놀랐을 것이다. 그러나 그것이 당신의 목소리가 다른 사람들에게 들리는 방식이다. 그 이유는 소리가 파동을 통해 이동하기 때문이다.

다른 사람이 말을 할 때, 그 음파는 공기를 통해서 이동한다. 그것들이 당신의 귀에 도달하면, 당신은 그것들을 듣는다. 그러나 당신이 말을 할 때, 그 음파는 또한 당신의 머리뼈들을 통과하여 이동한다. 그래서 그것들은 두 가지 다른 경로로 당신의 귀에 도달하고, 이것은 당신의 목소리를 더 낮고 더 선명하게 들리게 만든다.

반면에, 당신이 자신의 목소리가 녹음된 것을 들을 때는 그 음파가 오직 공기 중으로만 이동하고 있다. 그래서 당신의 목소리는 더 높고 더 약하게 들린다. 이러한 이유로, 많은 사람들이 자신의 목소리가 녹음된 것을 듣는 것을 좋아하지 않는다.

구문 해설

① Do you remember **the first time you heard** a recording of your own voice?
→ 「the first time+주어+동사의 과거형」은 '처음으로 ~가 …했을 때'의 의미이다.

② You were probably surprised by [**how** it sounded].
→ how는 '~하는 방법[방식]'이라는 의미의 관계부사로, 〈방법〉을 나타낸다. 선행사 the way와 관계부사 how는 같이 쓸 수 없으므로, 둘 중 하나는 반드시 생략한다.

③ The reason is [**that** sound travels in waves].
→ that은 명사절을 이끄는 접속사로, [ ]는 문장의 보어 역할을 한다.

⑦ So they reach your ears in two different ways, [**which** makes your voice sound lower and stronger].
→ [ ]는 앞 절의 내용을 부연 설명하는 계속적 용법의 관계대명사절로, '그리고 그것은[이는]'이라고 해석한다. 계속적 용법의 관계대명사는 관계대명사 앞에 콤마(,)를 쓴다.

3

본책 • pp. 72-73

정답 1 ② 2 ⑤ 3 ③ 4 move, liquid

문제 해설

1 척추의 디스크가 낮 동안 받은 중력의 영향으로 납작해져서 아침보다 저녁에 키가 더 작아진다는 내용의 글이므로, 제목으로는 ② '중력은 우리를 더 작아지게 만들 수 있다'가 가장 알맞다.
① 당신의 척추를 건강하게 유지하기 ③ 우리는 중력 없이 살 수 있을까?
④ 척추의 중요한 기능들 ⑤ 당신의 척추에 왜 많은 뼈가 있는가

2 키는 하루 중 언제 측정하는지에 따라 다르다는 내용의 (C), 저녁보다 아침에 키가 더 크다는 내용의 (B), 그 이유는 척추가 디스크로 연결된 작은 뼈들을 포함하기 때문이라는 내용의 (A)의 흐름이 알맞다.

3 빈칸 앞에서 누워 있을 때는 중력이 더 이상 뼈들이 디스크를 짓누르게 만들지 않는다고 했으므로, 빈칸에는 ③ '더 두꺼운'이 가장 알맞다.
① 더 무른 ② 더 딱딱한 ④ 더 짧은 ⑤ 더 강한

4 문장 ⑤-⑥을 통해 알 수 있다.

디스크는 당신의 척추가 여러 방향으로 움직이게 해 준다. 이것은 그것들이 무르고 액체를 함유하고 있기 때문이다.

본문 직독 직해

① How tall are you? / ④ Surprisingly, / your answer depends on / what time of day / you
당신은 얼마나 큰가 / 놀랍게도 / 당신의 대답은 ~에 달려 있다 / 하루 중 몇 시에 / 당신이
measure yourself. / ③ It may sound strange, / but you're actually taller / in the morning /
자신을 측정하는지 / 이상하게 들릴 수도 있다 / 그러나 당신은 실제로 더 크다 / 아침에
than you are / in the evening. / ② This is because / your spine contains / 33 small bones / that
당신이 그런 것보다 / 저녁에 / 이것은 ~ 때문이다 / 당신의 척추는 포함한다 / 33개의 작은 뼈를
are connected / by discs. / ⑤ These discs are soft / and contain liquid. / ⑥ They allow / your
연결된 / 디스크들에 의해 / 이러한 디스크들은 무르다 / 그리고 액체를 함유한다 / 그것들은 ~하게 한다
spine to easily move / in many directions. /
당신의 척추가 쉽게 움직이게 / 많은 방향으로

⑦ During the day, / gravity pulls / the bones of your spine / downward. / ⑧ They squeeze
낮 동안에는 중력이 잡아당긴다 당신의 척추의 뼈들을 아래쪽으로 그것들은 디스크들을

the discs / and make them flatter. / ⑨ As a result, / you become / up to one centimeter /
짓누른다 그리고 그것들을 더 납작하게 만든다 결과적으로 당신은 된다 (최고) 1센티미터까지

shorter. / ⑩ When you lie down / to sleep, / however, / gravity no longer causes / the bones to
더 작아지게 당신이 누울 때 자기 위해 그러나 중력은 더 이상 야기하지 않는다 뼈들이

squeeze the discs. / ⑪ The discs get thicker, / and you gain back / your lost height. /
디스크들을 짓누르도록 디스크들은 더 두꺼워진다 그리고 당신은 되찾는다 당신의 잃어버린 키를

본문 해석

당신은 키가 얼마나 큰가? (C) 놀랍게도, 당신의 대답은 하루 중 몇 시에 자신을 측정하는지에 따라 다르다. (B) 이상하게 들릴 수도 있지만, 당신은 실제로 저녁보다 아침에 키가 더 크다. (A) 이것은 당신의 척추에 디스크들로 연결된 33개의 작은 뼈가 있기 때문이다. 이러한 디스크들은 무르고 액체를 함유하고 있다. 그것들은 당신의 척추가 여러 방향으로 쉽게 움직이게 해 준다.

낮 동안에는 중력이 당신의 척추의 뼈들을 아래로 잡아당긴다. 그것들은 디스크들을 짓눌러 더 납작하게 만든다. 결과적으로 당신은 (최고) 1센티미터까지 더 작아지게 된다. 그러나 당신이 자려고 누울 때, 중력은 더 이상 뼈들이 디스크들을 짓누르게 만들지 않는다. 디스크들은 더 두꺼워지고, 당신은 잃어버렸던 키를 되찾는다.

구문 해설

② **This is because** your spine contains *33 small bones* [*that* are connected by discs].
→ this is because ~는 '이것은 ~ 때문이다'의 의미로, 뒤에 이유에 해당하는 내용이 온다.
→ [ ]는 선행사 33 small bones를 수식하는 주격 관계대명사절이다.
→ are connected는 '연결된다'의 의미로, 「be+p.p.」의 수동태이다.

④ Surprisingly, your answer depends on [what time of day you measure yourself].
→ [ ]는 「의문사+주어+동사」의 간접의문문으로, 동사구 depends on의 목적어 역할을 한다.

⑥ They **allow your spine to** easily **move** in many directions.
→ 「allow+목적어+to-v」는 '~가 …하게 하다'의 의미이다.

⑧ They squeeze the discs and **make them flatter**.
→ 「make+목적어+형용사」는 '~을 …하게 만들다'의 의미이다.

⑩ When you lie down to sleep, however, gravity **no longer** *causes the bones to squeeze* the discs.
→ no longer는 '더 이상 ~ 아닌'의 의미이다.
→ 「cause+목적어+to-v」는 '~가 …하게 야기하다'의 의미이다.

본책 • pp. 74-75

4

정답 1 ② 2 ② 3 ③ 4 (1) F (2) F

문제 해설

1 맛을 느끼는 데 있어 미각과 후각이 함께 역할을 한다는 내용의 글이므로, 주제로는 ② '음식 맛을 느끼는 데 사용되는 감각들'이 가장 알맞다.
[문제] 글의 주제로 가장 알맞은 것은?
① 막힌 코를 치료하는 방법

③ 기본적인 맛의 여러 가지 종류

④ 신경 세포의 기능들

⑤ 뇌와 코의 관계

2 '맛의 나머지는 냄새를 맡는 것에서 온다'는 주어진 문장은 혀의 미뢰가 기본적인 맛만 인식한다는 내용의 문장 ④와 냄새가 코로 가서 맛을 느끼게 하는 과정을 설명하는 내용의 문장 ⑤ 사이인 ②의 위치가 가장 알맞다.

[문제] 다음 문장이 들어갈 위치로 가장 알맞은 곳은?

3 문장 ⑤-⑥에서 냄새가 코로 가서 신경 세포를 자극하여 뇌로 정보를 전달한다고 했고, 문장 ⑦-⑧에서 코가 막히면 점액 때문에 맛을 잘 느낄 수 없다고 했으므로, 냄새가 신경 세포에 이르지 못하여 신경 세포를 자극하지 못한다는 것을 알 수 있다. 따라서, 빈칸에는 ③ '~에 이르다[닿다]'가 가장 알맞다.

[문제] 글의 빈칸에 들어갈 말로 가장 알맞은 것은?

① 느끼다 ② 만들어 내다 ④ 다시 세우다 ⑤ 만족시키다

4 (1) 문장 ④에서 미뢰는 신맛을 포함하여 기본적인 맛을 인식한다고 했다.

(2) 문장 ⑨-⑩에서 코를 잡는 것은 쓴 약 맛을 피하는 데 효과가 없다고 했다.

[문제] 글의 내용과 일치하면 T, 그렇지 않으면 F를 쓰시오.

(1) 혀의 미뢰는 신맛을 인식하지 못한다.

(2) 코를 잡으면 쓴맛을 피할 수 있다.

본문 직독 직해

① When you have / a stuffed nose, / you cannot taste well. / ② Why is this? / ③ It is because / your nose helps you taste. / ④ The taste buds / on your tongue / only recognize basic tastes, / such as sweet, sour, bitter, and salty. / The rest of the taste / comes from smelling. / ⑤ When you eat something, / the scent of the food / goes into your nose / and / stimulates the nerve cells / in it. / ⑥ Then / these send information / about the taste / to the brain. / ⑦ However, / when your nose is stuffed, / the scent cannot reach / the nerve cells / because of the mucus. / ⑧ So / you cannot taste the food / well. /

당신이 가질 때 / 막힌 코를 / 당신은 맛을 잘 느낄 수 없다 / 이것은 왜일까 / 그것은 ~ 때문이다 / 당신의 코가 당신이 맛을 느끼는 것을 돕기 / 미뢰는 / 당신 혀의 / 오직 기본적인 맛을 인식할 수 있다 / 단맛, 신맛, 쓴맛, 그리고 짠맛과 같은 / 맛의 나머지는 / 냄새를 맡는 것에서 온다 / 당신이 무언가를 먹을 때 / 음식의 냄새는 / 당신의 코로 간다 / 그리고 / 신경 세포들을 자극한다 / 그것(코) 안에 있는 / 그러면 / 이것들은 정보를 보낸다 / 맛에 관한 / 뇌로 / 그러나 / 당신의 코가 막혔을 때 / 냄새는 도달하지 못한다 / 신경 세포에 / (코에서 나오는) 점액 때문에 / 그래서 / 당신은 음식의 맛을 느낄 수 없다 / 잘

⑨ Then, / does holding your nose work / when you want to avoid / tasting bitter medicine? / ⑩ It does not / because we don't use / our sense of smell / when tasting bitter flavors! /

그러면 / 당신의 코를 잡는 것이 효과가 있을까 / 당신이 피하고 싶을 때 / 쓴 약 맛을 / 느끼는 것을 그것은 아니다 / 우리가 이용하지 않기 때문에 / 우리의 후각을 / 쓴 맛을 맛볼 때

본문 해석

당신이 코가 막혔을 때, 당신은 맛을 잘 느낄 수 없다. 이것은 왜일까? 그것은 당신의 코가 당신이 맛을 느끼는 것을 돕기 때문이다. 당신 혀의 미뢰는 오직 단맛, 신맛, 쓴맛, 그리고 짠맛과 같은 기본적인 맛만 인식할 수 있다. 맛의 나머지는 냄새를 맡는 것에서 온다. 당신이 무언가를 먹을 때, 음식의 냄새는 당신의 코로 가서 그것 안에 있는 신경 세포들을 자극한다. 그러면 이것들은 맛에 관한 정보를 뇌로 보낸다. 그러나 당신의 코가 막혔을 때, (코에서 나오는) 점액 때문에 냄새가 신경 세포에 도달하지 못한다. 그래서 당신은 음식 맛을 잘 느낄 수 없다.

그러면, 당신이 쓴 약 맛을 느끼는 것을 피하고 싶을 때 당신의 코를 잡는 것이 효과가 있을까? 우리가 쓴 맛을

맛볼 때 우리의 후각을 이용하지 않기 때문에 그것은 아니다!

구문 해설

③ **It is because** your nose *helps you taste.*

→ it is because ~는 '그것은 ~ 때문이다'의 의미이다.

→ 「help + 목적어 + 동사원형[to-v]」은 '~가 …하는 것을 돕다'의 의미이다.

⑤ … , the scent [of the food] **goes** into your nose and **stimulates** the nerve cells in *it*.

→ [ ]는 앞의 명사 the scent를 수식하는 전치사구이다.

→ 동사 goes와 stimulates가 접속사 and에 병렬 연결되어 있다.

→ it은 앞에 있는 your nose를 가리킨다.

⑦ … , the scent cannot reach the nerve cells **because of** the mucus.

→ 「because of + 명사(구)」는 '~ 때문에'의 의미이다.

⑨ Then, does **holding your nose** work when you want to *avoid tasting* bitter medicine?

→ holding your nose는 주어 역할을 하는 동명사구이다.

→ 「avoid + v-ing」는 '~하는 것을 피하다'의 의미로, avoid의 목적어로 동명사가 쓰인다.

⑩ … we don't use our sense of smell **when** (**we are**) tasting bitter flavors!

→ when은 '~할 때'의 의미로, 〈때〉를 나타내는 접속사이다. 시간의 접속사 when 뒤에 「주어 + be동사」가 생략되었다.

Review Test

본책 • pp. 76-77

정답 1 ④ 2 1) measure 2) stimulate 3 ④ 4 1) 손가락이 매우 민감해서 2) 종이 가장자리가 고르지 않아서 5 ⑤ 6 which makes your voice sound lower and stronger 7 ③ 8 height

문제 해설

1 ④ flat: 납작한

2 1) '어떤 것의 정확한 크기를 찾다'라는 의미의 단어는 'measure(측정하다)'이다.
2) '신체에서 반응을 만들어 내다'라는 의미의 단어는 'stimulate(자극하다)'이다.

3 빈칸 앞에는 손가락에 많은 통증 수용기가 있어 종이에 베었을 때 통증 신호가 뇌로 전달된다고 했고, 빈칸 뒤에는 우리가 고통을 크게 느끼게 된다는 결과가 언급되었으므로, 빈칸에는 ④ 'As a result(그 결과)'가 적절하다.
① 그러나 ② 게다가 ③ 예를 들어 ⑤ 반면에

4 종이에 베인 손가락의 상처가 많이 아픈 두 가지 이유는 손가락이 매우 민감하고 종이 가장자리가 고르지 않기 때문이라고 언급되었다.

5 ⑤ 녹음된 자신의 목소리는 더 높고 약하게 들린다고 했다.

6 앞 절을 선행사로 하는 계속적 용법의 관계대명사 which를 쓰고, '~을 …하게 만들다'라는 의미의 「make+목적어+동사원형」 구문을 이용한다.

7 '결과적으로 당신은 1센티미터까지 더 작아지게 된다'는 내용의 주어진 문장은 낮 동안 중력으로 인해 디스크들이 짓눌려 더 납작해진다는 문장 다음인 ③에 오는 것이 가장 자연스럽다.

8 어떤 사람 또는 어떤 것의 맨 아래에서 맨 위까지의 거리

Section
07 Marketing

본책 • pp. 80-81

1

정답 1 ⑤ 2 ① 3 (1) F (2) T (3) F 4 rely, first, anchor

문제 해설

1 물건 구매 시 처음 본 물건을 닻으로 두고 비교하게 된다는 닻 내림 효과에 관한 글이므로, 제목으로는 ⑤ '첫 경험이 어떻게 제품에 대한 우리의 의견을 형성하는가'가 가장 알맞다.
① 사람들이 더 낮은 가격으로 흥정하는 이유 ② 왜 구매 결정은 매우 어려운가
③ 한 유명한 제품에 얽힌 역사 ④ 회사가 신제품을 개발하는 방법

2 비싼 물건을 먼저 본 후 그것보다 저렴한 물건을 발견하게 되면, 그 물건이 여전히 예산을 초과하더라도 처음 본 것 보다는 저렴하기 때문에 좋은 거래처럼 보인다는 것이 자연스럽다. 그러므로 빈칸에는 ① '좋은 거래'가 가장 알맞다.
② 잘못된 선택 ③ 전체 계획 ④ 흥미로운 물건 ⑤ 더 높은 품질의 상품

3 (1) 문장 ⑦에서 처음 발견한 정보가 닻에 해당된다고 했다.
(2) 문장 ⑨-⑩에 언급되어 있다.
(3) 문장 ⑪에서 많은 식당들은 값비싼 요리를 메뉴의 맨 위에 놓는다고 했다.

4 사람들은 그들이 처음 발견한 정보에 크게 의존한다. 이 정보는 닻이라고 불린다.

본문 직독 직해

① Imagine / seeing an expensive item / in a store. / ② Then / you see an item / that is
상상해 보아라 비싼 물건을 본다고 가게에서 그런 다음 당신은 물건을 발견한다
similar but cheaper. / ③ The cheaper item is still over your budget. / ④ But / it seems like a
비슷하지만 더 싼 그 더 저렴한 물건도 여전히 당신의 예산을 초과한다 하지만 그것이 좋은
good deal. / ⑤ This is called / the anchoring effect. /
거래처럼 보인다 이것은 불린다 닻 내림 효과라고

⑥ The anchoring effect happens / because of the way people process information. / ⑦ They
그 닻 내림 효과는 발생한다 사람들이 정보를 처리하는 방식 때문에 그들은
usually rely the most / on the information / that they find first / —the "anchor." / ⑧ Once they
보통 가장 많이 의존한다 정보에 처음 그들이 찾은 닻에 일단 그들이
have an anchor, / they compare other things to it. /
닻을 갖게 되면 그들은 다른 것들을 그것과 비교한다

⑨ The anchoring effect can be a powerful tool / for selling products. / ⑩ That is because /
닻 내림 효과는 강력한 도구가 될 수 있다 제품을 판매하는 (그것은) ~이기 때문이다
it can change / the way customers think. / ⑪ For example, / many restaurants place a few
그것은 바꿀 수 있다 고객이 생각하는 방식을 예를 들어 많은 식당들은 몇 가지
expensive dishes / at the top of their menu. / ⑫ Customers see these items / first. / ⑬ So, / the
값비싼 요리를 놓는다 메뉴의 맨 위에 고객들은 이 상품들을 본다 먼저 그래서
other dishes seem cheap / even if they really aren't. /
나머지 요리들은 저렴해 보인다 비록 실제로 그렇지 않더라도

본문 해석

가게에서 비싼 물건을 본다고 상상해 보아라. 그런 다음 당신은 비슷하지만 더 싼 물건을 발견한다. 그 더 저렴한 물건도 여전히 당신의 예산을 초과한다. 하지만 그것이 좋은 거래처럼 보인다. 이것은 닻 내림 효과라고 불린다.

그 닻 내림 효과는 사람들이 정보를 처리하는 방식 때문에 발생한다. 그들은 보통 그들이 처음 찾은 정보인 '닻'에 가장 많이 의존한다. 일단 그들이 닻을 갖게 되면, 그들은 다른 것들을 그것과 비교한다.

닻 내림 효과는 제품을 판매하는 강력한 도구가 될 수 있다. 그것은 닻 내림 효과가 고객이 생각하는 방식을 바꿀 수 있기 때문이다. 예를 들어, 많은 식당들은 메뉴의 맨 위에 몇 가지 값비싼 요리를 놓는다. 고객들은 이 상품들을 먼저 본다. 그래서 나머지 요리들은 비록 실제로 그렇지 않더라도 저렴해 보인다.

구문 해설

① Imagine [**seeing** an expensive item in a store].
→ [ ]는 동사 Imagine의 목적어 역할을 하는 동명사구이다.

④ But it **seems like** a good deal.
→ seem like은 '~처럼 보이다, ~인 것 같다'의 의미이다.

⑥ The anchoring effect happens because of **the way** [(how) people process information].
→ [ ]는 선행사 the way를 수식하는 관계부사절이다. 선행사 the way와 관계부사 how는 함께 쓸 수 없다.

⑦ They usually rely the most on **the information** [**that** they find first] —the "anchor."
→ [ ]는 선행사 the information을 수식하는 목적격 관계대명사절이다.

⑩ That is because **it** can change *the way* [(how) customers think].
→ it은 The anchoring effect를 가리킨다.
→ [ ]는 선행사 the way를 수식하는 관계부사절이다. 선행사 the way와 관계부사 how는 함께 쓸 수 없다.

2

본책 • pp. 82-83

정답 1 ④ 2 ③ 3 ③ 4 parade, crowd, reason

문제 해설

1 다른 사람들이 사는 물건을 따라 사지 말고 자신에게 필요한 물건을 구매해야 한다는 요지의 글이다.

2 '곧, 점점 더 많은 사람들이 모였고, 그들은 큰 무리를 형성했다'는 주어진 문장은 사람들이 음악 소리를 들었을 때 악대차를 따라갔다는 문장 ⑤와 대부분의 사람들이 왜 그 무리에 합류했는지 이유를 몰랐다는 문장 ⑥ 사이인 ③의 위치에 들어가는 것이 가장 자연스럽다.

3 많은 사람들이 그 제품을 사용하고 있다는 점을 호소하는 ③이 편승 효과를 이용한 광고 문구로 가장 알맞다.

4 보기 | 상황 군중, 무리 행렬, 거리 행진 이유

과거에, 악대차는 거리 행진들에서 사용되었다. 그것들은 악단을 실어 나르고, 사람들은 그것들을 따라갔다. 무리가 더 커지면서, 더 많은 사람들이 이유를 모르는 채 종종 무리에 합류했다. 오늘날 '편승 효과'라는 용어는 단지 남들이 그것을 하고 있기 때문에 사람들이 어떤 것을 할 때 사용된다.

본문 직독 직해

① When a product becomes popular, / do you buy it / even if you do not need it? /
어떤 상품이 인기 있어지면 당신은 그것을 사는가 당신이 그것이 필요 없음에도 불구하고

② If so, / you are experiencing / the "bandwagon effect." /
만약 그렇다면 당신은 경험하고 있다 '편승 효과'를

③ The term comes from / American parades. / ④ In the past, / bandwagons would carry a
그 용어는 ~에서 유래한다 미국의 거리 행진들 과거에 악대차는 악단을 실어 나르곤 했다

band. / ⑤ When people heard the music, / they followed the bandwagon. / Soon, / more and
사람들이 그 음악 소리를 들었을 때 그들은 악대차를 따라갔다 곧 점점 더

more people gathered, / and / they formed a big crowd. / ⑥ But / most of them did not know /
많은 사람들이 모였다 그리고 그들은 큰 무리를 형성했다 그러나 그들 중 대부분은 몰랐다

why they had joined the crowd. /
왜 그들이 그 무리에 합류했는지

⑦ These days, / the term "bandwagon effect" is used / to describe the act / of people /
요즘에는 '편승 효과'라는 용어는 사용된다 행동을 묘사하는 데 사람들이

doing something / just because others are doing it. / ⑧ We can see this / in our daily lives. /
무언가를 하는 단지 다른 사람들이 그것을 하고 있기 때문에 우리는 이것을 볼 수 있다 우리의 일상생활에서

⑨ Advertisements / that say things like / "Ten bottles are sold / every second" / also use this
광고는 ~와 같은 것들을 말하는 열 병이 팔린다 매초에 또한 이 효과를

effect. / ⑩ But / you should not buy things / just because others do. / ⑪ Make sure / you buy
이용한다 그러나 당신은 물건을 사서는 안 된다 단지 다른 사람들이 그러기(사기) 때문에 반드시 ~해라 당신이

items / only when you need them! /
물건을 사도록 오직 당신이 그것들이 필요할 때만

본문 해석

어떤 상품이 인기 있어지면, 당신은 그것이 필요 없음에도 불구하고 그것을 사는가? 만약 그렇다면, 당신은 '편승 효과(bandwagon effect)'를 경험하고 있다.

그 용어는 미국의 거리 행진들에서 유래한다. 과거에, 악대차는 악단을 실어 나르곤 했다. 사람들이 그 음악 소리를 들었을 때, 그들은 악대차를 따라갔다. 곧, 점점 더 많은 사람들이 모였고, 그들은 큰 무리를 형성했다. 그러나 그들 중 대부분은 그들이 왜 무리에 합류했는지 몰랐다.

요즘에는, '편승 효과'라는 용어는 단지 다른 사람들이 그것을 하고 있기 때문에 사람들이 무언가를 하는 행위를 묘사하는 데 사용된다. 우리는 우리의 일상생활에서 이것을 볼 수 있다. "매초에 열 병씩 팔립니다"와 같은 것들을 말하는 광고들 또한 이 효과를 이용한다. 그러나 단지 다른 사람들이 그런다고(산다고) 해서 물건을 사서는 안 된다. 반드시 오직 당신이 그것들이 필요할 때만 물건을 사도록 해라!

구문 해설

① When a product **becomes popular**, do you buy it *even if* you do not need it?
- 「become+형용사」는 '~해지다'의 의미이다.
- even if ~는 '~에도 불구하고'의 의미인 접속 어구이다.

④ In the past, bandwagons **would** carry a band.
- would는 '~하곤 했다'의 의미인 조동사로, 〈과거의 습관〉을 나타낸다.

⑥ But most of them did not know [why they *had joined* the crowd].
- [ ]는 「의문사+주어+동사」의 간접의문문으로, 동사 know의 목적어 역할을 한다.
- had joined는 과거완료(had+p.p.)로, 기준이 되는 과거 시점(did not know)보다 먼저 일어난 일임을 나타낸다.

⑦ These days, the term "bandwagon effect" **is used to describe** the act of *people* [*doing* something just because others are doing it].
- 「be used+to-v」는 '~하는 데 사용되다'의 의미이다.
- [ ]는 전치사 of의 목적어 역할을 하는 동명사구이다. people은 동명사(doing)의 의미상의 주어이다.

⑨ ***Advertisements*** [*that* say things like "Ten bottles are sold every second"] also **use** this effect.

→ 문장의 주어는 Advertisements이고, 동사는 use이다.

→ [ ]는 선행사 Advertisements를 수식하는 주격 관계대명사절이다.

본책 • pp. 84-85

3

정답 1 ② 2 ④ 3 ④ 4 (1) F (2) T

문제 해설

1 거울 뉴런으로 인해 다른 사람을 보면 그들의 감정, 행동을 따라 하게 된다는 내용의 글이므로, 제목으로는 ② '보고 느껴라: 거울 뉴런이 작용하는 방법'이 가장 알맞다.

① 식품 브랜드의 최악의 속임수　③ 마케팅 전문가가 돈을 버는 방법들

④ 거울 뉴런이 기억을 돕는 방법　⑤ TV를 너무 많이 보는 것은 뉴런에 해롭다

2 거울 뉴런의 작용을 햄버거를 먹는 광고 모델을 예로 설명하는 내용 중에, 사람들은 햄버거에 많은 다른 것들을 넣는다는 내용의 (d)는 흐름과 무관하다.

3 다른 사람들의 행동을 보면 그 행동을 따라 하게 된다는 거울 뉴런이 작동하는 방식에 대해서 설명하는 문장으로, 빈칸에는 ④ '당신이 실제로 그것을 직접 하고 있는 것처럼'이 가장 알맞다.

① 당신이 위험에 처한 것처럼

② 그것이 익숙한 이미지인 것처럼

③ 다른 것에 집중함으로써

⑤ 그 행동의 이유를 알아냄으로써

4 (1) 문장 ④-⑤에서 다른 사람들이 무언가를 하는 것을 보기만 해도 그 행동을 따라하게 되고, 이것이 거울 뉴런이 작동하는 방법이라고 했다.

(2) 문장 ⑨-⑬에 언급되어 있다.

(1) 거울 뉴런은 당신이 직접 행동을 할 때만 작동한다.

(2) 광고는 거울 뉴런을 사용하여 시청자가 보는 것을 원하게 만들 수 있다.

본문 직독 직해

① Have you ever seen a TV advertisement / that really grabbed your attention? / ② Did it make you feel / like the person in it? / ③ If so, / you might have been influenced / by mirror neurons / in the brain. / ④ When you see someone doing something, / your brain's mirror neurons react / as if you were actually doing it / yourself. / ⑤ This can even cause you to copy / what you have seen. / ⑥ Marketing experts try / to use this effect. /

당신은 TV 광고를 본 적이 있는가 / 정말로 당신의 관심을 붙잡는 / 그것이 당신을 느끼게 했는가 / TV 광고 속의 사람처럼 / 만약 그렇다면 / 당신은 영향을 받은 것일지도 모른다 / 거울 뉴런에 의해 / 뇌의 / 당신이 누군가가 무언가를 하는 것을 볼 때 / 당신의 뇌 속 거울 뉴런은 반응한다 / 당신이 그것을 실제로 하고 있는 것처럼 / 직접 / 이것은 심지어 당신을 따라 하게 할 수도 있다 / 당신이 본 것을 / 마케팅 전문가들은 노력한다 / 이 효과를 사용하려고

⑦ For example, / imagine there is a TV advertisement / for a hamburger. / ⑧ The

예를 들어 / TV 광고가 있다고 상상해 보아라 / 햄버거의

advertisement may show the model / taking a bite of the hamburger. / ⑨ Due to mirror
그 광고는 모델을 보여줄 수 있다 햄버거를 한입 먹는 거울 뉴런 때문에

neurons, / people who watch the advertisement may start / to copy the model. / ⑩ Without
광고를 본 사람들은 시작할지도 모른다 그 모델을 따라 하기 그것을

even noticing it, / they might imitate / the model's emotions and facial expressions. /
알아채지도 못하고 그들은 모방할 수도 있다 모델의 감정과 표정을

(⑪ People put lots of different things / on hamburgers. /) ⑫ Viewers may feel / like they have
사람들은 많은 다른 것들을 넣는다 햄버거에 아마 시청자들은 느낄 것이다 그들이

bitten the hamburger. / ⑬ As a result, / the advertisement makes them want the real thing! /
햄버거를 베어 물은 것처럼 결과적으로 광고는 그들이 실제인 것을 원하게 만든다

본문 해석

당신은 정말로 당신의 관심을 붙잡는 TV 광고를 본 적이 있는가? 그것이 당신을 TV 광고 속의 사람처럼 느끼게 했는가? 만약 그렇다면, 당신은 뇌의 거울 뉴런에 의해 영향을 받았을지도 모른다. 당신이 누군가가 무언가를 하는 것을 볼 때, 당신의 뇌 속 거울 뉴런이 당신이 실제로 그것을 직접 하고 있는 것처럼 반응한다. 이것은 심지어 당신으로 하여금 당신이 본 것을 따라 하게 할 수도 있다. 마케팅 전문가들은 이 효과를 사용하려고 노력한다.

예를 들어, 햄버거의 TV 광고가 있다고 상상해 보아라. 그 광고는 햄버거를 한 입 먹는 모델을 보여줄 수 있다. 거울 뉴런 때문에 광고를 본 사람들은 그 모델을 따라 하기 시작할지도 모른다. 그들은 그것을 알아채지도 못하고 모델의 감정과 표정을 모방할 수도 있다. (사람들은 햄버거에 많은 다른 것들을 넣는다.) 시청자들은 아마 그들이 햄버거를 베어 물은 것처럼 느낄 것이다. 결과적으로, 광고는 그들이 실제인 것을 원하게 만든다!

구문 해설

① **Have** you ever **seen** *a TV advertisement* [*that* really grabbed your attention]?
→ have been은 '한 적이 있다'의 의미로, 〈경험〉을 나타내는 현재완료(have[has]+p.p.)이다.
→ [ ]는 선행사 a TV advertisement를 수식하는 주격 관계대명사절이다.

② Did it **make you feel** *like* the person in it?
→ 「make+목적어+동사원형」은 '~을 …하게 만들다'의 의미이다.
→ like는 '~와 마찬가지로, ~와 (똑)같이'의 의미인 전치사로 쓰였다.
→ it은 a TV advertisement를 가리킨다.

④ When you **see someone doing** something, your brain's mirror neurons react *as if you were* actually *doing* it yourself.
→ 「see+목적어+v-ing」는 '~가 …하고 있는 것을 보다'의 의미이다.
→ 「as if+주어+were/일반동사의 과거형」은 가정법 과거로 '마치 ~인 것 처럼'의 의미이다.

⑦ For example, imagine [(**that**) there is a TV advertisement for a hamburger].
→ [ ]는 동사 imagine의 목적어 역할을 하는 명사절로, 접속사 that이 생략되었다.

⑧ The advertisement may show the model [**taking** a bite of the hamburger].
→ [ ]는 the model을 수식하는 현재분사구이다.

⑨ Due to mirror neurons, **people** [**who** watch the advertisement] may *start to copy* the model.
→ [ ]는 선행사 people을 수식하는 주격 관계대명사절이다.
→ 「start+to-v[v-ing]」는 '~하기 시작하다'의 의미이다.

⑩ **Without** even **noticing** it, they might imitate *the model's emotions* and *facial expressions*.
→ 「without+v-ing」는 '~하지 않은 채'의 의미이다.
→ 명사구 the model's emotions와 facial expressions가 접속사 and로 병렬 연결되어 있다.

⑬ As a result, the advertisement **makes them want** the real thing!
→ 「make+목적어+동사원형」은 '~을 …하게 만들다'의 의미이다.

본책 • pp. 86-87

4

정답 1 ④ 2 ② 3 senses 4 음식의 모습, 냄새, 소리

문제 해설

1 식당들이 음식의 맛뿐만 아니라 시각, 청각, 후각 등을 이용해 손님을 만족시킨다는 내용의 글로, 제목으로는 ④ '손님들을 끌어당기는 것: 맛있는 음식은 충분하지 않다'가 가장 알맞다.
[문제] 글의 제목으로 가장 알맞은 것은?
① 훌륭한 요리사가 되는 방법 ② 외식의 새로운 트렌드
③ 식당을 여는 것에 대한 몇 가지 조언들 ⑤ 맛있는 음식: 식당의 가장 중요한 것

2 빈칸 앞에서 다른 감각들이 음식을 경험하는 데 영향을 끼친다고 했고, 빈칸이 있는 문장에서 전체적인 경험이 좋은 경우에 대해 이야기하고 있으므로, 빈칸에는 ② '음식을 더욱 더 즐긴다'가 가장 알맞다.
[문제] 글의 빈칸에 들어갈 말로 가장 알맞은 것은?
① 음식에 집중하지 않는다 ③ 음식의 질을 존중한다
④ 그들의 감각의 중요성을 안다 ⑤ 음식의 맛이 중요하다고 생각하지 않는다

3 '우리 주위에 있는 것들에 관해 신체가 정보를 얻는 방법들'의 의미를 가진 단어는 senses(감각들)이다.
[문제] 다음 영영 뜻풀이에 해당하는 단어를 글에서 찾아 쓰시오.

4 문장 ⑨에 언급되어 있다.
[문제] 글의 밑줄 친 these가 의미하는 것은 무엇인가? 우리말로 쓰시오.

본문 직독 직해

① It is Friday night. / ② You enter / your favorite steak restaurant. / ③ You can smell /
금요일 밤이다 / 당신은 들어간다 / 당신이 매우 좋아하는 스테이크 식당에 / 당신은 냄새를 맡을 수 있다
the delicious food. / ④ There is an open kitchen, / so / you can see the chef cooking. /
맛있는 음식의 / 개방된 주방이 있다 / 그래서 / 당신은 요리사가 요리하고 있는 것을 볼 수 있다
⑤ He puts a piece of meat / on the hot grill. / ⑥ It makes a sizzling sound / and / turns brown. /
그는 고기 한 점을 놓는다 / 뜨거운 석쇠 위에 / 그것은 지글거리는 소리는 낸다 / 그리고 / 갈색이 된다
⑦ All of these things / make your mouth water. /
이 모든 것들은 / 당신의 입에 군침이 돌게 한다

⑧ Many restaurants know / that tasty food is not enough / to attract customers. /
많은 식당들이 안다 / 맛있는 음식이 충분하지 않다는 것을 / 고객을 끌기에
⑨ The sights, smells, and sounds / of the food / all / affect a customer's experience. / ⑩ So /
모습, 냄새, 그리고 소리 / 음식의 / 모두 / 고객의 경험에 영향을 미친다 / 그래서
restaurants use these / to get more customers. / ⑪ If the entire experience is good, / customers
식당들은 이것들을 이용한다 / 더 많은 고객들을 얻기 위해 / 만약 전체적인 경험이 좋다면 / 고객들은

enjoy the food / even more! /
음식을 즐긴다 더욱 더

⑫ So / when you visit / your favorite restaurant, / do not just taste the food. / ⑬ Pay
그러므로 당신이 방문할 때 당신이 매우 좋아하는 식당을 단지 음식만 맛보지 마라 ~에

attention to / how the restaurant satisfies / your other senses. / ⑭ Keep / your eyes, ears, and
주목하라 그 식당이 만족시키는 방법 당신의 다른 감각들을 두어라 당신의 눈과 귀와

nose open / for a sizzling experience! /
코를 열어 둔 채로 지글거리는 (음식) 경험을 위해

본문 해석

금요일 밤이다. 당신은 당신이 매우 좋아하는 스테이크 식당에 들어간다. 당신은 맛있는 음식 냄새를 맡을 수 있다. 개방된 주방이 있어서, 당신은 요리사가 요리하고 있는 것을 볼 수 있다. 그는 고기 한 점을 뜨거운 석쇠 위에 놓는다. 그것은 지글거리는 소리를 내고 갈색이 된다. 이 모든 것들은 당신의 입에 군침이 돌게 한다.

많은 식당들이 맛있는 음식이 고객을 끌기에 충분하지 않다는 것을 안다. 음식의 모습, 냄새, 그리고 소리 모두가 고객의 경험에 영향을 미친다. 그래서 식당들은 더 많은 고객들을 얻기 위해 이것들을 이용한다. 만약 전체적인 경험이 좋다면, 고객들은 음식을 더욱 더 즐긴다!

그러므로 당신이 매우 좋아하는 식당에 방문할 때, 단지 음식만 맛보지 마라. 그 식당이 당신의 다른 감각들을 만족시키는 방법에 주목하라. 지글거리는 (음식) 경험을 위해 당신의 눈과 귀와 코를 열어 두어라!

구문 해설

④ There is an open kitchen, so you can **see the chef cooking.**
→ 「see + 목적어 + v-ing」는 '~가 …하고 있는 것을 보다'의 의미이다.

⑦ **All of these things *make* your mouth *water.***
→ 「all of + 명사」는 뒤에 오는 명사에 수를 일치시키므로, 복수형 동사 make가 쓰였다.
→ 「make + 목적어 + 동사원형」은 '~가 …하게 하다'의 의미이다.

⑧ Many restaurants know [**that** tasty food is not *enough to attract* customers].
→ that은 명사절을 이끄는 접속사로, [ ]는 동사 know의 목적어 역할을 한다.
→ 「enough + to-v」는 '~하기에 충분한'의 의미이다.

⑪ If the entire experience is good, customers enjoy the food **even** more!
→ even은 '더욱, 훨씬'의 의미로, 비교급(more)을 강조한다.

⑬ Pay attention to [**how** the restaurant satisfies your other senses].
→ [ ]는 전치사 to의 목적어 역할을 하는 관계부사절로, how는 '~하는 방법[방식]'의 의미이다. 방법을 나타내는 선행사 the way와 관계부사 how는 같이 쓸 수 없으므로, 둘 중 하나는 반드시 생략한다.

⑭ **Keep your eyes, ears, and nose open** for a sizzling experience!
→ 「keep + 목적어 + 형용사」는 '~을 …한 상태로 두다'의 의미이다.

Review Test

정답 1 ④ 2 1) ⓒ 2) ⓐ 3) ⓑ 3 ⑤ 4 1) T 2) T 5 ③ 6 advertisement 7 ④
8 how the restaurant satisfies your other senses

문제 해설

1 ④ describe: 묘사하다

2 1) sizzle((음식이) 지글거리는 소리를 내다): ⓒ (기름에) 구워지는 음식의 소리를 내다
2) affect(영향을 미치다): ⓐ 무언가 또는 누군가에게 변화를 야기하다
3) term(용어): ⓑ 특정한 단어나 어구

3 ⑤는 '좋아하다'라는 의미의 동사로 쓰였고, 본문과 나머지 선택지는 모두 '~같이, ~처럼'이라는 의미의 전치사로 쓰였다.
① 그는 바람처럼 달린다. ② 이것은 초콜릿 같은 맛이 난다.
③ 그녀는 그녀의 엄마처럼 보인다. ④ 그는 사자처럼 싸웠다.
⑤ 그들은 주말마다 하이킹 가는 것을 좋아한다.

4 1) 과거에 악대차의 악단 음악 소리를 듣고 사람들이 무리 지어 따라다녔고, 그들 중 대부분은 그들이 왜 무리에 합류했는지 몰랐다고 했다.
2) '편승 효과'는 다른 사람들이 무언가를 하고 있기 때문에 그것을 따라서 하는 행위를 묘사하는 데 사용된다고 했다.

5 빈칸 앞 문장에서 모델이 햄버거를 먹는 TV 광고를 거울 뉴런의 예로 들었고, 빈칸 뒤에서 그 광고를 본 사람들이 그 모델을 따라 하게 된다고 했다. 따라서, 빈칸에는 이유를 나타내는 ③ '~때문에'가 알맞다.
① ~에도 불구하고 ② 제외하고 ④ 대신에 ⑤ ~와 달리

6 제품 판매를 돕기 위해 대중에게 소개되는 것

7 주어진 문장은 '그것은 지글거리는 소리를 내고 갈색이 된다'는 내용으로, It이 a piece of meat을 가리키므로, ④에 오는 것이 가장 자연스럽다.

8 선행사 the way가 생략된 관계부사절이 와야 하고, 관계부사 뒤에 모든 문장 성분을 갖춘 절이 와야 하므로 「how+주어+동사」의 어순으로 쓴다.

Section **08** Origins

본책 • pp. 92-93

1

정답 1 ③ 2 ④ 3 (1) T (2) F 4 remove, clear

문제 해설

1 투명 테이프가 발명된 과정에 관한 글이므로, 주제로는 ③ '어떻게 스카치테이프가 발명되었는지'가 가장 알맞다.
① 왜 자동차가 보통 단 한 가지 색인지 ② 셀로판의 여러 다른 용도
④ 왜 접착제가 테이프보다 훨씬 더 강력한지 ⑤ 새로운 종류의 자동차 페인트의 발명

2 '그러나 차에서 접착제를 완전히 제거하는 것이 거의 불가능했다.'는 내용의 주어진 문장은 붙여진 종이가 제거되었을 때 차가 두가지 색이 된다는 문장 ⑥과 그래서 한 남자가 해결책을 찾기로 결심했다는 문장 ⑦ 사이에 오는 것이 가장 알맞다.

3 (1) 문장 ①에 언급되어 있다.
(2) 문장 ⑧, ⑨를 통해 Drew가 발명한 종이테이프가 대단한 성공이었음을 알 수 있다.

4

보기	제거하다	붙이다	색칠된	투명한

과거에는, 자동차를 두 가지 다른 색으로 칠하는 것이 어려웠다. 그래서 한 남자가 제거하기 쉬운 종이테이프를 발명했다. 이후에, 그는 셀로판을 가지고 실험해서 투명한 테이프 또한 발명했다.

본문 직독 직해

① In the 1920s, / cars / with two different colors of paint / were popular. / ② Unfortunately, / this made life difficult / for car painters. /
1920년대에 / 자동차들 / 두 가지 다른 색의 페인트가 칠해진 / 인기 있었다 / 안타깝게도 / 이것은 삶을 힘들게 만들었다 / 도장공들에게

③ First, / they painted the car / one color. / ④ Next, / they glued paper / over the parts / of the car / that had to stay / the original color. / ⑤ Finally, / they painted the car / a second color. / ⑥ When the paper was removed, / the car was two colors. / However, / it was nearly impossible / to completely remove the glue / from the cars. / ⑦ So / a man / named Richard Gurley Drew / decided / to find a solution. / ⑧ Two years later, / he invented paper tape / that could be removed / cleanly and easily. /
먼저 / 그들은 차를 칠했다 / 한 가지 색으로 / 다음으로 / 그들은 종이를 붙였다 / 부분들 위에 / 차의 / 유지되어야 했던 / 원래의 색으로 / 마지막으로 / 그들은 차를 칠했다 / 두 번째 색으로 / 종이가 제거되었을 때 / 차는 두 가지 색이었다 / 그러나 / 거의 불가능했다 / 접착제를 완전히 제거하는 것은 / 차에서 / 그래서 / 한 남자가 / Richard Gurley Drew라는 이름의 / 결심했다 / 해결책을 찾기로 / 2년 후에 / 그는 종이테이프를 발명했다 / 제거될 수 있는 / 깨끗하고 쉽게

⑨ It was a great success, / but Drew wasn't satisfied. / ⑩ He began experimenting / with cellophane, / a new thin, clear plastic material / used for packaging. / ⑪ In 1930, / he invented the first clear tape. / ⑫ Today / we know his invention / as "Scotch tape." /
그것은 대단한 성공이었다 / 그러나 Drew는 만족하지 않았다 / 그는 실험하기 시작했다 / 셀로판을 가지고 / 새로운 얇고 투명한 플라스틱 물질인 / 포장에 쓰이는 / 1930년에 / 그는 최초의 투명한 테이프를 발명했다 / 오늘날 / 우리는 그의 발명품을 알고 있다 / '스카치테이프'로

본문 해석

1920년대에는 두 가지 다른 색의 페인트가 칠해진 자동차들이 인기 있었다. 안타깝게도, 이것은 자동차 도장공들의 삶을 힘들게 만들었다.

먼저, 그들은 차를 한 가지 색으로 칠했다. 다음으로, 그들은 차에서 원래의 색으로 유지되어야 하는 부분들 위에 종이를 붙였다. 마지막으로, 그들은 차를 두 번째 색으로 칠했다. 종이가 제거되었을 때, 차는 두 가지 색이었다. 그러나 차에서 접착제를 완전히 제거하는 것이 거의 불가능했다. 그래서 Richard Gurley Drew라는 이름의 한 남자는 해결책을 찾기로 결심했다. 2년 후에, 그는 깨끗하고 쉽게 제거될 수 있는 종이테이프를 발명했다.

그것은 대단한 성공이었지만, Drew는 만족하지 않았다. 그는 셀로판, 즉 포장에 쓰이는 새로운 얇고 투명한 플라스틱 물질을 가지고 실험하기 시작했다. 그는 1930년에 최초의 투명한 테이프를 발명했다. 오늘날 우리는 그의 발명품을 '스카치테이프'라고 알고 있다.

구문 해설

① In the 1920s, **cars** [with two different colors of paint] **were** popular.
→ 문장의 주어가 cars로 복수 명사이므로, 복수형 동사 were가 쓰였다.
→ [ ]는 cars를 수식하는 전치사구이다.

④ Next, they glued paper over **the parts of the car** [**that** had to *stay the original color*].
→ [ ]는 선행사 the parts of the car를 수식하는 주격 관계대명사절이다.
→ 「stay+명사」는 '~로 유지되다'의 의미이다.

㉤ However, **it** was nearly impossible **to completely *remove the glue from the cars*.**
→ it은 가주어이고, to completely remove 이하가 진주어이다.
→ 「remove A from B」는 'A를 B로부터 제거하다'의 의미이다.

⑦ So a man [**named** Richard Gurley Drew] decided to find a solution.
→ [ ]는 a man을 수식하는 과거분사구이다.

⑩ He **began experimenting** with *cellophane*, [a new thin, clear plastic material {used for packaging}].
→ 「begin+v-ing[to-v]」는 '~하기 시작하다'의 의미이다.
→ cellophane과 [ ]는 동격 관계이다.
→ { }는 a new thin, clear plastic material을 수식하는 과거분사구이다.

2

본책 • pp. 94-95

정답 1 ② 2 ① 3 (1) F (2) T 4 sailors, ill

문제 해설

1 '날씨 아래에 있는(under the weather)'이라는 관용어의 기원 및 의미에 관한 글이므로, 주제로는 ② '나쁜 날씨가 어떻게 한 관용구에 영감을 주었는가'가 가장 알맞다.
① 선원들이 자주 병에 걸리는 이유 ③ 새로운 관용구를 배우는 것이 어려운 이유
④ 항해에서 멀어지는 추세의 이면에 있는 이론 ⑤ 아플 때 스스로 기분을 좋게 하는 방법

2 빈칸 앞 문장에는 '날씨 아래에 있는(under the weather)'이라는 관용어가 뱃멀미에 관해서 말할 때만 사용되었다고 했고, 빈칸 다음 문장에는 오늘날 그 관용어가 모든 종류의 질병에 사용될 수 있다고 했으므로, 빈칸에는 ① '더 넓은'이 가장 알맞다.
② 좁은 ③ 숨겨진 ④ 이상한 ⑤ 전통적인

3 (1) 문장 ⑥-⑦에서 배가 움직여서 아픈 선원들은 휴식을 취하고 나아지기 위해 갑판 아래로 갔다고 했다.
(2) 문장 ⑪에 언급되어 있다.

4 '날씨 아래에 있는(under the weather)'이라는 관용어의 기원에 대한 한 가지 이론은 아팠을 때 배의 갑판 아래로 갔었던 선원들로부터 유래했다는 것이다.

본문 직독 직해

① If you are feeling a bit unwell, / you may say / that you're "under the weather." / ② What does our health have to do with the weather? / ③ There are several common theories / about the origin of this idiom. /
만약 당신이 조금 아프다면 / 당신은 말할지도 모른다 / '날씨 아래에 있는'이라고 / 우리의 건강이 날씨와 어떤 관계가 있을까 / 몇 가지 일반적인 이론이 있다 / 이 관용어의 기원에 대한

④ One popular theory suggests / that it came from the language of sailors. / ⑤ When the weather was bad, / the sea would be rough. / ⑥ This made the boat move / a lot, / which often made sailors ill. / ⑦ They had to go / below deck / to rest and get better. / ⑧ That meant / they were literally under the bad weather / taking place above deck. /
한 인기 있는 이론은 시사한다 / 그것이 선원들의 언어로부터 왔다고 / 날씨가 나쁠 때 / 바다는 거칠었다 / 이것은 배를 움직이게 만들었고 / 많이 / 이것은 종종 선원들을 아프게 했다 / 그들은 가야만 했다 / 갑판 아래로 / 휴식을 취하고 나아지기 위해 / 그것은 의미했다 / 그들이 문자 그대로 나쁜 날씨 아래에 있다는 것을 / 갑판 위에서 일어나는

⑨ At first, / the idiom was only used / to talk about seasickness. / ⑩ As time went on, / it took on a wider meaning. / ⑪ Today, / "under the weather" can be used / for any type of illness. /
처음에 / 그 관용어는 단지 사용되었다 / 뱃멀미에 대해 말할 때만 / 시간이 지나면서 / 그것은 더 넓은 의미를 가지게 되었다 / 오늘날 / '날씨 아래에 있는'은 사용될 수 있다 / 모든 종류의 질병에

본문 해석

만약 당신이 조금 아프다면, 당신은 '날씨 아래에 있는(under the weather)'이라고 말할지도 모른다. 우리의 건강이 날씨와 어떤 관계가 있을까? 이 관용어의 기원에 대한 몇 가지 일반적인 이론이 있다.

한 인기 있는 이론은 그것이 선원들의 언어로부터 왔다고 시사한다. 날씨가 나쁠 때, 바다는 거칠었다. 이것은 배를 많이 움직이게 만들었고, 이것은 종종 선원들을 아프게 했다. 그들은 휴식을 취하고 나아지기 위해 갑판 아래로 가야만 했다. 그것은 그들이 문자 그대로 갑판 위에서 일어나는 나쁜 날씨 아래에 있다는 것을 의미했다.

처음에 그 관용어는 단지 뱃멀미에 대해 말할 때만 사용되었다. 시간이 지나면서, 그것은 더 넓은 의미를 가지게 되었다. 오늘날, '날씨 아래에 있는'은 모든 종류의 질병에 사용될 수 있다.

구문 해설

① If you are **feeling a bit unwell**, you may say [*that* you're "under the weather."]
→ 「feel+형용사」는 '~하게 느끼다'의 의미이다. 부사 a bit이 형용사 unwell을 수식하고 있다.
→ [ ]는 동사 say의 목적어 역할을 하는 명사절이다.

② What does our health **have to do with** the weather?
→ have to do with는 '~와 관계가 있다'의 의미이다.

③ There are several common theories [about the origin of this idiom].
→ [ ]는 several common theories를 수식하는 전치사구이다.

④ One popular theory suggests [**that** it came from the language of sailors].
→ [ ]는 동사 suggests의 목적어 역할을 하는 명사절이다.

⑥ This **made the boat move** a lot, [*which* often made sailors ill].
→ 「make+목적어+동사원형」은 '~을 …하게 만들다'의 의미이다.
→ [ ]는 앞 절의 내용을 부연 설명하는 계속적 용법의 관계대명사절로, '그리고 그것은[이는]'이라고 해석한다. 계속적 용법의 관계대명사는 관계대명사 앞에 콤마(,)를 쓴다.
→ 「make+목적어+형용사」는 '~을 …하게 만들다'의 의미이다.

⑦ They **had to go** below deck *to rest* and *(to) get better*.
→ 「had to+동사원형」은 「have to+동사원형」의 과거형으로, '~해야 했다'의 의미이다.
→ to rest와 (to) get better는 〈목적〉을 나타내는 부사적 용법의 to부정사로, 접속사 and로 병렬 연결되어 있다.

⑧ That meant [(**that**) they were literally under the bad weather {*taking* place above deck}].
→ [ ]는 동사 meant의 목적어 역할을 하는 명사절로, 접속사 that이 생략되었다.
→ { }는 the bad weather를 수식하는 현재분사구이다.

⑨ At first, the idiom **was** only **used to talk** about seasickness.
→ 「be used+to-v」는 '~하는 데 사용되다'의 의미이다.

⑪ Today, "under the weather" **can be used** for any type of illness.
→ can be used는 '사용될 수 있다'라는 의미로, 조동사와 함께 쓰인 수동태이다. 조동사 뒤에는 동사원형이 오므로, be동사의 원형인 be를 써서 「조동사+be+p.p.」로 나타낸다.

3

본책 • pp. 96-97

정답 1 ② 2 ① 3 ② 4 ②

문제 해설

1 초승달 모양의 빵인 크루아상의 유래에 관해 설명한 글이므로, 제목으로는 ② '달 모양 빵의 유래'가 가장 알맞다.
① 오스만 제국의 제빵사들 ③ 오스트리아인들이 크루아상을 먹지 않는 이유
④ 크루아상: 하나의 빵, 다양한 모양 ⑤ 두 종류의 빵 사이의 전쟁

2 빈칸 앞에 사람들이 크루아상이 프랑스에서 비롯되었다고 생각한다는 내용이 오고, 빈칸 뒤에는 크루아상이 사실 오스트리아의 빵에 기반을 두고 있다는 내용이 이어지므로, 빈칸에는 역접의 의미를 나타내는 ① '그러나'가 가장 알맞다.
② 그러므로 ③ 게다가 ④ 예를 들어 ⑤ 다시 말해서

3 크루아상이 오스트리아의 빵인 킵펠에서 유래되었다는 내용 중에, 지구에서 보일 때 달의 모양이 매일 밤 변한다는 내용의 (b)는 글의 흐름과 무관하다.

4 ②: 문장 ⑨에서 오스만 제국 사람들이 도시의 벽 아래에 굴을 파고 있었다고 했다.
①은 문장 ⑦에, ③은 문장 ⑧-⑪에, ④는 문장 ⑫에, ⑤는 문장 ⑬에 언급되어 있다.

본문 직독 직해

① Many people assume / that the croissant comes from France. / ② However, / it is actually
많은 사람들은 생각한다 크루아상이 프랑스에서 비롯되었다고 그러나 그것은 사실 ~에

based on / a type of Austrian bread, / the kipfel. / ③ Both the croissant and the kipfel / are
기반을 둔다 일종의 오스트리아 빵에 킵펠이라는 크루아상과 킵펠 둘 다

shaped / like a crescent moon. / (④ When it is viewed / from Earth, / the moon changes shape /
생겼다 초승달처럼 그것이 보일 때 지구에서 달은 모양이 변한다

night after night. /)
매일 밤

⑤ According to legend, / the kipfel was created / in 1683 / after Austria defeated / the
전설에 따르면 킵펠은 만들어졌다 1683년에 오스트리아가 패배시킨 후에

Ottoman Empire / in a battle. / ⑥ The Ottomans had surrounded / the city of Vienna. /
오스만 제국을 전쟁에서 오스만 제국 사람들은 둘러쌌었다 비엔나 도시를

⑦ Luckily, / the city was protected / by tall walls. / ⑧ One night, / an Austrian baker / heard
다행히 그 도시는 보호되고 있었다 높은 벽에 의해 어느 날 밤 한 오스트리아인 제빵사가

strange sounds / beneath his bakery. / ⑨ He realized / the Ottomans were digging a tunnel /
이상한 소리를 들었다 그의 빵집 아래에서 그는 알아챘다 오스만 제국 사람들이 굴을 파고 있다는 것을

under the city walls! / ⑩ He quickly alerted / the Austrian soldiers. / ⑪ The tunnel was
도시의 벽 아래에 그는 재빨리 알렸다 오스트리아 병사들에게 그 굴은

destroyed, / and the city was saved! /
파괴되었다 그리고 그 도시는 구해졌다

⑫ To celebrate, / he made some special bread. / ⑬ It was shaped / like the moon / on the
기념하기 위해 그는 어떤 특별한 빵을 만들었다 그것은 생겼었다 달처럼

Ottoman Empire's flag. / ⑭ Nearly 100 years later, / the kipfel was brought / to France, / where
오스만 제국의 국기 위의 거의 100년이 지난 후 킵펠은 들여져 왔다 프랑스로

it became the croissant. /
그곳에서 그것은 크루아상이 되었다

본문 해석

많은 사람들이 크루아상이 프랑스에서 비롯되었다고 생각한다. 그러나, 그것은 사실 킵펠(kipfel)이라는 일종의 오스트리아 빵에 기반을 두고 있다. 크루아상과 킵펠 둘 다 초승달처럼 생겼다. (지구에서 보일 때 달은 매일 밤 모양이 변한다.)

전설에 따르면, 킵펠은 오스트리아가 전쟁에서 오스만 제국을 패배시킨 후 1683년에 만들어졌다. 오스만 제국 사람들이 비엔나 도시를 둘러쌌었다. 다행히, 그 도시는 높은 벽으로 보호되고 있었다. 어느 날 밤, 한 오스트리아인 제빵사가 자신의 빵집 아래에서 이상한 소리를 들었다. 그는 오스만 제국 사람들이 도시의 벽 아래에 굴을 파고 있다는 것을 알아챘다! 그는 재빨리 오스트리아 병사들에게 알렸다. 그 굴은 파괴되었고, 도시는 지켜졌다.

(이를) 기념하기 위해, 그는 어떤 특별한 빵을 만들었다. 그것은 오스만 제국의 국기에 있는 달처럼 생겼었다. 거의 100년이 지난 후, 킵펠은 프랑스로 들여져 왔고, 그곳에서 그것은 크루아상이 되었다.

구문 해설

① Many people assume [**that** the croissant comes from France].
→ [ ]는 동사 assume의 목적어 역할을 하는 명사절이다.

② However, it **is** actually **based on** *a type of Austrian bread, the kipfel.*
→ be based on ~은 '~에 기반을 두다'의 의미이다.
→ a type of Austrian bread와 the kipfel은 동격 관계이다.

③ **Both the croissant and the kipfel are** shaped like a crescent moon.

→ 「both A and B」는 'A와 B 둘 다'의 의미로, 복수 취급하므로 복수형 동사 are가 쓰였다.

⑥ The Ottomans **had surrounded** the city of Vienna.

→ had surrounded는 과거완료(had + p.p.)로, 과거 시점(문장 ⑤의 defeated)보다 먼저 일어난 일임을 나타낸다.

⑭ … , the kipfel **was brought to** *France*, [*where* it became the croissant].

→ 「A be brought to B」는 「bring A to B(A를 B로 가져오다[들여오다])」의 수동태 표현으로, 'A가 B로 들여져 오다'의 의미이다.

→ where는 선행사 France를 부연 설명하는 계속적 용법의 관계부사이다.

본책 • pp. 98-99

4

정답 1 ① 2 ③ 3 사람들이 보통 무기를 오른손에 들었기 때문에 4 carrying, hidden

문제 해설

1 사람들이 왜 악수를 하기 시작했는지에 관한 글이므로, 제목으로는 ① '악수의 유래'가 가장 알맞다.
[문제] 글의 제목으로 가장 알맞은 것은?
② 전 세계의 안부 인사 ③ 고대의 무기 찾기
④ 손짓으로 의사소통하기 ⑤ 사람들은 왜 오른손을 사용할까?

2 기원전 5세기경의 그림들이 악수하는 사람들을 보여준다는 내용의 (B), 그 그림들 중 다수가 병사들을 보여준다는 내용의 (A), 그래서 일부 전문가들은 악수가 무기를 확인하는 방법이었다고 생각한다는 내용의 (C)의 흐름이 알맞다.
[문제] 문장 (A)~(C)의 순서로 가장 알맞은 것은?

3 문장 ⑪에 언급되어 있다.
[문제] 사람들이 보통 오른손으로 악수를 했던 이유는 무엇인가? 우리말로 쓰시오.

4 [문제] 다음 빈칸에 알맞은 단어를 상자에서 골라 쓰시오.

파는	들고 있는	숨겨진	강력한

과거에는, 사람들이 자신이 무기를 들고 있지 않다는 것을 보여주기 위해 악수를 했다. 흔드는 동작은 숨겨진 무기를 드러내기 위해 사용되었다.

본문 직독 직해

① When two people meet, / they often shake hands. / ② Today / this seems perfectly normal. / ③ But / why did people start / grabbing each other's hands / and shaking them / in the first place? /
두 사람이 만나면 / 그들은 종종 악수를 한다 / 오늘날 / 이것은 지극히 평범해 보인다 / 그러나 / 왜 사람들은 시작했을까 / 서로의 손을 잡는 것을 / 그리고 그것들을 흔드는 것을 / 처음에

④ It is believed that / it started / in ancient times. / ⑥ Paintings / from as early as the fifth century BC / show people / shaking hands. / ⑤ Many of these paintings / show
~라고 믿어진다 / 그것은 시작되었다 / 고대에 / 그림들은 / 기원전 5세기만큼 일찍이[5세기경의] / 사람들을 보여준다 / 악수하고 있는 / 이러한 그림들 중 다수가 / 병사들을

soldiers. / ⑦ So / some experts think / shaking hands was a way / of checking for weapons. /
보여준다 그래서 일부 전문가들은 생각한다 악수가 방법이었다고 무기를 확인하는

⑧ A person with a weapon / in his or her hand / couldn't grab / another person's hand. /
무기가 있는 사람은 그 혹은 그녀의 손에 잡을 수 없었다 다른 사람의 손을

⑨ Also, / people sometimes hid weapons / in their sleeves. / ⑩ If someone did this, /
또한 사람들은 때때로 무기를 숨겼다 자신의 소매 속에 만약 누군가 이렇게 했다면

moving the person's hand / up and down / would reveal the weapon. / ⑪ Since people usually
그 사람의 손을 움직이는 것은 위 아래로 무기를 드러나게 했을 것이다 사람들은 보통

carried weapons / in their right hands, / it was common / to always use the right hand / in a
무기를 들었기 때문에 그들의 오른손에 일반적이었다 항상 오른손을 사용하는 것이

handshake. / ⑫ Eventually, / this became / a gesture of peace / between two people / who were
악수할 때 결국 이것은 ~가 되었다 평화의 제스처가 두 사람 사이에

meeting. /
만나고 있는

본문 해석

두 사람이 만나면 그들은 종종 악수를 한다. 오늘날 이것은 지극히 평범해 보인다. 그러나 왜 사람들은 처음에 서로의 손을 잡고 흔들기 시작했을까?

그것은 고대에 시작되었다고 믿어진다. (B) 기원전 5세기경의 그림들은 악수하고 있는 사람들을 보여준다. (A) 이러한 그림들 중 다수가 병사들을 보여준다. (C) 그래서 일부 전문가들은 악수가 무기를 확인하는 방법이었다고 생각한다. 손에 무기를 든 사람은 다른 사람의 손을 잡을 수 없었다.

또한, 사람들은 때때로 자신의 소매 속에 무기를 숨겼다. 만약 누군가 이렇게 했다면, 그 사람의 손을 위 아래로 움직이는 것은 무기를 드러나게 했을 것이다. 사람들은 보통 무기를 오른손에 들었기 때문에, 악수를 할 때 항상 오른손을 사용하는 것이 일반적이었다. 결국 이것은 만나고 있는 두 사람 사이에 평화의 제스처가 되었다.

구문 해설

③ But why did people start **grabbing** each other's hands and **shaking** them in the first place?
→ 동사 start의 목적어 역할을 하는 동명사 grabbing과 shaking이 접속사 and로 병렬 연결되어 있다.

④ **It** is believed [**that** it started in ancient times].
→ It은 가주어, [ ]가 진주어이다.

⑥ **Paintings** [from *as early as* the fifth century BC] **show** people shaking hands.
→ 문장의 주어는 Paintings이며, 동사는 show이다. [ ]는 앞의 명사 Paintings를 수식하는 전치사구이다.
→ 「as + 형용사[부사]의 원급 + as」는 '~만큼 …한[하게]'라는 의미의 원급 비교이다.
→ shaking hands는 people을 수식하는 현재분사구이다.

⑩ **If** someone did this, [*moving* the person's hand up and down] would reveal the weapon.
→ if는 '만약 ~라면'의 의미로, 〈조건〉을 나타내는 접속사이다.
→ [ ]는 주어 역할을 하는 동명사구이다.

⑪ **Since** people usually carried weapons in their right hands, *it* was common *to always use the right hand in a handshake*.
→ since는 '~이기 때문에'의 의미인 접속사이다.
→ it은 가주어, to always use 이하가 진주어이다.

⑫ Eventually, this became a gesture of peace between **two people** [**who** were meeting].
→ [ ]는 선행사 two people을 수식하는 주격 관계대명사절이다.

Review Test

본책 • pp. 100-101

정답 1 ② 2 ③ 3 ③ 4 모든 종류의 질병 5 the city was protected by tall walls 6 ②
7 ④ 8 소매 속에 무기를 숨기는 것

문제 해설

1 ② invention: 발명

2 revealed(드러내 보였다)와 반대 의미의 단어는 ③ 'hid(숨겼다)'이다.

> 그 개는 이빨을 드러내 보이고 나에게 으르렁거렸다.

① 보여주었다 ② 사용했다 ④ 보호했다 ⑤ 깨달았다

3 날씨가 안 좋을 때 바다가 거칠었다는 (B)가 먼저 오고, 거친 바다가 선원들을 아프게 했다는 (A)가 다음에 온 후, 선원들이 갑판 아래에 가서 쉬어야 했다는 (C)로 이어지는 것이 자연스럽다.

4 모든 종류의 질병에 대해 말할 때 사용될 수 있다고 했다.

> 오늘날에 '날씨 아래에 있는(under the weather)'은 무엇에 관해 말하는 데 사용되는가?

5 「be+p.p.」 형태의 수동태 구문을 쓴다.

6 오스트리아가 전쟁에서 오스만 제국을 이긴 후, 상대국의 국기에 있는 달과 같은 모양의 특별한 빵을 만들었다는 것은 전쟁의 승리를 기념하기 위해서였을 것이므로, 빈칸에는 ② '기념하기 위해'가 알맞다.

① 우연히 ③ 실수로 ④ 벌로 ⑤ 화가 나서

7 악수가 무기를 확인하는 방법이었을 것이라는 내용 중에, '일부 문화에서는 병사들이 월급으로 소금을 지급받았다.'는 (d)는 글의 흐름과 무관하다.

8 바로 앞 문장에 언급되어 있다.

Section 09 Sports & Entertainment

본책 • pp. 104-105

1

정답 1 ② 2 ④ 3 ③ 4 (1) pitch (2) spectators (3) decisions

문제 해설

1 지금과 달랐던 과거의 야구 규칙에 관한 글이므로, 제목으로는 ② '과거 야구의 이상한 규칙들'이 가장 알맞다.
① 현대 야구의 규칙 ③ 야구: 가장 어려운 경기
④ 야구에는 왜 심판이 있을까? ⑤ 야구를 하는 새로운 방법 찾기

2 빈칸 뒤쪽에 과거의 야구 규칙이 어떻게 달랐는지에 대한 예가 나오고 있으므로, 빈칸에는 ④ '오늘날의 규칙들과 매우 달랐다'가 가장 알맞다.
① 너무 복잡해서 이해할 수 없었다 ② 경기를 공정하게 하는 데 도움이 됐다
③ 현재의 규칙보다 훨씬 엄격했다 ⑤ 대부분의 다른 스포츠의 규칙과 유사했다

3 오늘날과 달랐던 과거의 야구 규칙을 설명한 내용 뒤에, 심판의 역할이 또다른 차이점이라는 내용의 (B), 오늘날 심판은 규칙을 시행하여 중립적인 역할을 한다는 내용의 (C), 하지만 과거에는 심판이 판정을 관중에게 요청하기도 했다는 내용의 (A)로 이어지는 흐름이 가장 알맞다.

4 **19세기의 야구 규칙**

누가	그들이 할 수 있었던 것
타자	그들은 낮거나 높은 (1) 투구를 요구할 수 있었다.
심판	그들은 (2) 관중들에게 그들이 (3) 결정을 내리는 것을 도와달라고 요청할 수 있었다.

본문 직독 직해

① The game of baseball is played / by two teams of nine players. / ② A player from one team throws a small ball. / ③ Then / a player from the other team tries to hit it / with a bat. /
야구 경기는 진행된다 / 9명의 선수로 이루어진 두 팀에 의해 / 한 팀의 선수가 작은 공을 던진다 / 그리고 / 다른 팀의 선수가 그것을 치려고 한다 / 방망이로

④ Baseball has been popular / for more than 150 years. / ⑤ However, / some of the rules / in the 19th century / were very different / from the rules of today. /
야구는 인기가 있어왔다 / 150년이 넘는 기간 동안 / 하지만 / 규칙들 중 일부는 / 19세기의 / 매우 달랐다 / 오늘날의 규칙들과

⑥ For example, / batters could request the kind of pitch / they wanted. / ⑦ They would ask the pitchers / to throw the ball / either high or low. / ⑨ Another difference was the role of the umpires. / ⑩ Today, / they play a neutral role / by enforcing the rules. / ⑧ But / in the past / they would sometimes ask spectators / for help / in making decisions. / ⑪ That doesn't sound very fair, / does it? / ⑫ Fortunately, / these rules were later changed. /
예를 들어 / 타자들은 투구의 종류를 요청할 수 있었다 / 그들이 원하는 / 그들은 투수들에게 요청했었다 / 공을 던지도록 / 높거나 낮게 / 또 다른 차이점은 심판의 역할이었다 / 오늘날 / 그들은 중립적인 역할을 한다 / 규칙을 시행함으로써 / 하지만 / 과거에 / 그들은 때때로 관중들에게 요청하기도 했다 / 도움을 / 결정을 내리는 데 / 그것은 매우 공정하게 들리지 않는다 / 그렇지 않은가 / 다행히도 / 이 규칙들은 나중에 바뀌었다

본문 해석

야구 경기는 9명의 선수로 이루어진 두 팀에 의해 진행된다. 한 팀의 선수가 작은 공을 던진다. 그리고 다른 팀의 선수가 방망이로 그것을 치려고 한다. 야구는 150년이 넘는 기간 동안 인기가 있어왔다. 하지만 19세기의 규칙

들 중 일부는 오늘날의 규칙들과 매우 달랐다.

예를 들어, 타자들은 그들이 원하는 투구의 종류를 요청할 수 있었다. 그들은 투수들에게 높거나 낮게 공을 던지도록 요청했었다. (B) 또 다른 차이점은 심판의 역할이었다. (C) 오늘날, 그들은 규칙을 시행함으로써 중립적인 역할을 한다. (A) 하지만 과거에는 때때로 관중들에게 결정을 내리는 데 도움을 요청하기도 했다. 그것은 매우 공정하게 들리지 않는다, 그렇지 않은가? 다행히도, 이 규칙들은 나중에 바뀌었다.

구문 해설

③ Then a player [from the other team] **tries to hit** it with a bat.
→ [ ]는 a player를 수식하는 전치사구이다.
→ 「try+to-v」는 '~하려고 노력하다'의 의미이다.

④ Baseball **has been** popular for more than 150 years.
→ has been은 '~해 왔다'의 의미로, 「have[has]+p.p.」 형태의 〈계속〉을 나타내는 현재완료이다.

⑥ For example, batters could request **the kind of pitch** [(**which**[**that**]) they wanted].
→ [ ]는 선행사 the kind of pitch를 수식하는 목적격 관계대명사절로, 관계대명사 which[that]가 생략되었다.

⑦ They would **ask** the pitchers **to throw** the ball *either high or low*.
→ 「ask+목적어+to-v」는 '~에게 …하는 것을 요청하다'의 의미이다.
→ 「either A or B」는 'A나 B 둘 중 하나'의 의미이다.

⑪ That doesn't **sound very fair**, *does it*?
→ 「sound+형용사」는 '~하게 들리다'의 의미이다. 부사 very는 형용사 fair를 수식한다.
→ does it은 부가의문문으로, 앞의 절이 부정문이므로 부가의문문은 긍정의 형태를 쓴다.

2

본책 • pp. 106-107

정답 1 ② 2 ⑤ 3 surface 4 공연이 물 안과 물 주변에서 이루어지기 때문에

문제 해설

1 거대한 수영장이 있는 라스베이거스의 극장에서 진행되는 물 쇼에 관한 글이므로, 제목으로는 ② '라스베이거스의 물 쇼'가 가장 알맞다.
① 영어에서 사용되는 프랑스어 단어들 ③ 물속에서 의사소통하는 방법
④ 캐나다에서 가장 인기 있는 쇼 ⑤ 라스베이거스: 세상에서 가장 습한 곳

2 ⑤: 문장 ⑫에서 연기자들이 물속에서 공기 호스를 이용해서 호흡한다고 했다.
①은 문장 ③에, ②는 문장 ⑥에, ③은 문장 ⑧에, ④는 문장 ⑩에 언급되어 있다.

3 '물이나 땅 부분의 맨 위 층'이라는 의미를 가진 단어는 surface(표면)다.

4 문장 ⑤에 언급되어 있다.

본문 직독 직해

① Did you know / that there is a theater / in Las Vegas / that has a giant pool? / ② This is /
당신은 알고 있었는가 / 극장이 있다는 것을 / 라스베이거스에 / 거대한 수영장을 가지고 있는 / 이것은 ~이다
where the show *O* is performed. / ③ It was created / by a Canadian circus. / ④ *O* sounds like
O 쇼가 공연되는 곳 / 그것은 만들어졌다 / 캐나다 서커스단에 의해 / O는

eau, / the French word / for water. / ⑤ This name is fitting / because the show takes place / in
eau처럼 들린다 프랑스어 단어 물에 해당하는 이 이름은 잘 어울린다 그 쇼가 이루어지기 때문에

and around water. /
물 안과 주변에서

⑥ Eighty-five world-class acrobats, swimmers, and divers / use the giant pool / in their
85명의 세계적인 수준의 곡예사, 수영선수, 그리고 다이버들이 그 거대한 수영장을 이용한다 그들의

performances. / ⑦ Gymnasts leap / through the air / on floating stages. / ⑧ Divers jump / into
공연에서 체조 선수들은 뛰어오른다 공중으로 떠 있는 무대들 위에서 다이버들은 뛴다

the pool / from breathtaking heights. / ⑨ Teams of swimmers / move gracefully together /
수영장 안으로 숨 막히는 높이에서 수영 선수들의 팀들이 함께 우아하게 움직인다

underwater. / ⑩ They dance / to the music / that plays / through underwater speakers. /
물속에서 그들은 춤을 춘다 음악에 맞추어 재생되는 수중 스피커를 통해

⑪ There are also many scuba divers / in the water / at all times. / ⑫ They help / the performers
많은 스쿠버 다이버들 또한 있다 물속에 항상 그들은 돕는다 연기자들이

use air hoses / to breathe / beneath the surface / of the pool. /
공기 호스를 사용하는 것을 호흡하기 위해 수면 아래에서 수영장의

⑬ If you visit Las Vegas / someday, / how about seeing / this amazing show? /
당신이 라스베이거스에 방문한다면 언젠가 보는 것이 어떤가 이 놀라운 쇼를

본문 해석

당신은 라스베이거스에 거대한 수영장이 있는 극장이 있다는 것을 알고 있었는가? 이곳은 O 쇼가 공연되는 곳이다. 그것은 캐나다 서커스단에 의해 만들어졌다. O는 물에 해당하는 프랑스어 단어인 eau처럼 들린다. 이 이름은 잘 어울리는데, 왜냐하면 그 쇼가 물 안과 물 주변에서 이루어지기 때문이다.

85명의 세계적인 수준의 곡예사와 수영 선수, 그리고 다이버들이 그들의 공연에서 그 거대한 수영장을 이용한다. 체조 선수들은 떠 있는 무대들 위에서 공중으로 뛰어오른다. 다이버들은 숨이 막히는 높이에서 수영장 안으로 뛰어든다. 수영 선수 팀들이 물속에서 함께 우아하게 움직인다. 그들은 수중 스피커를 통해 재생되는 음악에 맞추어 춤을 춘다. 또한 물속에는 항상 많은 스쿠버 다이버들이 있다. 그들은 연기자들이 수영장의 수면 아래에서 호흡하기 위해 공기 호스를 사용하는 것을 돕는다.

당신이 언젠가 라스베이거스에 방문한다면, 이 놀라운 쇼를 보는 것이 어떤가?

구문 해설

① Did you know [**that** there is *a theater* in Las Vegas {*that* has a giant pool}]?

→ that은 명사절을 이끄는 접속사로, [ ]는 동사 know의 목적어 역할을 한다.

→ { }는 선행사 a theater를 수식하는 주격 관계대명사절이다.

② This is (**the place**) [**where** the show *O* is performed].

→ [ ]는 〈장소〉를 나타내는 선행사를 수식하는 관계부사절로, 선행사 the place가 생략되었다. 관계부사의 선행사가 time, place 등과 같이 일반적인 명사일 경우 선행사를 생략할 수 있다.

④ *O* sounds like ***eau*, the French word for water**.

→ *eau*와 the French word for water는 동격 관계이다.

⑩ They dance to **the music** [**that** plays through underwater speakers].

→ [ ]는 선행사 the music을 수식하는 주격 관계대명사절이다.

⑫ They **help the performers use** air hoses *to breathe* beneath the surface of the pool.

→ 「help + 목적어 + 동사원형[to-v]」은 '~가 …하는 것을 돕다'의 의미이다.

➜ to breathe는 '호흡하기 위해'의 의미로, 〈목적〉을 나타내는 부사적 용법의 to부정사이다.

⑬ If you visit Las Vegas someday, **how about seeing** this amazing show?

➜ 「how about+v-ing」는 '~하는 것은 어때?'의 의미로 〈제안〉을 나타낸다.

본책 • pp. 108-109

3

정답 1 ④ 2 ④ 3 ①, ⑤ 4 war dance, spirit

문제 해설

1 뉴질랜드의 전통 춤 하카에 관해 설명하는 글이므로, 제목으로는 ④ '뉴질랜드의 전통 춤'이 가장 알맞다.

① 전통적인 마오리식 럭비 ② 스포츠가 된 춤

③ 고대 뉴질랜드에서의 한 전쟁 ⑤ 한 럭비팀의 재미있는 축하 행사

2 ④: 발 구르기는 하카 춤의 동작으로 언급되지 않았다.

①, ②, ③, ⑤는 문장 ⑥에 언급되어 있다.

3 문장 ⑦-⑧에 언급되어 있다.

4 문장 ②-④와 ⑪-⑬에 언급되어 있다.

> 하카는 마오리의 전통적인 출전의 춤이다. 오늘날 그것은 그들의 정신과 힘의 상징이다. 그것은 뉴질랜드의 국가 대표 럭비팀에 의해 공연된다.

본문 직독 직해

① The All Blacks are / New Zealand's national rugby team. / ② Before every international match, / they perform / a famous war dance. / ③ It is known as the *haka*. / ④ The *haka* is a tradition / of the Maori. / ⑤ The Maori lived in New Zealand / before the Europeans arrived. / ⑥ *Haka* dancers chant / and slap their bodies / while opening their eyes wide / and sticking out their tongues. /

올 블랙스는 ~이다 / 뉴질랜드의 국가 대표 럭비팀 / 매 국제 경기 전에 / 그들은 춘다 / 유명한 출전의 춤을 / 그것은 하카라고 알려져 있다 / 하카 춤은 전통이다 / 마오리족의 / 마오리족은 뉴질랜드에서 살았다 / 유럽인들이 도착하기 전에 / 하카 무용수들은 구호를 외친다 / 그리고 자신의 몸을 철썩 때린다 / 눈을 크게 뜨는 동안 / 그리고 혀를 내미는

⑦ In the past, / the dance was performed / to scare the enemy / before a battle. / ⑧ It was also used / to ask the war god for help. / ⑨ Over time, / however, / it became / more of a social event. / ⑩ Performing the *haka* / brought people together. / ⑪ It showed / their spirit and strength. / ⑫ Today you can see the *haka* / at many events, / including weddings and funerals. / ⑬ But the best place / to see the *haka* / is at an All Blacks rugby match! /

과거에는 / 이 춤은 추어졌다 / 적을 겁주기 위해 / 전투 전에 / 그것은 또한 사용되었다 / 전쟁의 신에게 도움을 구하는 데 / 시간이 지나면서 / 그러나 / 그것은 ~이 되었다 / 사회적인 행사에 더 가까운 것 / 하카 춤을 추는 것은 / 사람들을 연합시켰다 / 그것은 보여주었다 / 그들의 정신과 힘을 / 오늘날 당신은 하카 춤을 볼 수 있다 / 많은 행사에서 / 결혼식과 장례식을 포함한 / 그러나 최적의 장소는 / 하카 춤을 볼 수 있는 / 올 블랙스 럭비 경기에서다

본문 해석

올 블랙스(All Blacks)는 뉴질랜드의 국가 대표 럭비팀이다. 매 국제 경기 전에, 그들은 유명한 출전의 춤을 춘다. 그것은 하카라고 알려져 있다. 하카 춤은 마오리족의 전통이다. 마오리족은 유럽인들이 (뉴질랜드에) 도착하기 전에 뉴질랜드에서 살았다. 하카 춤을 추는 사람들은 눈을 크게 뜨고 혀를 내밀면서 구호를 외치고 자신의 몸을 철썩 때린다.

과거에 이 춤은 전투 전에 적을 겁주기 위해 추어졌다. 그것은 또한 전쟁의 신에게 도움을 구하는 데 사용되었다. 그러나 시간이 지나면서, 그것은 사회적인 행사에 더 가까운 것이 되었다. 하카 춤을 추는 것은 사람들을 연합시켰다. 그것은 그들의 정신과 힘을 보여주었다. 오늘날 당신은 결혼식과 장례식을 포함한 많은 행사에서 하카 춤을 볼 수 있다. 그러나 하카 춤을 볼 수 있는 최적의 장소는 올 블랙스 럭비 경기이다!

구문 해설

③ It **is known as** the *haka*.
→ be known as ~는 '~로 알려지다'의 의미이다.

⑥ *Haka* dancers chant and slap their bodies **while** (**they are**) *opening* their eyes wide and *sticking out* their tongues.
→ while은 '~하는 동안'의 의미로, 〈때〉를 나타내는 접속사이다. 접속사 while 뒤에 「주어+be동사」가 생략되었다.
→ 현재분사 opening과 sticking out이 접속사 and로 병렬 연결되어 있다.

⑦ In the past, the dance was performed **to scare** the enemy before a battle.
→ to scare는 '겁주기 위해'라는 의미로, 〈목적〉을 나타내는 부사적 용법의 to부정사이다.

⑧ It **was** also **used to** ***ask*** *the war god* ***for*** *help*.
→ 「be used+to-v」는 '~하는 데 사용되다'의 의미이다.
→ 「ask A for B」는 'A에게 B를 부탁하다, 요청하다'의 의미이다. the war god이 A, help가 B에 해당한다.

⑩ **Performing the *haka*** brought people together.
→ Performing the *haka*는 주어 역할을 하는 동명사구이다.

⑬ But the best place **to see** the *haka* is [at an All Blacks rugby match]!
→ to see는 the best place를 수식하는 형용사적 용법의 to부정사이다.
→ [ ]는 보어 역할을 하는 전치사구이다.

본책 • pp. 110-111

4

정답 1 ③ 2 ① 3 ① 4 (1) T (2) F

문제 해설

1 두 개의 서로 다른 월드컵 트로피에 관해 설명하는 글이므로, 제목으로는 ③ '하나의 토너먼트의 두 가지 트로피'가 가장 알맞다.
[문제] 글의 제목으로 가장 알맞은 것은?
① 쥘 리메: 트로피 디자이너 ② 브라질을 패배시킨 규칙
④ 스포츠 트로피는 어떻게 만들어지는가 ⑤ 가장 위대한 월드컵 챔피언들

2 '그러나 두 개의 다른 월드컵 트로피가 있다'는 내용의 주어진 문장은 첫 번째 월드컵 트로피인 쥘 리메 트로피에 대한 설명이 나오기 전인 ①에 들어가는 것이 가장 알맞다.
[문제] 다음 문장이 들어갈 위치로 가장 알맞은 곳은?

3 쥘 리메 트로피의 특별한 규칙을 설명하면서 한 팀이 월드컵에서 세 번 우승하면 트로피를 영원히 가질 수 있었다고 했다. 빈칸 앞에서 브라질이 세 번째 우승을 했다고 했으므로, 빈칸에는 ① '쥘 리메 트로피를 받았다'가 가장 알

맞다.

[문제] 글의 빈칸에 들어갈 말로 가장 알맞은 것은?

② 특별한 규칙을 바꾸라는 말을 들었다　　③ 트로피를 다시 차지할 수 없었다

④ 트로피의 복제품을 받을 수 있었다　　⑤ FIFA 월드컵 트로피를 받았다

4 (1) 문장 ②-③에 언급되어 있다.

(2) 문장 ⑧에서 FIFA 월드컵 트로피는 어떤 팀도 보유할 수 없다고 했다.

[문제] 글의 내용과 일치하면 T, 그렇지 않으면 F를 쓰시오.

(1) 쥘 리메 트로피는 1930년에 처음으로 수여되었다.

(2) FIFA 월드컵 트로피는 현재 브라질의 소유이다.

본문 직독직해

① The most famous sports trophy / in the world / is given / to the winner / of the World Cup soccer tournament / every four years. / However, / there are two different World Cup trophies. /
가장 유명한 스포츠 트로피는 / 세계에서 / 주어진다 / 우승자에게 / 월드컵 축구 토너먼트의 / 4년마다 / 그러나 / 두 개의 다른 월드컵 트로피가 있다

② The first is the Jules Rimet Trophy. / ③ It was awarded / to the World Cup winner / from 1930 to 1970. / ④ Each winning team / kept the trophy / for four years / before giving it / to the next winner. / ⑤ However, / there was a special rule /—if a team won the World Cup / three times, / they could keep the trophy / forever. / ⑥ In 1970, / Brazil won the World Cup / for the third time / and / was given / the Jules Rimet Trophy. /
첫 번째는 쥘 리메 트로피이다 / 그것은 수여되었다 / 월드컵 우승자에게 / 1930년에서 1970년까지 / 각각의 우승 팀은 / 그 트로피를 가지고 있었다 / 4년 동안 / 그것을 주기 전에 / 다음 우승자에게 / 그러나 / 특별한 규칙이 있었다 / 만약 한 팀이 월드컵에서 우승했다면 / 세 번 / 그들은 그 트로피를 보유할 수 있었다 / 영원히 / 1970년에 / 브라질이 월드컵에서 우승했다 / 세 번째로 / 그리고 / 받았다 / 쥘 리메 트로피를

⑦ After this, / a new trophy / —the FIFA World Cup Trophy— / was designed, / and / the special rule was changed. / ⑧ Now, / no team can keep / the FIFA World Cup Trophy. / ⑨ Instead, / they get / a copy of the trophy. /
이후에 / 새로운 트로피가 / FIFA 월드컵 트로피 / 고안되었다 / 그리고 / 그 특별한 규칙은 바뀌었다 / 이제 / 어떤 팀도 보유할 수 없다 / FIFA 월드컵 트로피를 / 대신에 / 그들은 받는다 / 트로피의 복제품을

본문 해석

세계에서 가장 유명한 스포츠 트로피는 4년마다 월드컵 축구 토너먼트 우승자에게 주어진다. 그러나 두 개의 다른 월드컵 트로피가 있다.

첫 번째는 쥘 리메 트로피이다. 그것은 1930년부터 1970년까지 월드컵 우승자에게 수여되었다. 각각의 우승 팀은 그 트로피를 다음 우승자에게 주기 전에 4년 동안 가지고 있었다. 그러나 특별한 규칙이 있었다. 만약 한 팀이 월드컵에서 세 번 우승했다면, 그들은 그 트로피를 영원히 보유할 수 있었다. 1970년에 브라질이 월드컵에서 세 번째로 우승했고 쥘 리메 트로피를 받았다.

이후에 새로운 트로피인 FIFA 월드컵 트로피가 고안되었고, 그 특별한 규칙은 바뀌었다. 이제 어떤 팀도 FIFA 월드컵 트로피를 보유할 수 없다. 대신에, 그들은 트로피의 복제품을 받는다.

구문 해설

① The most famous sports trophy in the world **is given** to the winner of the World Cup soccer tournament *every four years*.

→ is given은 '주어진다'의 의미로, 「be+p.p.」의 수동태이다.

→ 「every+기간」은 '~마다'의 의미이다.

③ It was awarded to the World Cup winner **from 1930 to 1970**.

→ 「from A to B」는 'A부터 B까지'의 의미이다.

⑥ In 1970, Brazil **won** the World Cup for the third time and ***was given*** the Jules Rimet Trophy.

→ 동사 won과 was given이 접속사 and로 병렬 연결되어 있다.

→ 「A be given B」는 「give A B(A에게 B를 주다)」의 수동태 표현으로 'A가 B를 받다'라는 의미이다. Brazil이 A, the Jules Rimet Trophy가 B에 해당한다.

Review Test

본책 • pp. 112-113

정답 1 ⑤ 2 ② 3 fitting 4 They help the performers use air hoses 5 ③ 6 정신과 힘 7 ⑤ 8 a copy

문제 해설

1 leap(뛰다)와 비슷한 의미의 단어는 ⑤ 'jump(뛰다)'이다.

> 나는 고양이가 2층 창문에서 뛰어오르는 것을 보았다.

① 철썩 때리다 ② 치다 ③ 요구하다 ④ 공연하다

2 giant(거대한)와 반대 의미의 단어는 ② 'tiny(작은)'이다.

> 저 거대한 동상 앞에서 사진을 찍자.

① 고대의 ③ 도움이 되는 ④ 비슷한 ⑤ 젖은

3

> 상황이나 목적에 맞는

4 '~가 …하는 것을 돕다'의 의미인 「help+목적어+동사원형」을 이용한다.

5 빈칸 앞에는 하카 춤의 목적이 전투 전에 적을 겁주기 위해서와 전쟁의 신에게 도움을 구하는 데 사용되었다고 했고, 빈칸 뒤에는 시간이 지나면서 하카 춤이 사회적인 행사에 더 가까운 것이 되었다고 했으므로, 빈칸에는 ③ 'however(그러나)'가 알맞다.

① 그러므로 ② 그 결과 ④ 예를 들면 ⑤ 다시 말하면

6 하카 춤은 사람들을 함께 연합시켜 정신과 힘을 보여준다고 했다.

> Q. 사회적인 행사에서 하카 춤이 보여주는 두 가지는 무엇인가?

7 ⑤ 디자인에 관한 내용은 언급되지 않았다.

8

> 1930년부터 1970년까지 쥘 리메 트로피가 사용되었고, 브라질은 세 번 우승한 후 그것을 보유하게 되었다. 지금은 FIFA 월드컵 트로피가 사용되며, 어떤 팀도 영원히 그 트로피를 보유할 수 없다. 우승팀은 대신 트로피의 복제품을 받는다.

1

본책 • pp. 116-117

정답 1 ③ 2 비올라가 바이올린보다는 깊은 소리를 내지만 첼로만큼은 깊은 소리를 내지 않는 것 3 ④ 4 ③

문제 해설

1 바이올린과 비올라를 비교하여 설명하는 내용의 글이므로, 주제로는 ③이 가장 알맞다.

2 문장 ⑦에 언급되어 있다.

3 바이올린과 비올라의 활을 비교하는 내용 중에 바이올린이 나무로 만들어진다는 내용의 (d)는 글의 흐름과 무관하다.

4 ③: 문장 ⑥, ⑦에서 바이올린이 높은 음조를 내고, 비올라는 더 깊은 소리를 낸다고 했다.
①은 문장 ①에, ②는 문장 ④에, ④는 문장 ⑩에, ⑤는 문장 ⑭에 언급되어 있다.

본문 직독 직해

① The violin and the viola are both orchestral stringed instruments. / ② However, / there are a few differences / between them. / ③ Most violins are around 35 centimeters long. / ④ On the other hand, / the viola can be 45 centimeters long. /
바이올린과 비올라는 둘 다 오케스트라의 현악기이다 / 하지만 / 몇 가지 차이점이 있다 / 그들 사이에는 / 대부분의 바이올린은 약 35센티미터 길이이다 / 반면 / 비올라는 45센티미터 길이가 될 수 있다

⑤ The sounds of the two instruments are also different. / ⑥ The violin has a very high pitch. / ⑦ The viola produces a deeper sound / than the violin, / but not as deep as the cello. / ⑧ That places the viola / in the middle of the stringed instrument family. /
두 악기의 소리도 다르다 / 바이올린은 매우 높은 음조를 가지고 있다 / 비올라는 더 깊은 소리를 낸다 / 바이올린보다 / 그러나 첼로만큼 깊지는 않다 / 그것은 비올라를 위치시킨다 / 현악기군의 중간에

⑨ The instruments' bows are also different. / ⑩ Violin bows are lighter than bows for violas. / ⑪ Furthermore, / the part of the bow / that is held in the hand, / known as the "frog," / is also different. / ⑫ On a violin bow, / the frog is pointy. / (⑬ Basically, / a violin is made of wood. /) ⑭ However, / on a viola bow, / it has a round shape. /
악기의 활도 다르다 / 바이올린 활은 비올라의 활보다 더 가볍다 / 더욱이 / 활의 부분 / 손에 잡히는 / '프로그'로 알려진 / 또한 다르다 / 바이올린 활에서 / 프로그는 뾰족하다 / 기본적으로 / 바이올린은 나무로 만들어진다 / 그러나 / 비올라 활에서 / 그것은 둥근 모양이다

본문 해석

바이올린과 비올라는 둘 다 오케스트라의 현악기이다. 하지만, 그들 사이에는 몇 가지 차이점이 있다. 대부분의 바이올린은 약 35센티미터 길이이다. 반면, 비올라는 45센티미터 길이가 될 수 있다.

두 악기의 소리도 다르다. 바이올린은 매우 높은 음조를 가지고 있다. 비올라는 바이올린보다 더 깊은 소리를 내지만, 첼로만큼 깊지는 않다. 그것은 비올라를 현악기군의 중간에 위치시킨다.

악기의 활도 다르다. 바이올린 활은 비올라의 활보다 더 가볍다. 더욱이, '프로그'로 알려진 손에 잡히는 활의 부분도 다르다. 바이올린 활에서 프로그는 뾰족하다. (기본적으로, 바이올린은 나무로 만들어진다.) 그러나 비올라 활에서 그것은 둥근 모양이다.

구문 해설

⑤ **The sounds** [of the two instruments] **are** also different.
→ 전치사구 [ ]의 수식을 받는 문장의 주어 The sounds가 복수 명사이므로 복수 동사 are가 쓰였다.

⑩ Violin bows are **lighter than** bows for violas.
→ 「형용사의 비교급+than」은 '~보다 더 …한'의 의미이다.

⑪ Furthermore, ***the part of the bow*** [**that** is held in the hand], known as the "frog," *is* also different.
→ [ ]는 선행사 the part of the bow를 수식하는 주격 관계대명사절이다.
→ 문장의 주어가 the part of the bow이며, the part는 전치사구 of the bow의 수식을 받고 있으므로, 단수 명사 the part에 맞춰 단수 동사 is가 쓰였다.

⑬ Basically, a violin **is made of** wood.
→ 「be made of」는 '~로 만들어지다'의 의미이다.

2

본책 • pp. 118-119

정답 1 ⑤ 2 ② 3 ③ 4 (1) F (2) F

문제 해설

1 한 장소를 각기 다른 시간에 여러 번 그려 빛의 변화를 담아내는 모네의 화풍과 그 때문에 생긴 사건에 관한 글이므로, 제목으로는 ⑤ '모네의 화풍으로 인해 야기된 재미있는 상황'이 가장 알맞다.
① 모네의 그림을 사랑한 판사 ② 모네: 수련을 사랑한 화가
③ 모네와 프랑스 미술의 발달 ④ 모네의 화풍을 변화시킨 경험

2 사람들이 법정에 가져온 그림들이 모두 모네의 진품이었던 이유를 설명하기 위해 모네의 화풍을 언급하는 부분이다. 빈칸 뒤에 모네가 하루 중 각기 다른 시간에 그의 정원에 있는 수련을 약 250점 그렸다는 예시로 보아, 빈칸에는 ② '같은 장소'가 가장 알맞다.
① 부유한 사람들 ③ 각기 다른 풍경들 ④ 다양한 물체들 ⑤ 각기 다른 꽃들

3 문장 ⑨-⑪에 언급되어 있다.

4 (1) 문장 ⑧에서 판사는 사람들이 가져온 모든 그림이 모네의 진품이라고 말했다고 했다.
(2) 문장 ⑩에서 모네의 작품들이 하루 중 각기 다른 시간에 그의 정원에 있는 수련을 보여준다고 했다.

본문 직독 직해

① Claude Monet was / a famous French painter. / ② Here is an interesting story / about
클로드 모네는 ~였다 / 유명한 프랑스 화가 / 여기에 흥미로운 이야기가 있다
his paintings. / ③ One day, / several people brought paintings / to court. / ④ Each of them
그의 그림들에 관한 / 어느 날 / 몇몇 사람들이 그림들을 가져왔다 / 법정으로 / 그들 각자는
said / their painting had been painted / by Monet. / ⑤ All of the paintings / showed / the
말했다 / 자신의 그림이 그려졌다고 / 모네에 의해 / 그 그림들 모두는 / 보여주었다
same scene, / but / each one was a little different. / ⑥ They wanted / the judge to decide /
같은 풍경을 / 그러나 / 각각은 조금 달랐다 / 그들은 원했다 / 판사가 결정해 주기를
which one was really painted / by Monet. / ⑦ The judge knew a lot / about art. / ⑧ After he
어떤 것이 정말 그려졌는지 / 모네에 의해 / 그 판사는 많이 알고 있었다 / 미술에 대해 / 그가

looked at the paintings, / he said, / "They all were!" /
그 그림들을 본 후에 그는 말했다 그것들 모두입니다

⑨ Monet painted the same place / at different times / of the day / to capture / the change
모네는 같은 장소를 그렸다 각기 다른 시간에 하루의 담아내기 위해 빛의 변화를

of light. / ⑩ For example, / his most famous works of art / show water lilies / in his garden /
예를 들어 그의 가장 유명한 미술 작품들은 수련들을 보여준다 그의 정원에 있는

at different times / of the day. / ⑪ He made / about 250 / of these water lily paintings! /
각기 다른 시간에 하루 중 그는 만들었다 약 250점을 이 수련 그림들의

본문 해석

클로드 모네는 유명한 프랑스 화가였다. 여기에 그의 그림들에 관한 흥미로운 이야기가 있다. 어느 날, 몇몇 사람들이 법정으로 그림들을 가져왔다. 그들 각자는 자신의 그림이 모네에 의해 그려졌다고 말했다. 그 그림들은 모두 같은 풍경을 보여주고 있었지만, 각각은 조금 달랐다. 그들은 어떤 것이 정말 모네에 의해 그려진 것인지 판사가 결정해 주기를 원했다. 그 판사는 미술에 대해 많이 알고 있었다. 그가 그 그림들을 본 후에, 그는 "그것들 모두입니다!"라고 말했다.

모네는 빛의 변화를 담아내기 위해 하루 중 각기 다른 시간에 같은 장소를 그렸다. 예를 들어, 그의 가장 유명한 미술 작품들은 하루 중 각기 다른 시간에 그의 정원에 있는 수련들을 보여준다. 그는 약 250점의 이 수련 그림들을 그렸다!

구문 해설

④ Each of them said [(**that**) their painting *had been painted* by Monet].
→ [ ]는 동사 said의 목적어 역할을 하는 명사절로, 접속사 that이 생략되었다.
→ had been painted는 「had been+p.p.」 형태의 과거완료 수동태로, '그려졌었다'의 의미이다. 특정 과거 시점(said)보다 먼저 일어난 일을 나타내기 위해 과거완료 시제를 썼다.

⑥ They **wanted the judge to decide** [which one was really painted by Monet].
→ 「want+목적어+to-v」는 '~가 …하기를 원하다'의 의미이다.
→ [ ]는 동사 decide의 목적어 역할을 하는 간접의문문이다.

⑧ After he looked at the paintings, he said, "They all **were**!"
→ were 다음에 really painted by Monet가 생략되었다. 생략해도 의미 파악이 가능하다면 반복되는 말은 생략하는 경우가 많다.

⑨ Monet painted the same place at different times of the day **to capture** the change of light.
→ to capture는 '담아내기 위해'의 의미로, 〈목적〉을 나타내는 부사적 용법의 to부정사이다.

본책 • pp. 120-121

3

정답 1 ⑤ 2 ④ 3 ① 4 instrument, strings

문제 해설

1 건물과 자연 공간을 이용해서 만든 거대한 현악기인 Earth Harp에 관한 글이므로, 제목으로는 ⑤ '건물과 자연을 하프로 바꾸다'가 가장 알맞다.
① 지구가 만드는 음악 ② 좋은 하프를 고르는 방법
③ 유명한 음악가가 되는 방법 ④ 하프는 어떻게 만들어지고 연주되는가

2 주어진 문장은 '현들은 하부로부터 수백 미터나 뻗어 있다'는 내용으로, 무대에 놓인 악기의 하부를 설명한 문장 ⑦과 현이 여러 장소의 꼭대기에 길게 연결되는 것을 설명한 문장 ⑧ 사이인 ④의 위치가 가장 알맞다.

3 ①: 문장 ⑤를 통해 알 수 있다.
②: 문장 ⑥에서 나무로 된 큰 하부를 갖고 있다고 했다.
③: 문장 ⑧에서 계곡의 꼭대기에도 부착된다고 했다.
④: 문장 ⑨에서 악기의 하부에 가까이 선다고 했다.
⑤: 문장 ⑫에서 일반 하프보다 깊은 소리를 낸다고 했다.

4 문장 ①-②, ⑧, 그리고 2번 문제의 주어진 문장에 언급되어 있다.

Earth Harp는 긴 현들을 빌딩, 극장 또는 자연 공간에 부착함으로써 만들어진 악기이다.

본문 직독 직해

① Do you know / what the longest stringed instrument in the world is? / ② It is the Earth
당신은 아는가 세상에서 가장 긴 현악기가 무엇인지 그것은 Earth
Harp. / ③ Musician William Close / invented it / in 1999. / ④ He turns / buildings and natural
Harp이다 음악가 William Close가 그것을 발명했다 1999년에 그는 바꾼다 빌딩과 자연
spaces / into enormous harps. / ⑤ The Earth Harp is still listed / in the Guinness World
공간들을 거대한 하프로 Earth Harp는 여전히 등재되어 있다 기네스 세계 기록에
Records / as the longest stringed instrument. /
가장 긴 현악기로서

⑥ The harp has / a large wooden base. / ⑦ This is usually set / on a stage. / Strings
그 하프는 갖고 있다 나무로 된 큰 하부를 이것은 보통 놓인다 무대 위에 현들은
stretch / from the base / for hundreds of meters. / ⑧ They are attached / to the tops / of
뻗어 있다 하부로부터 수백 미터에 걸쳐 그것들은 부착된다 꼭대기에
theaters, buildings, and even valleys. /
극장과 빌딩, 그리고 심지어 계곡의

⑨ The musician stands / on the stage / near the base of the instrument. / ⑩ He wears
그 음악가는 선다 무대 위에 그 악기의 하부 가까이 그는
cotton gloves / coated with sticky resin. / ⑪ He runs his hands / along the strings / and causes /
면장갑을 낀다 끈적끈적한 송진이 묻은 그는 그의 손을 움직인다 그 현들을 따라 그리고 야기한다
them to vibrate. / ⑫ This makes a beautiful sound / that is much deeper / than that of a
그것(현)들이 진동하도록 이것은 아름다운 소리를 낸다 훨씬 더 깊은
normal harp. /
일반 하프의 그것(소리)보다

본문 해석

당신은 세상에서 가장 긴 현악기가 무엇인지 아는가? 그것은 Earth Harp이다. 음악가 William Close가 1999년에 그것을 발명했다. 그는 빌딩과 자연 공간들을 거대한 하프로 바꾼다. Earth Harp는 여전히 가장 긴 현악기로 기네스 세계 기록에 등재되어 있다.

그 하프는 나무로 된 큰 하부를 갖고 있다. 이것은 보통 무대 위에 놓인다. 현들은 하부로부터 수백 미터나 뻗어 있다. 그것들은 극장과 빌딩, 그리고 심지어 계곡의 꼭대기에 부착된다.

그 음악가는 무대 위에서 악기의 하부에 가까이 선다. 그는 끈적끈적한 송진이 묻은 면장갑을 낀다. 그는 현들을 따라 그의 손을 움직이고 그것(현)들을 진동하게 한다. 이것은 일반 하프의 그것(소리)보다 훨씬 더 깊은 아름다운 소리를 낸다.

구문 해설

① Do you know [what the longest stringed instrument in the world is]?
→ [ ]는 동사 know의 목적어 역할을 하는 간접의문문이다.

④ He **turns** buildings and natural spaces **into** enormous harps.
→ 「turn A into B」는 'A를 B로 바꾸다'의 의미이다.

⑧ **They** *are attached to* the tops of theaters, buildings, and even valleys.
→ They는 2번 문제에 주어진 문장의 Strings를 가리킨다.
→ 「A be attached to B」는 「attach A to B(A를 B에 부착하다)」의 수동태 표현으로, 'A가 B에 부착되다'의 의미이다.

⑩ He wears cotton gloves [**coated** with sticky resin].
→ [ ]는 cotton gloves를 수식하는 과거분사구이다.

⑫ This makes **a beautiful sound** [**that** is *much* deeper than that of a normal harp].
→ [ ]는 선행사 a beautiful sound를 수식하는 주격 관계대명사절이다.
→ much는 '훨씬, 더욱'의 의미로 비교급을 강조하는 부사이다. even, still, a lot, far도 비교급을 강조할 때 쓸 수 있다.
→ that은 the sound를 대신하는 대명사이다.

본책 • pp. 122-123

4

정답 1 ④ 2 그림을 먼지로부터 보호하기 위해 여러 겹의 니스가 그림에 덧칠해진 것 3 (1) F (2) T
4 nickname, night, removed

문제 해설

1 (A) 빈칸 앞에 〈야경〉이라는 이름의 렘브란트의 작품을 소개하고, 빈칸 뒤에 그 이름이 공식적인 이름은 아니라는 내용이 오므로 빈칸에는 However(하지만)가 가장 알맞다.
(B) 빈칸 앞에서 사람들이 그 작품을 〈야경〉이라는 별명으로 불렀지만 그 별명이 잘못된 것으로 밝혀졌다는 내용이 오고, 빈칸 뒤에 그 작품이 밤 풍경이 전혀 아니라는 내용이 오므로 Actually(사실)가 가장 알맞다.
[문제] 빈칸 (A)와 (B)에 들어갈 말로 가장 알맞은 것은?
① 그러므로 … 놀랍게도 ② 그러므로 … 사실
③ 그러나 … 유사하게 ⑤ 결과적으로 … 유사하게

2 문장 ⑧에 언급되어 있다.
[문제] 글의 밑줄 친 This가 의미하는 것은 무엇인가? 우리말로 쓰시오.

3 (1) 문장 ⑪에서 1940년대에 그림의 색이 원래 상태로 복원되었다고 했다.
(2) 문장 ⑫에 언급되어 있다.
[문제] 글의 내용과 일치하면 T, 그렇지 않으면 F를 쓰시오.
(1) 사람들은 그림의 원래 색을 복원하는 데 실패했다.
(2) 어떤 사람들은 그 별명을 'Day Watch'로 바꾸려고 했다.

4 [문제] 다음 빈칸에 알맞은 단어를 상자에서 골라 쓰시오.

제거하다	별명	밤	복원[복구]하다

〈야경〉은 렘브란트의 그림의 별명이다. 사람들은 그 그림이 밤 풍경을 보여준다고 생각했다. 하지만, 사실 그것은 여러 겹의 니스 때문에 어두워졌다. 니스가 제거되었지만, 그것은 여전히 〈야경〉이라고 불린다.

본문 직독 직해

① In a painting, / a group of armed people / gather together / at night. / ② It is *Night*
한 그림 속에 한 무리의 무장한 사람들이 함께 모여 있다 밤에 그것은

Watch, / one of Rembrandt's most famous works. / ③ However, / *Night Watch* / is not its
〈야경〉이다 렘브란트의 가장 유명한 작품들 중 하나인 그러나 〈야경〉은 그것의

official name. / ④ Its real name / is very long. / ⑤ So / people started / using the name / *Night*
공식적인 이름이 아니다 그것의 진짜 이름은 매우 길다 그래서 사람들은 시작했다 이름을 사용하기

Watch / because it seemed to describe / the painting / well. / ⑥ However, / it turns out / that
〈야경〉이라는 그것이 설명하는 것 같았기 때문에 그 그림을 잘 하지만 밝혀진다

the nickname is wrong! / ⑦ Actually, / it is not a night scene / at all! /
그 별명이 잘못된 것으로 사실 그것은 밤 풍경이 아니다 전혀

⑧ After Rembrandt's death, / layers of varnish / were added / to the painting / to protect
렘브란트의 사망 후에 여러 겹의 니스가 덧칠해졌다 그림에 그것을 보호하기

it / from dirt. / ⑨ This made / the painting / look dark. / ⑩ Naturally, / people thought / the
위해 먼지로부터 이것은 만들었다 그 그림을 어두워 보이게 자연스럽게 사람들은 생각했다

painting showed / a nighttime event. / ⑪ In the 1940s, / however, / the layers of varnish /
그 그림이 보여 준다고 밤에 일어난 일을 1940년대에 하지만 여러 겹의 니스가

were removed / and / the colors were restored / to their original condition. / ⑫ Soon, / there
제거되었다 그리고 색들은 복원되었다 원래 상태로 곧

were efforts / to change its nickname / to "Day Watch." / ⑬ But / its original nickname / was
노력들이 있었다 그것의 별명을 변경하려는 'Day Watch'로 하지만 그것의 원래 별명이

already famous, / so / the painting is still called / *Night Watch* / to this day! /
이미 유명했다 그래서 그 그림은 여전히 불린다 〈야경〉이라고 지금까지도

본문 해석

한 그림 속에, 밤에 한 무리의 무장한 사람들이 함께 모여 있다. 그것은 렘브란트의 가장 유명한 작품들 중 하나인 〈야경(夜警)〉이다. 그러나, 〈야경〉은 그것의 공식적인 이름은 아니다. 그것의 진짜 이름은 매우 길다. 그래서 사람들은 그것이 그 그림을 잘 설명하는 것 같았기 때문에 〈야경〉이라는 이름을 사용하기 시작했다. 하지만, 그 별명은 잘못된 것으로 밝혀진다! 사실, 그것은 밤 풍경이 전혀 아니다!

렘브란트의 사망 후에, 그것을 먼지로부터 보호하기 위해 여러 겹의 니스가 그림에 덧칠해졌다. 이것은 그 그림이 어두워 보이게 했다. 자연스럽게, 사람들은 그 그림이 밤에 일어난 일을 보여준다고 생각했다. 하지만, 1940년대에 여러 겹의 니스가 제거되었고, 색들은 그것들의 원래 상태로 복원되었다. 곧, 그것의 별명을 'Day Watch'로 변경하려는 노력들이 있었다. 하지만 그것의 원래 별명이 이미 유명해서, 그 그림은 지금까지도 여전히 〈야경〉이라고 불린다!

구문 해설

⑤ So people **started using** the name *Night Watch* because it *seemed to describe* the painting well.

➜ 「start+v-ing[to-v]」는 '~하기 시작하다'의 의미이다.

➜ 「seem+to-v」는 '~인 것 같다, ~인 것처럼 보이다'의 의미이다.

⑥ However, **it** turns out [**that** the nickname is wrong]!

→ it은 가주어이고, [ ]가 진주어이다.

⑦ Actually, it is **not** a night scene **at all**!

→ not ~ at all은 '전혀 ~ 아니다'의 의미이다.

⑧ … , layers of varnish **were added to** the painting *to protect* it from dirt.

→ 「A be added to B」는 「add A to B(A를 B에 더하다[첨가하다])」의 수동태 표현으로, 'A가 B에 더해지다[첨가되다]'라는 의미이다.

→ to protect는 '보호하기 위해'의 의미로, 〈목적〉을 나타내는 부사적 용법의 to부정사이다.

→ 「protect A from B」는 'A를 B로부터 보호하다'의 의미이다.

⑨ This **made the painting** *look dark*.

→ 「make + 목적어 + 동사원형」은 '~가 …하게 하다'의 의미이다.

→ 「look + 형용사」는 '~하게 보이다'의 의미이다.

Review Test

본책 • pp. 124-125

정답 1 ③ 2 1) instrument 2) restore 3 ③ 4 there are a few differences between them
5 ⑤ 6 court 7 ⑤ 8 소리

문제 해설

1 ③ turn out: ~인 것으로 드러나다[밝혀지다]

2 1) '음악을 연주하는 데 사용되는 물건'이라는 의미의 단어는 'instrument(악기)'이다.
2) '어떤 것을 정상의 상태로 되돌리다'라는 의미의 단어는 'restore(복원[복구]하다)'이다.

3 ① 바이올린은 보통 35센티미터이고 비올라는 보통 45센티미터로, 바이올린이 보통 10cm 더 짧다.
② 비올라는 바이올린보다는 깊은 소리를 내지만, 첼로만큼 깊은 소리는 내지 못한다고 했다.
④ 바이올린의 활이 비올라의 활보다 가볍다고 했다.
⑤ 비올라의 활에서 프로그는 둥근 모양을 가지고 있다고 했다.

4 '~가 있다'는 「there is[are] ~」 구문을 쓰며, 복수형 주어(differences)가 이어지므로 there are를 이용하여 쓴다.

5 사람들이 판사에게 모네가 그린 진짜 그림이 무엇인지 판별해 달라고 했다는 내용의 (C), 판사가 미술에 대해 많이 알고 있었다는 내용의 (B), 그 판사가 사람들이 가지고 있는 그림이 모두 진짜라고 답해주었다는 내용의 (A)로 이어지는 흐름이 가장 자연스럽다.

6 범죄가 판결되는 건물이나 방

7 attach A to B: A를 B에 붙이다 (A be attached to B: A가 B에 부착되다)

8 일반 하프의 소리와 Earth 하프의 소리를 비교하는 문장으로, 문맥상 the sound(소리)를 가리킨다.

독해

Reading TUTOR 리딩튜터

10단계 초·중·고등 독해 프로그램
STARTER 1 | 2 | 3
JUNIOR 1 | 2 | 3 | 4
수능 입문 | 기본 | 실력 (예정)

1316 READING

기초부터 내신까지 중학 독해 완성
Level 1 | Level 2 | Level 3
1316 Grammar | 1316 Listening

JUNIOR READING EXPERT

앞서가는 중학생들을 위한 원서형 독해 교재
Level 1 | Level 2 | Level 3 | Level 4
Junior Listening Expert | Reading Expert

READING Inside

중상위권 대상의 통합교과 원서형 독해서
Starter | Level 1 | Level 2 | Level 3
Grammar Inside

듣기

능률 중학영어 듣기 모의고사 22회

전국 16개 시·도 교육청 주관
영어듣기평가 실전대비서
Level 1 | Level 2 | Level 3

1316 LISTENING

기초부터 실전까지 중학 듣기 완성
Level 1 | Level 2 | Level 3
1316 Grammar | 1316 Reading

JUNIOR LISTENING EXPERT

앞서가는 중학생들을 위한 원서형 듣기 교재
Level 1 | Level 2 | Level 3 | Level 4
Junior Reading Expert

수능 · 기타

첫번째 수능영어

한 발 앞서 시작하는
중학생을 위한 수능 대비서
기본 | 유형 | 실전

능률중학영어

문법, 독해, 쓰기, 말하기를
함께 배우는 중학 영어 종합서
예비중 | 중1 | 중2 | 중3

열중16강

문법과 독해를 완성하는 특강용 교재
문법 Level 1 | Level 2 | Level 3
문법+독해 Level 1 | Level 2 | Level 3

NE능률 영어교육연구소

NE능률 영어교육연구소는 전문성과 탁월성을 기반으로
영어 교육 트렌드를 선도합니다.

Reading TUTOR 리딩튜터 Junior 2

펴 낸 날	2024년 10월 5일 (초판 1쇄)
펴 낸 이	주민홍
펴 낸 곳	(주)NE능률
지 은 이	NE능률 영어교육연구소
개발책임	김지현
개 발	조은영, 권영주, 김영아, 최리
영문교열	Patrick Ferraro, Julie Tofflemire, Keeran Murphy
디자인책임	오영숙
디 자 인	안훈정, 오솔길
제작책임	한성일
등록번호	제1-68호
I S B N	979-11-253-4760-6

대표전화	02 2014 7114
홈페이지	www.neungyule.com
주 소	서울시 마포구 월드컵북로 396(상암동) 누리꿈스퀘어 비즈니스타워 10층

Section 01

Fashion

1 왜 잠그지 않는 거야!

in common	공통으로
suit	명 정장
bottom	형 맨 아래에 있는
button	명 단추 동 단추를 잠그다
theory	명 이론
practical	형 현실적인, 실용적인 (practice 명 실천; 관행, 관례)
fit	동 맞다
tightly	부 단단히, 꽉
especially	부 특히
interesting	형 흥미로운
rule	동 통치하다
elegant	형 우아한
popular	형 인기 있는 (popularity 명 인기)
court	명 법정; 궁정
overweight	형 과체중인
respect	명 존경
set a trend	유행을 창조하다

2 작은 삼각형의 비밀

own	동 소유하다
at least	적어도
comfortable	형 편안한 (↔ uncomfortable 형 불편한)
sweatshirt	명 운동복 상의[맨투맨 티]
notice	동 의식하다, (보거나 듣고) 알다
collar	명 칼라, 옷깃
industry	명 (특정 분야의) 산업
stitch	명 스티치, 바늘땀

stretchable	형 신축성이 있는
material	명 직물, 옷감
waistband	명 (치마 · 바지의) 허리 밴드
a pair of	한 벌의, 한 쌍의
shorts	명 반바지
extra	형 여분의
cloth	명 천, 옷감 (clothing 명 의류 clothes 명 옷, 의복)
purpose	명 목적, 용도
sweat	동 땀을 흘리다 명 땀
soak up	~을 빨아들이다, 흡수하다
discomfort	명 불편, 불쾌
control	동 통제하다, 조절하다
fashionable	형 유행하는
due to	~ 덕분에, ~로 인해
improvement	명 향상
sportswear	명 운동복
necessary	형 필요한

3 이 단추의 용도가 뭐야?

wonder	동 궁금해하다
sleeve	명 소매
origin	명 기원, 출신
unclear	형 불분명한
painful	형 고통스러운
wipe one's nose	~의 콧물을 닦다
habit	명 습관
come up with	찾아내다, 생각해 내다
clever	형 영리한
rather	부 다소
cruel	형 잔인한

solution	명 해결책
metal	형 금속의
sew	동 바느질하다 (sew–sewed–sewn/sewed)
rough	형 거친
scratch	동 긁다
handkerchief	명 손수건
equipment	명 장비, 용품
material	명 재료
battle	명 전투, 투쟁
unexpected	형 예상 밖의
trouble	명 문제

4 수염을 기르려면 세금을~

beard	명 (턱)수염
pay	동 지불하다
rule	명 규칙; 통치, 지배
powerful	형 강력한
shave	동 면도하다
introduce	동 소개하다; 도입하다
law	명 법, 법률
military	형 군사의
system	명 제도, 체제
tax	명 세금
token	명 표시, 징표
hire	동 고용하다
collect	동 모으다; 징수하다
refuse	동 거부하다
unusual	형 특이한
influence	명 영향

Section 02

Culture

1 파인애플은 맛있기만 한 게 아니야

culture	명 문화
consider	동 고려하다; 여기다
symbol	명 상징
European	명 유럽인 형 유럽의
trip	명 여행
unusual	형 특이한
outside	명 겉(면) (↔ inside 명 안(쪽))
pinecone	명 솔방울
unique	형 특이한
environment	명 환경
successfully	부 성공적으로
cultivate	동 경작하다, 재배하다
rare	형 드문
guest	명 손님
host	명 주인, 주최자 동 주최하다
decoration	명 장식
dish	명 요리
value	동 소중하게 생각하다
tragic	형 비극적인

2 무시무시한 음력 7월!

superstitious	형 미신을 믿는 (superstition 명 미신)
gate	명 출입문
spirit	명 영혼
return	동 돌아오다[가다]
earth	명 지구; 세상, 이승
ghost	명 귀신, 유령

get married	결혼하다
burn	동 (불이) 타오르다; 태우다
paper money	지폐
comfort	명 안락; 위로, 위안
light	명 빛; 등
monthly	형 매월의
tradition	명 전통
careful	형 주의 깊은
lesson	명 교훈

3 빗자루를 왜 뛰어넘지?

wedding	명 결혼(식)
typical	형 전형적인
custom	명 관습, 풍습
broom	명 빗자루
MC	명 사회자 (master of ceremonies)
mean	동 뜻하다, 의미하다 (mean – meant – meant)
African American	형 아프리카계 미국인의
marriage	명 결혼
ban	동 금지하다
slave	명 노예
secretly	부 비밀스럽게, 몰래
symbolize	동 상징하다
sweep	동 (빗자루 등으로) 쓸다, 털다
link	동 연결하다, 잇다
modern	형 현대의
origin	명 기원, 유래
importance	명 중요성

4 태국 원숭이는 복도 많네!

prepare	동 (음식을) 준비하다, 마련하다

vegetable	명 채소, 야채
in front of	~ 앞에
temple	명 사찰, 신전
for free	무료로
join	동 참여하다
unfortunately	부 불행하게도, 유감스럽게도
thank	동 감사하다, 감사를 표하다
local	형 지역의, 현지의
good luck	행운
set up	~을 마련하다
buffet	명 뷔페
make a wish	소원을 빌다

Section 03 Food

1 바나나보다 중요해질지도 몰라!

crisis	명 위기
worse	형 더 나쁜 (worsen 동 악화되다)
climate	명 기후
up to	~까지
regularly	부 정기적으로
solution	명 해결책
plant	명 식물
staple food	주식
unlike	전 ~와 달리
root	명 뿌리
stem	명 줄기
benefit	명 혜택
quickly	부 빨리

harvest	동 수확하다
season	명 계절
diseas	명 질병
easily	부 쉽게
despite	전 ~에도 불구하고
danger	명 위험
cause	명 원인
hunger	명 굶주림, 기아
locally	부 생산지에서
crop	명 작물
extinct	형 멸종된
national	형 국가의, 전국적인
dish	명 요리
product	명 상품, 제품
worldwide	부 전 세계에

2 버터가 다 떨어졌다고요? 걱정 마세요!

fill	동 채우다
jar	명 병
heavy cream	유지가 많은 크림
shake	동 흔들다
thicken	동 걸쭉해지다, 짙어지다
mixture	명 혼합물
fat	명 지방
molecule	명 분자
stick together	함께 뭉치다
eventually	부 결국
form	동 형성되다
lump	명 덩어리
place	동 놓다[두다]

bowl	명 그릇
rinse	동 씻다
at least	적어도
finally	부 마침내
take out	꺼내다
squeeze	동 짜다[쥐다]
go bad	썩다, 나빠지다
homemade	형 집에서 만든, 손수 만든
origin	명 기원, 근원

3 실수가 나쁜 것만은 아니야~

popular	형 인기 있는
invent	동 발명하다
by accident	우연히 (= accidentally)
bake	동 굽다
forget	동 잊어버리다
ingredient	명 재료
rise	동 오르다; (빵 · 케이크 등이) 부풀다
serve	동 (음식을) 제공하다, 대접하다
tofu	명 두부
by mistake	실수로
elderly	형 나이가 지긋한, 연로한
chew	동 씹다 (chewy 형 쫄깃쫄깃한)
soybean	명 콩, 대두
complain	동 불평하다
tasteless	형 맛없는
cool down	식다
recipe	명 조리법
injure	동 (사고로) 부상을 입히다
a pair of	한 쌍의

4 식당 인테리어에 이런 비밀이!

secret	명 비밀
common	형 흔한; 공통의
study	명 공부; 연구
excited	형 들뜬, 흥분한
cause	동 야기하다
reduce	동 줄이다
appetite	명 식욕
calm	형 차분한
actually	부 실제로는, 사실은
link	동 연결하다
think of A as B	A를 B로 생각하다[여기다]
nature	명 자연
freshness	명 신선함 (fresh 형 신선한)
healthy	형 건강한; 건강에 좋은

Section 04 Nature & Environment

1 4초면 충분해요

Antarctica	명 남극 대륙
run	동 달리다; 이어지다
chin	명 턱
survive	동 살아남다 (survival 명 생존)
condition	명 상태; 《복수형》 환경
unusual	형 특이한, 드문
period	명 기간
second	명 (시간 단위인) 초
each day	날마다

add up to	결국 ~되다
lay	동 놓다; (알을) 낳다 (lay – laid – laid)
protect	동 보호하다
at all times	항상
awake	형 깨어 있는
daytime	명 낮 (시간)
danger	명 위험 (dangerous 형 위험한)
species	명 (생물 분류의 기본 단위) 종(種)
secure	형 안심하는; 안전한
uncomfortable	형 불편한

2 어질어질 꽃 냄새

bright	형 밝은
grow	동 자라다, 성장하다
up to	~까지
finish	동 끝내다
bloom	동 (꽃이) 피다, 꽃을 피우다
sweet	형 달콤한
perfume	명 향수
scent	명 향기
terrible	형 끔찍한
rot	동 썩다
meat	명 고기
to make matters worse	설상가상으로
beetle	명 딱정벌레
fly	동 날다 명 파리
colorful	형 형형색색의, 알록달록한
common	형 흔한

3 무지개색으로 빛나는 해변

be full of	~로 가득 차다
throw	동 던지다, 버리다(throw - threw - thrown)
garbage	명 쓰레기 (= trash)
including	전 ~을 포함하여
be known as	~로 알려져 있다
take care of	~을 돌보다; ~을 처리하다
by oneself	혼자
wave	명 파도
break down	~을 부수다
tiny	형 아주 작은
smooth	형 매끄러운
jewelry	명 보석류
sparkle	동 반짝이다
government	명 정부
clean up	~을 치우다[청소하다]
area	명 지역
remove	동 제거하다, 치우다
remain	동 남아 있다
get rid of	~을 처리하다[없애다]
cover	동 가리다, 덮다
process	명 과정

4 친환경 도시, 쿠리치바

pollution	명 오염
come together	(하나로) 합치다, (함께) 모이다
environment	명 환경
exchange	명 교환 동 교환하다, 주고받다
bring	동 가져오다
receive	동 받다

school supplies	학용품
in return	보상으로, 답례로
plant	동 심다
grass	명 풀, 잔디
green	형 녹색의; 친환경적인
feature	명 특징
attraction	명 끌림; 명소
suffer from	~로 고통받다
poverty	명 빈곤
overcome	동 극복하다
destination	명 목적지
in exchange for	~와 교환으로, ~ 대신에

Section 05 Psychology

1 왜 자꾸 늦을까?

law	명 법; 법칙
complete	동 완료하다
miss	동 놓치다
deadline	명 기한, 마감 기한
happen	동 발생하다
ability	명 능력
unexpected	형 예기치 않은
event	명 사건, 일
delay	명 지연, 지체
avoid	동 피하다
compare A with B	A와 B를 비교하다
current	형 현재의
past	형 지난

realistic	형 현실적인
extra	형 추가의
meet	동 만나다; (기한 등을) 지키다
useful	형 유용한
benefit	명 혜택, 이득

2 다 바꾸고 싶어!

stuff	명 것, 물건
French	형 프랑스의
philosopher	명 철학자
in comparison	~와 비교하여
robe	명 예복[가운]
replace	동 대신하다; 바꾸다
end up with	결국 ~하게 되다
prevent	동 막다, 방지하다
purchase	동 구매하다 명 구매
fit	동 (모양 · 크기가 어떤 사람 · 사물에) 맞다
match	동 어울리다, (색깔 · 무늬 · 스타일이 서로) 맞다
reveal	동 드러내다[밝히다]
organize	동 준비하다; 정리하다
possession	명 (주로 복수로) 소유물
trendy	형 최신 유행의
lead	동 이끌다
a series of	일련의

3 분명히 집중했는데?

find	동 찾다; ~라고 생각하다
experience	동 경험하다
handle	동 다루다
experiment	명 실험
meaning	명 의미

generally	부 일반적으로
familiar	형 익숙한, 친숙한
name	동 이름을 지어 주다; 이름을 대다
recognize	동 인식하다
hold on to	~을 고수하다, 계속 보유하다
calm	동 진정시키다
stimulate	동 자극하다
slow down	~을 늦추다

4 조금만 더 도와줘~

ask	동 부탁하다, 요청하다
playground	명 운동장, 놀이터
corner	명 (길)모퉁이
far	형 먼 부 멀리 (far – farther – farthest)
pattern	명 (정형화된) 양식, 패턴
repeat	동 반복되다
arrive	동 도착하다
technique	명 기법
classic	형 전형적인, 대표적인
strategy	명 전략
sale	명 《복수형》 영업(부)
salesperson	명 판매원
prevent	동 막다
request	명 요청
focus on	~에 집중하다
lead to	~로 이어지다
difference	명 차이
favor	명 부탁
work	동 일하다; 효과가 있다
trick	명 비결, 요령

trade	명 영업, 장사
limited	형 제한된, 한정된
edition	명 판
product	명 상품, 제품
honest	형 정직한, 솔직한
continue	동 계속하다

Section 06 Body & Health

1 얕보면 안 되는 이것

cut	동 베다 (cut-cut-cut) 명 (베인) 상처
pain	명 아픔, 통증 (painful 형 아픈)
cause	동 ~을 야기하다[초래하다]
minor	형 작은[가벼운]
injury	명 부상
hurt	동 다치게[아프게]하다
sensitive	형 세심한; 민감한
signal	명 신호
organ	명 기관
edge	명 끝, 가장자리
uneven	형 평평하지 않은; 고르지 않은
microscope	명 현미경
rough	형 고르지 않은, 거친
damage	동 손상을 주다
treat	동 대하다; 치료하다
sense	동 감지하다
mild	형 가벼운, 순한
intense	형 극심한, 강렬한
expected	형 예상되는

preventable	형 예방할 수 있는

2 이게 정말 내 목소리라니!

recording	명 녹음(된 것) (record 동 녹음하다)
sound	동 (소리가) 들리다 명 소리, 음
travel	동 (빛 · 소리 등이) 이동하다, 나아가다
wave	명 파동
reach	동 도달하다
bone	명 뼈
strong	형 (목소리가) 강한, 선명한
weak	형 (빛 · 소리 등이) 약한
form	동 형성하다
method	명 방법
improve	동 개선하다
design	명 디자인; 설계; 구조

3 키가 줄어들고 있다고?

spine	명 척추
contain	동 포함하다, 함유하다
connect	동 연결하다
disc	명 원반; (등뼈나 목뼈의) 디스크
depend on	~에 의존하다; ~에 달려 있다
measure	동 측정하다, 재다
soft	형 부드러운; 무른
liquid	명 액체
allow	동 허락하다, 가능하게 하다
direction	명 방향
gravity	명 중력
downward	부 아래쪽으로
squeeze	동 짜내다; 짓누르다

flat	형 납작한 (flat – flatter – flattest)
gain	동 얻다
lost	형 잃어버린
height	명 키, 높이
function	명 기능
thick	형 두꺼운 (thick – thicker – thickest)

4 맛을 느끼려면 협력이 필요해

stuffed	형 (코가) 막힌
taste	동 맛을 느끼다 명 맛
tongue	명 혀
recognize	동 알아보다, 인식하다
basic	형 기본적인
sweet	형 달콤한
sour	형 신, 시큼한
bitter	형 맛이 쓴
salty	형 짠
scent	명 향기, 냄새
stimulate	동 자극하다
work	동 효과가 있다; 기능하다
avoid	동 피하다
medicine	명 약
flavor	명 맛, 풍미
rest	명 나머지
rebuild	동 다시 세우다
satisfy	동 만족시키다

Section 07 Marketing

1 닻이 걸렸다!

imagine	동 상상하다
budget	명 예산, 비용
anchor	동 닻을 내리다 명 닻
effect	명 효과
process	동 처리하다
information	명 정보
rely on	~에 의존하다
compare A to B	A를 B와 비교하다
powerful	형 강력한
too	명 도구
product	명 상품, 제품
customer	명 고객
dish	명 요리
even if	(비록) ~일지라도
bargain	동 협상[흥정]하다
invent	동 발명하다
experience	명 경험
shape	동 (어떤) 모양으로 만들다; 형성하다
choice	명 선택
entire	형 전체의
object	명 물건

2 친구 따라 물건을 산다고?

term	명 용어
parade	명 행렬, 거리 행진
carry	동 나르다, 옮기다
band	명 악단, 악대

follow	동 따라가다
join	동 함께 하다[합류하다]
crowd	명 군중, 무리
describe	동 묘사하다
daily	형 매일의
advertisement	명 광고
sell	동 팔다 (sell – sold – sold)
second	명 초
gather	동 모이다
form	동 형성[구성]하다
situation	명 상황
reason	명 이유

3 나도 모르게 따라 하게 돼!

advertisement	명 광고
grab	동 붙잡다
attention	명 주의, 주목
influence	동 영향을 주다
mirror	명 거울
neuron	명 뉴런
brain	명 뇌
react	동 반응하다
copy	동 복사하다; 따라 하다
expert	명 전문가
take a bite	한 입을 베어 물다
notice	동 알아채다
imitate	동 모방하다
emotion	명 감정
facial expression	얼굴 표정
viewer	명 시청자

bite	동 물다 (bite-bit-bitten)
as a result	그 결과
trick	명 속임수
function	동 기능하다[작용하다]

4 지글거리는 스테이크

favorite	형 마음에 드는, 매우 좋아하는
steak	명 스테이크
piece	명 조각; 점
grill	명 그릴, 석쇠
sizzle	동 (음식이) 지글거리는 소리를 내다
water	동 물을 주다; 군침이 돌다
tasty	형 맛있는 (= delicious)
attract	동 끌다, 유인하다
sight	명 시력; 모습
affect	동 영향을 미치다
satisfy	동 만족시키다
sense	명 감각
trend	명 동향, 추세
eat out	외식하다
focus on	~에 집중하다
respect	동 존중하다
quality	명 질
importance	명 중요성

Section 08 Origins

1 스카치테이프가 자동차와 관계가 있다고?

popular	형 인기 있는
unfortunately	부 불행하게도
glue	동 (접착제로) 붙이다 명 접착제
stay	동 유지하다, ~인 채로 있다
original	형 원래의
remove	동 없애다, 제거하다
decide	동 결심하다
solution	명 해결책
success	명 성공
satisfied	형 만족하는
experiment	동 실험하다
cellophane	명 셀로판
clear	형 분명한; 투명한
material	명 재료, 물질
packaging	명 포장, 포장재
invent	동 발명하다 (invention 명 발명품)
use	명 용도
nearly	부 거의
impossible	형 불가능한
completely	부 완전히

2 날씨 아래에 있다는 것은?

unwell	형 몸이 편치 않은, 아픈
have to do with	~와 관계가 있다
several	형 몇몇의
common	형 흔한
theory	명 이론

origin	명 기원, 유래
idiom	명 관용어
come from	~에서 비롯되다
language	명 언어
sailor	명 선원 (sailing 명 배 타기)
ill	형 아픈 (illness 명 병)
below	전 아래에
deck	명 (배의) 갑판
rest	동 쉬다
get better	좋아지다, 호전되다
mean	동 의미하다 (mean–meant–meant)
literally	부 문자 그대로
take place	일어나다
above	전 위에
seasickness	명 뱃멀미
inspire	동 영감을 주다

3 달을 닮은 빵

assume	동 (당연한 것으로) 여기다, 생각하다
croissant	명 크루아상
be based on	~에 기반을 두다
shaped	형 ~ 모양[형태]의, 생긴 (shape 명 형태, 모양)
view	동 보다
legend	명 전설
create	동 만들다
defeat	동 패배시키다
empire	명 제국
battle	명 싸움, 전투
surround	동 둘러싸다
protect	동 보호하다

beneath	전 ~ 아래에
realize	동 알아채다
dig	동 파다
alert	동 알리다
soldier	명 병사
destroy	동 파괴하다
save	동 구하다
celebrate	동 기념하다
flag	명 기, 깃발
bring	동 가져오다 (bring – brought – brought)

4 오른손 좀 확인해 보겠습니다~

shake hands	악수하다 (shake – shook – shaken)
perfectly	부 완전히, 지극히
normal	형 평범한, 정상적인
grab	동 붙잡다
in the first place	우선[먼저]; 처음에
ancient	형 고대의
expert	명 전문가
weapon	명 무기
hide	동 숨기다 (hide – hid – hidden)
sleeve	명 소매
reveal	동 밝히다; 드러내 보이다
carry	동 들고 다니다, 지니고 있다
handshake	명 악수
eventually	부 결국
gesture	명 몸짓, 제스처
peace	명 평화
greeting	명 안부 인사
communicate	동 의사소통을 하다
motion	명 동작

Section 09 Sports & Entertainment

1 세상에 이런 규칙이!

player	명 선수
throw	동 던지다
hit	동 치다
bat	명 방망이 (batter 명 타자)
request	동 요구하다
pitch	명 경기장; 투구 (pitcher 명 투수)
spectator	명 관중
make a decision	결정하다
difference	명 차이점
role	명 역할
enforce	동 집행[시행]하다
fair	형 공평한 (fairly 부 공평하게)
fortunately	부 운 좋게도
complex	형 복잡한
helpful	형 도움이 되는
strict	형 엄격한
current	형 현재의
similar	형 유사한

2 환상의 쇼에 당신을 초대합니다

giant	형 거대한
perform	동 공연하다 (performance 명 공연 performer 명 연기자)
circus	명 서커스단, 곡예단
fitting	형 잘 어울리는, 적합한
take place	개최되다, 일어나다

world-class	형 세계적 수준의
acrobat	명 곡예사
gymnast	명 체조 선수
leap	동 뛰어오르다
floating	형 떠 있는
stage	명 무대
breathtaking	형 숨이 막히는, 숨이 멎는 듯한
height	명 높이
gracefully	부 우아하게
underwater	부 물속에서 형 수중의
hose	명 호스
breathe	동 호흡하다
beneath	전 ~ 아래에
surface	명 표면, 수면
aquatic	형 물과 관련된
wet	형 젖은; 습한

3 럭비 선수들의 댄스 타임~

national	형 국가의, 국가적인
international	형 국제적인
match	명 경기
war dance	(전쟁 전에 추는) 출전의 춤
chant	동 구호를 외치다
slap	동 철썩 때리다
wide	부 크게 열어[뜨고]
stick out	~을 내밀다
tongue	명 혀
scare	동 겁주다
battle	명 전투
more of	~에 더 가까운 것, 오히려 ~

bring together	~을 연합[결속]시키다
spirit	명 정신, 영혼
strength	명 힘
funeral	명 장례식
ancient	형 고대의, 먼 옛날의
celebration	명 축하 행사
symbol	명 상징

4 아무나 가질 수 없어요

trophy	명 트로피
tournament	명 토너먼트
award	동 수여하다
keep	동 가지고 있다, 보유하다
design	동 만들다, 고안하다
copy	명 복제품
defeat	동 패배시키다
champion	명 챔피언, 우승자
unable	형 ~할 수 없는
belong to	~에게 속하다, ~의 소유이다

Section 10 Art

1 비슷하지만 다른 둘

orchestral	형 오케스트라[관현악단]의
pitch	명 경기장; 음의 높이
famil	명 가족; (같은 종류의) 집단, 군
bow	명 (바이올린 등을 켜는) 활
furthermore	부 더욱이
hold	동 잡다 (hold–held–held)

known as	~로 알려진
pointy	형 끝이 뾰족한
basically	부 근본적으로, 기본적으로

2 모두 진품이 맞아요

French	형 프랑스의, 프랑스인의
several	형 몇몇의, 여럿의
court	명 법정
scene	명 장면; 풍경
judge	명 판사
decide	동 결심하다; 결정하다
capture	동 포착하다, 담아내다
work	명 일; 작품
development	명 발달
humorous	형 재미있는
situation	명 상황
object	명 물건, 물체

3 제가 아는 그 악기가 맞나요?!

invent	동 발명하다
natural	형 자연의 (nature 명 자연)
enormous	형 거대한
list	동 (명부 · 목록 등에) 기입[기재]하다
wooden	형 나무로 된, 목재의
base	명 맨 아랫부분, 하부
set	동 (특정한 장소 · 위치에) 놓다 (set – set – set)
attach	동 부착하다, 붙이다
valley	명 계곡
instrument	명 기구; 악기
cotton	명 면직물

coat	동 칠하다, 입히다
sticky	형 끈적끈적한
run	동 (어떤 방향으로) 움직이다
along	전 ~을 따라
string	명 끈, 줄; 악기의 현[줄]
vibrate	동 진동하다
stretch	동 뻗어 있다

4 왜 이런 별명이?

armed	형 무장한, 무기를 든
gather	동 모이다
watch	명 감시, 망 보기
official	형 공식적인
describe	동 묘사하다, 설명하다
turn out	~인 것으로 드러나다[밝혀지다]
nickname	명 별명
death	명 죽음
layer	명 층, 겹
protect	동 보호하다
dirt	명 먼지
naturally	부 당연히, 자연스럽게
nighttime	명 야간, 밤
remove	동 제거하다
restore	동 복원[복구]하다
original	형 원래의
condition	명 상태
effort	명 노력

Word Review

Section 01 Fashion

다음 우리말은 영어로, 영어는 우리말로 쓰시오.

1 theory ____________
2 practical ____________
3 popular ____________
4 own ____________
5 notice ____________
6 extra ____________
7 wonder ____________
8 unclear ____________
9 cruel ____________
10 pay ____________
11 shave ____________
12 law ____________
13 단단히, 꽉 ____________
14 특히 ____________
15 우아한 ____________
16 편안한 ____________
17 통제하다, 조절하다 ____________
18 향상 ____________
19 기원, 출신 ____________
20 고통스러운 ____________
21 해결책 ____________
22 소개하다; 도입하다 ____________
23 군사의 ____________
24 고용하다 ____________

Section 02 Culture

다음 우리말은 영어로, 영어는 우리말로 쓰시오.

1 consider ______________________

2 unique ______________________

3 dish ______________________

4 spirit ______________________

5 burn ______________________

6 tradition ______________________

7 typical ______________________

8 mean ______________________

9 ban ______________________

10 in front of ______________________

11 unfortunately ______________________

12 set up ______________________

13 환경 ______________________

14 경작하다, 재배하다 ______________________

15 드문 ______________________

16 귀신, 유령 ______________________

17 주의 깊은 ______________________

18 교훈 ______________________

19 관습, 풍습 ______________________

20 상징하다 ______________________

21 중요성 ______________________

22 참여하다 ______________________

23 지역의, 현지의 ______________________

24 소원을 빌다 ______________________

Section 03 Food

다음 우리말은 영어로, 영어는 우리말로 쓰시오.

1 crisis ____________________

2 climate ____________________

3 benefit ____________________

4 fill ____________________

5 stick together ____________________

6 at least ____________________

7 invent ____________________

8 by accident ____________________

9 complain ____________________

10 common ____________________

11 reduce ____________________

12 nature ____________________

13 뿌리 ____________________

14 수확하다 ____________________

15 질병 ____________________

16 걸쭉해지다, 짙어지다 ____________________

17 씻다 ____________________

18 짜다 ____________________

19 잊어버리다 ____________________

20 오르다; (빵·케이크 등이) 부풀다 ____________________

21 (음식을) 제공하다, 대접하다 ____________________

22 들뜬, 흥분한 ____________________

23 차분한 ____________________

24 건강한; 건강에 좋은 ____________________

Section 04 Nature & Environment

다음 우리말은 영어로, 영어는 우리말로 쓰시오.

1 chin ____________________
2 unusual ____________________
3 protect ____________________
4 grow ____________________
5 to make matters worse ____________________
6 beetle ____________________
7 be full of ____________________
8 garbage ____________________
9 sparkle ____________________
10 pollution ____________________
11 exchange ____________________
12 overcome ____________________
13 살아남다 ____________________
14 기간 ____________________
15 안심하는; 안전한 ____________________
16 (꽃이) 피다, 꽃을 피우다 ____________________
17 향수 ____________________
18 형형색색의, 알록달록한 ____________________
19 던지다, 버리다 ____________________
20 ~을 돌보다; ~을 처리하다 ____________________
21 남아 있다 ____________________
22 풀, 잔디 ____________________
23 특징 ____________________
24 목적지 ____________________

Section 05 Psychology

다음 우리말은 영어로, 영어는 우리말로 쓰시오.

1 complete ____________________
2 ability ____________________
3 delay ____________________
4 philosopher ____________________
5 replace ____________________
6 end up with ____________________
7 handle ____________________
8 meaning ____________________
9 recognize ____________________
10 pattern ____________________
11 focus on ____________________
12 lead to ____________________
13 놓치다 ____________________
14 기한, 마감 기한 ____________________
15 피하다 ____________________
16 막다, 방지하다 ____________________
17 구매하다 ____________________
18 어울리다, (색깔·무늬·스타일이 서로) 맞다 ____________________
19 경험하다 ____________________
20 익숙한, 친숙한 ____________________
21 자극하다 ____________________
22 운동장, 놀이터 ____________________
23 도착하다 ____________________
24 비결, 요령 ____________________

Section 06 Body & Health

다음 우리말은 영어로, 영어는 우리말로 쓰시오.

1 pain ______

2 minor ______

3 edge ______

4 microscope ______

5 weak ______

6 form ______

7 spine ______

8 depend on ______

9 function ______

10 taste ______

11 basic ______

12 sour ______

13 베다; (베인) 상처 ______

14 부상 ______

15 세심한; 민감한 ______

16 극심한, 강렬한 ______

17 (빛·소리 등이) 이동하다, 나아가다 ______

18 도달하다 ______

19 방향 ______

20 중력 ______

21 잃어버린 ______

22 혀 ______

23 맛이 쓴 ______

24 향기, 냄새 ______

Section 07 Marketing

다음 우리말은 영어로, 영어는 우리말로 쓰시오.

1 imagine ______
2 process ______
3 rely on ______
4 carry ______
5 crowd ______
6 advertisement ______
7 grab ______
8 influence ______
9 react ______
10 attract ______
11 satisfy ______
12 quality ______
13 예산, 비용 ______
14 효과 ______
15 상품, 제품 ______
16 용어 ______
17 묘사하다 ______
18 상황 ______
19 주의, 주목 ______
20 전문가 ______
21 모방하다 ______
22 동향, 추세 ______
23 물을 주다; 군침이 돌다 ______
24 외식하다 ______

Section 08 Origins

다음 우리말은 영어로, 영어는 우리말로 쓰시오.

1 glue ______________
2 original ______________
3 material ______________
4 unwell ______________
5 idiom ______________
6 ill ______________
7 assume ______________
8 realize ______________
9 celebrate ______________
10 ancient ______________
11 hide ______________
12 gesture ______________
13 결심하다 ______________
14 성공 ______________
15 완전히 ______________
16 언어 ______________
17 쉬다 ______________
18 문자 그대로 ______________
19 둘러싸다 ______________
20 알리다 ______________
21 기, 깃발 ______________
22 무기 ______________
23 소매 ______________
24 밝히다; 드러내 보이다 ______________

Section 09 Sports & Entertainment

다음 우리말은 영어로, 영어는 우리말로 쓰시오.

1 spectator ____________________

2 make a decision ____________________

3 fair ____________________

4 giant ____________________

5 leap ____________________

6 surface ____________________

7 international ____________________

8 scare ____________________

9 funeral ____________________

10 award ____________________

11 keep ____________________

12 defeat ____________________

13 차이점 ____________________

14 역할 ____________________

15 집행[시행]하다 ____________________

16 무대 ____________________

17 숨이 막히는, 숨이 멎는 듯한 ____________________

18 높이 ____________________

19 전투 ____________________

20 축하 행사 ____________________

21 상징 ____________________

22 만들다, 고안하다 ____________________

23 ~할 수 없는 ____________________

24 ~에게 속하다, ~의 소유이다 ____________________

Section 10 Art

다음 우리말은 영어로, 영어는 우리말로 쓰시오.

1 furthermore ____________________

2 known as ____________________

3 scene ____________________

4 capture ____________________

5 humorous ____________________

6 natural ____________________

7 enormous ____________________

8 valley ____________________

9 sticky ____________________

10 gather ____________________

11 turn out ____________________

12 layer ____________________

13 끝이 뾰족한 ____________________

14 근본적으로, 기본적으로 ____________________

15 판사 ____________________

16 일; 작품 ____________________

17 물건, 물체 ____________________

18 (명부·목록 등에) 기입[기재]하다 ____________________

19 나무로 된, 목재의 ____________________

20 끈, 줄; 악기의 현[줄] ____________________

21 진동하다 ____________________

22 공식적인 ____________________

23 별명 ____________________

24 복원[복구]하다 ____________________

Word Review 정답

Section 01

1 이론 2 현실적인, 실용적인 3 인기 있는 4 소유하다 5 의식하다, (보거나 듣고) 알다 6 여분의 7 궁금해하다 8 불분명한 9 잔인한 10 지불하다 11 면도하다 12 법, 법률 13 tightly 14 especially 15 elegant 16 comfortable 17 control 18 improvement 19 origin 20 painful 21 solution 22 introduce 23 military 24 hire

Section 02

1 고려하다; 여기다 2 특이한 3 요리 4 영혼 5 (불이) 타오르다; 태우다 6 전통 7 전형적인 8 뜻하다, 의미하다 9 금지하다 10 ~ 앞에 11 불행하게도, 유감스럽게도 12 ~을 마련하다 13 environment 14 cultivate 15 rare 16 ghost 17 careful 18 lesson 19 custom 20 symbolize 21 importance 22 join 23 local 24 make a wish

Section 03

1 위기 2 기후 3 혜택 4 채우다 5 함께 뭉치다 6 적어도 7 발명하다 8 우연히 9 불평하다 10 흔한; 공통의 11 줄이다 12 자연 13 root 14 harvest 15 disease 16 thicken 17 rinse 18 squeeze 19 forget 20 rise 21 serve 22 excited 23 calm 24 healthy

Section 04

1 턱 2 특이한, 드문 3 보호하다 4 자라다, 성장하다 5 설상가상으로 6 딱정벌레 7 ~로 가득 차다 8 쓰레기 9 반짝이다 10 오염 11 교환; 교환하다, 주고받다 12 극복하다 13 survive 14 period 15 secure 16 bloom 17 perfume 18 colorful 19 throw 20 take care of 21 remain 22 grass 23 feature 24 destination

Section 05

1 완료하다 2 능력 3 지연, 지체 4 철학자 5 대신하다; 바꾸다 6 결국 ~하게 되다 7 다루다 8 의미 9 인식하다 10 (정형화된) 양식, 패턴 11 ~에 집중하다 12 ~로 이어지다 13 miss 14 deadline 15 avoid 16 prevent 17 purchase 18 match 19 experience 20 familiar 21 stimulate 22 playground 23 arrive 24 trick

Section 06

1 아픔, 통증 2 작은[가벼운] 3 끝, 가장자리 4 현미경 5 (빛·소리 등이) 약한 6 형성하다 7 척추 8 ~에 의존하다; ~에 달려 있다 9 기능 10 맛을 느끼다; 맛 11 기본적인 12 신, 시큼한 13 cut 14 injury 15 sensitive 16 intense 17 travel 18 reach 19 direction 20 gravity 21 lost 22 tongue 23 bitter 24 scent

Section 07

1 상상하다 2 처리하다 3 ~에 의존하다 4 나르다, 옮기다 5 군중, 무리 6 광고 7 붙잡다 8 영향을 주다 9 반응하다 10 끌다, 유인하다 11 만족시키다 12 질 13 budget 14 effect 15 product 16 term 17 describe 18 situation 19 attention 20 expert 21 imitate 22 trend 23 water 24 eat out

Section 08

1 (접착제로) 붙이다; 접착제 2 원래의 3 재료, 물질 4 몸이 편치 않은, 아픈 5 관용어 6 아픈 7 (당연한 것으로) 여기다, 생각하다 8 알아채다 9 기념하다 10 고대의 11 숨기다 12 몸짓, 제스처 13 decide 14 success 15 completely 16 language 17 rest 18 literally 19 surround 20 alert 21 flag 22 weapon 23 sleeve 24 reveal

Section 09

1 관중 2 결정하다 3 공평한 4 거대한 5 뛰어오르다 6 표면, 수면 7 국제적인 8 겁주다 9 장례식 10 수여하다 11 가지고 있다, 보유하다 12 패배시키다 13 difference 14 role 15 enforce 16 stage 17 breathtaking 18 height 19 battle 20 celebration 21 symbol 22 design 23 unable 24 belong to

Section 10

1 더욱이 2 ~로 알려진 3 장면; 풍경 4 포착하다, 담아내다 5 재미있는 6 자연의 7 거대한 8 계곡 9 끈적끈적한 10 모이다 11 ~인 것으로 드러나다[밝혀지다] 12 층, 겹 13 pointy 14 basically 15 judge 16 work 17 object 18 list 19 wooden 20 string 21 vibrate 22 official 23 nickname 24 restore